Game Day and God

Football, Faith, and Politics in the American South

☙

Sports and Religion Series

Edited by Joseph L. Price

MERCER
UNIVERSITY PRESS

Endowed by
TOM WATSON BROWN
and
THE WATSON-BROWN FOUNDATION, INC.

Game Day and God

Football, Faith, and Politics in the American South

ↁ

Eric Bain-Selbo

Mercer University Press
Macon, Georgia

MUP/H790

© 2009 Mercer University Press
1400 Coleman Avenue
Macon, Georgia 31207

Books published by Mercer University Press are printed on acid free
paper that meets the requirements of American National Standard for
Information Sciences—Permanence of Paper for Printed Library
Materials.

Mercer University Press is a member of Green Press initiative
(greenpressinitiative.org), a nonprofit organization working to help
publishers and printers increase their use of recycled paper and decrease
their use of fiber derived from endangered forests. This book is printed
on recycled paper.

The publisher extends thanks to Mr. Harris D. (Bud) Ford, Associate
Athletic Director, Media Relations, University of Tennessee Athletic
Department for providing the cover image from the 1998 National
Championship game at the Fiesta Bowl. Tennessee defeated Florida
State 23-16 in the game played Jan. 4, 1999. Leading the prayer is team
captain Al Wilson, linebacker from Jackson, Tennessee.

ISBN 13 978-0-88146-155-8

Library of Congress Cataloging-in-Publication Data
Bain-Selbo, Eric.
Game day and God : football, faith, and politics in the American south
/ Eric Bain-Selbo. -- 1st ed.
p. cm.
Includes bibliographical references and index.
ISBN-13: 978-0-88146-155-8 (hardback : alk. paper)
ISBN-10: 0-88146-155-5 (hardback : alk. paper)
1. Football--Religious aspects. 2. Football--Social aspects. I. Title.
GV959.B26 2009
796.3320973--dc22
2009024977

Contents

Dedicated to my loving mother, Florinne Selbo,
who moved me South as a boy, raised me right,
and took me to every practice and game
(and watched every game).

and

In memory of Stan Lusby,
my teacher and mentor at the University of Tennessee,
who believed I could achieve things I had not even begun to imagine,
and who was a very good man.

Preface

This book arose both from intellectual curiosity as a scholar and personal passion as a fan. I often had heard that college football in the South was a religion. So as a scholar of religion as well as a philosopher, I was curious about how true that assessment really was. I also am a proud graduate of the University of Tennessee, where I spent more joyous Saturdays than I probably deserved watching my beloved Volunteers do battle with Gators, Bulldogs, and others. I *like* the game of football, but I really *love* game day. I love the rituals and the colors and the energy of the crowd. When the band stops at the bottom of "the Hill" on its march to the stadium and plays "Rocky Top" while thousands of fans sing along, I am not ashamed to say that I get choked up. I daresay that when I first introduced my children to this scene, I probably even had a tear in my eye.

Given my background and what led me to write this book, it should not be surprising that some of it comes across as celebrating this phenomenon. As a scholar and a reflective fan, however, I also am aware of its shortcomings and the reader will find a critical element to my treatment of the subject, especially in the latter chapters. In the end, I hope this work is of interest to scholars—particularly those in religious studies—but also to fans. I tried to limit the academic jargon and to explain concepts or theories so that the educated reader but non-academic could get something out of it.

I have many people to thank for helping me along the way. Many thanks to Marc Jolley and everyone at Mercer University Press who helped bring this book to fruition. Marc committed to the idea of the book (and my doing it) long before he knew whether or not I could pull it off. I appreciate his confidence and take the book's publication as confirmation that his confidence was well placed. Thanks to Joseph Price, series editor, for his support as well. His feedback and encouragement were quite valuable. Many thanks to all the fans who filled out survey cards, spoke with me, and occasionally provided sustenance (chicken wings, barbecue, burgers, beer, and more). I truly experienced their Southern hospitality and learned so much from them. I also must thank the numerous faculty and university officials who helped along the way. Media relations at the University of Tennessee, University of Georgia, Louisiana State University, University of Alabama, and University of Mississippi provided a wealth of information and even field passes to games, providing a unique perspective from which to watch the fans during the game. Faculty and other representatives at these institutions also took the time to hear about my research and to provide their feedback. Some even provided me with opportunities to share my work with their students and local communities. A special thank you to the good people at the Paul W. Bryant Museum, especially Ken Gaddy and Taylor Watson, for the time they took with me and for allowing me to pore through boxes and boxes of correspondence.

As I have done with previous works, I enlisted a few friends and colleagues as readers of drafts of chapters. I feel deeply indebted to them for the time and care they put into reading those chapters. I greatly respect them as scholars and friends. They are Gary Grieve-Carlson, Owen Moe, and Jeffrey Robbins—all from my previous institution, Lebanon Valley College. I also must thank LVC and various members of the faculty grants committee for two years of funding to travel South for game-day experiences and to observe and interview fans. Some of my colleagues thought this was the biggest boondoggle they had ever seen (it was pretty sweet), so I thank the members of the grants committee for seeing the value of this project and funding my efforts. I also appreciate the support I have received from my current institution, Western Kentucky University, particularly the media relations office, which has helped to publicize my work.

Finally, I must thank my family. My wife, Laura, probably has heard more stories about college football than she would care to hear for the rest of her life. She nevertheless has been very supportive, especially as I have taken off to conduct research and to share it at numerous conferences and public settings. My children, Zach and Hannah, have borne their father's obsession with this project (and with Tennessee football!) with patience well beyond their years. I have enjoyed sharing stories with them and hope that in years to come this book might teach them something about college football, the South, religion, and myself. I must note, too, that Zach even helped with some of the research at a Tennessee game, and I hope that it will be as fond a memory for him as it is for me.

I will not summarize here the contents of the book. The table of contents should be descriptive enough for that. While the chapters can stand alone, I would advise reading them in order. I think the book does *build* toward its conclusion. Or maybe that is just me…

Foreword

Southerners' devotion to football often begins with support for their local high school team. As their enthusiasm intensifies and merges with that of other partisans, their collective excitement galvanizes communities from the shores of the Atlantic to the plains of Texas. At one end of the Southern spectrum lies Summerville, South Carolina, where former coach John McKissick won the most games in American high school football history during his forty-plus-year career there. Even among the devout Evangelicals in coastal Carolina, he was revered almost equally with God and Southern history. And on the western edges of the South, in Odessa, Texas, the Permian High Panthers often challenged for the championship of Texas High School football. That team's stadium is well known for making "Friday Night Lights" burn brighter than nearby churches' Sunday morning candles. While Southerners' football passion often starts with their allegiance to local high school teams, it is in their nearly blind devotion to collegiate teams that their religious fervor is manifest most clearly.

Commonplace among Southerners are perceptions and assertions about the religious significance of collegiate football throughout the region. Foremost among the pundits who make such statements are coaches, athletes, politicians, and authors. Former Alcorn State University football coach Marino Casem, for instance, observed the region's distinct devotion to football in contrast to fans' fondness for the game in other areas of the country. "In the East," he noted, "college football is a cultural attraction. On the West Coast, it is a tourist attraction. In the Midwest, it is cannibalism. But in the South," he concluded, "it is religion." Somewhat similarly, author Willie Morris, a native of Yazoo, Mississippi, remarked that although Americans generally like football, Southerners celebrate it as "a folk ritual touching on religiosity," with Saturday serving as "a holy day." With a hint of envy about the prominence given to football over other sports, former Atlanta Braves' pitcher Steve Stone, who also served as Harry Caray's side-kick on the Cubs' broadcasts during the 1990s, resonated with these sentiments, observing that Southern football not only climaxes each week's activities, but that it also orders the entire year. According to Stone, sports' fans in the South "say there are only two seasons: fall football and spring football."

Throughout the South, one's reverence for collegiate football is often measured in the depth of one's allegiance to an SEC team. In Alabama, for example, former Senator Jeremiah Denton recognized the extreme devotion engendered by Bear Bryant, and he explained that Alabamians "believe that on the eighth day the Lord created the Crimson Tide."[1] And according to one of Bryant's coaching successors for the Tide, Bill Curry, "Nothing in Alabama rivals football in importance," not even religion. When Curry first took over the head coaching job at Alabama, he received death threats because he was perceived as an outsider, a Yellow Jacket from Georgia Tech. Concerned about the welfare of the Curry family, their former pastor in Atlanta called their house and spoke to Curry's wife Carolyn, who assured him that they were fine. "We have learned that football is a religion over here," she joked. "Oh no, Carolyn," the minister responded. "It's a lot more important than that."[2]

While these representative commentators have quipped about Southerners' fervent fascination with football, scholars have also analyzed the importance of Willie Morris' recognition that Saturday—the day for collegiate football—is a holy day. In particular, Edwin Cady's *The Big Game* explores how collegiate sports rivalries, especially in football, reflect and orient American life. Using a different literary scheme in two seminal works, *Reading Football* and *King Football*, Michael Oriard examines the

---

[1] All of these remarks can be found in Barbara Binswanger and Jim Charlton, ed., *On the Night the Hogs Ate Willie and Other Quotations on All Things Southern* (New York: Dutton, 1994) 130-33.

[2] Bill Curry, "Bama-Auburn a Year-Round Affair," EPSN.com: College Football, posted November 19, 2004; archived at http://sports.espn.go.com/espn/print?id+1925995&type=Columnist&imagesPrint=off.

cultural myths that shape Americans' embrace of football, and he analyzes the media's transformation of those myths.

Now Eric Bain-Selbo extends and challenges the initial insights of these cultural analyses of collegiate football in his creative work *Gameday and God*. Bain-Selbo focuses on the way that collegiate football in the South—specifically, in its paragon conference, the SEC—generates a denomination of civil religion. He demonstrates how the myths, rituals, and symbols associated with SEC football develop and solidify fans' loyalty to their favorite team. In turn, then, Bain-Selbo shows how their allegiance clarifies their identity and creates a cohesive community in which political differences are tolerated, ignored, or overcome; in which social standing beyond team support is deemed irrelevant; and in which racial discord is set aside or surmounted.

With vivid details derived from his own field research (which required him to attend home games at most of the SEC member universities) and with the personal touch of extended family (which, of course, is a distinct "cousin" characteristic of Southern culture), Bain-Selbo demonstrates how that which is ordinary—a football game—can facilitate an experience of the extraordinary by examining the rituals associated with the game (such as fans' tail-gate parties and their reverence for players' paraphernalia, or relics). Drawing upon cultural theorists ranging from Karl Marx and Emile Durkheim to René Girard and Robert Bellah, and upon religious studies scholars such as Mircea Eliade and Wayne Proudfoot, Bain-Selbo scores a victory in this impressive work, not only for appreciating the significance of Southern collegiate football but also for expanding our understanding of the dynamics of religious life.

Joseph L. Price
Editor, Sports and Religion series

1

Bulldogs, and Marches, and Bear! Oh, My! The Morphology of the Sacred in College Football in the South

Michael Oriard, whose research on football and American culture and consciousness is helpful in coming to understand the role that football plays in the American South, writes that while the locus of college football power and even the "primary breeding ground" of the top players has shifted from the East Coast to the Midwest and now to the South, this has occurred "without an accompanying myth or folklore" in the latter region.[1] While he is right that this shift has occurred, he is wrong to believe that there is no "accompanying myth or folklore." Not only is there myth, folklore, and legend in Southern college football, there are also symbols, rituals, and a sense of sacrality that permeate the religious experience that is Southern college football.

It certainly is platitudinous to say today that it is hard to define what religion is. Obviously, there are the easy cases. The church, synagogue, temple, and mosque down the street would seem likely places to see something like religion happening. It does not take long, though, to complicate what otherwise seems quite simple. While specific liturgies and the ideas they express are stereotypically religious, is everything that happens down the street religious? Are bingo night, the monthly potluck dinner, and the parenting group religious just because they meet in a house of worship? Even with all that is happening down the street, could other activities in other places provide people with the same benefits?

---

[1] Michael Oriard, *King Football: Sport & Spectacle in the Golden Age of Radio & Newsreels, Movies & Magazines, the Weekly & the Daily Press* (Chapel Hill: University of North Carolina Press, 2001) 368.

Indeed, can college football provide the kind of social and psychological "goods" that religion historically has provided? If college football is part of the civil religion of the American South, then what in particular is religious about it? In this chapter, I will begin to answer these questions by looking at the morphology of the sacred in Southern college football.

The Meaning(s) of the Sacred

What is "the morphology of the sacred"? Morphology refers to the study or analysis of the different forms something might take. In this case, morphology concerns the different forms in which the sacred might manifest itself. But what is the sacred? Answering this question is as difficult as determining what religion is. Clearly the two are related. For our purposes, let us assume that the sacred is the power or source or motivating element of religious behavior and the ultimate object of religious thought.

In the most basic sense, the sacred is that which is not profane. The root of the word profane (and, by the way, fanatic or fan) is found in the Latin word *fanum*, meaning temple. The temple is where religious activity is carried out. Profane means that which is in front of or outside the temple. In other words, that which is not sacred. But can we define or describe the sacred in any way other than as the opposite of the profane?

Mircea Eliade, the renowned twentieth-century scholar of comparative religion, whose work is often cited by scholars writing about sports and religion, equates the sacred with the real. He writes, "The sacred is preeminently the *real*, at once power, efficacy, the source of life and fecundity. Religious man's desire to live *in the sacred* is in fact equivalent to his desire to take up his abode in objective reality, not to let himself be paralyzed by the never-ceasing relativity of purely subjective experiences, to live in a real and effective world, and not in an illusion."[2] As the real, the

---

[2] Mircea Eliade, *The Sacred & the Profane: The Nature of Religion*, translated by Willard R. Trask (New York: Harcourt Brace Jovanovich, 1959) 28 (emphasis original).

sacred is that which is significant rather than insignificant, meaningful rather than meaningless. It is that which infuses our lives with purpose and value. Participation in a specific ritual, for example, adds a depth or quality to life that is not there outside the ritual (that is, in profane existence). Consequently, the sacred makes profane existence bearable. It is something greater than us, which means that it is not "purely subjective." Thus, the sacred is identified with the transcendent—that which is beyond any single individual. Transcendence is a quality or characteristic of the sacred.

Can sport be sacred? While a more extensive treatment of this question can be found in the conclusion, obviously there are many scholars, myself included, who believe it can. As William J. Morgan claims, "It is in terms of being that the essential structures of sport are rendered intelligible as incisive meaning forms. The ontological sphere [the sphere of the real] of sport is unveiled in its cultural-artistic form and ultimately in its religious development. As a stirring cultural force, sport shares with the other forms of culture a transcendent pursuit."[3]

The transcendent pursuit is of something greater than the athlete or spectator. Morgan concludes that the "distinguishing character of sport, then, is to be found in its transcendental locus, being [that which transcends the particular individual], in which spirit is unfolded in the primacy of the lived situation."[4] Within the same volume that Morgan's essay appears, Howard Slusher argues, "Like religion, sport offers its 'followers' a grouping of myths, symbols and rituals that facilitate the total experience…. The spirit of man, in sport and religion, is an exercise of personal venture into the scientifically unknown. The arenas and coliseums are little more than shrines for *spiritual* activity. They allow man to escape

---

[3] William J. Morgan, "An Existential Phenomenological Analysis of Sport as a Religious Experience," in *Religion and Sport: The Meeting of the Sacred and Profane,* ed. Charles Prebish (Westport CT: Greenwood Press, 1993) 120.

[4] Ibid., 133.

the boredom of everyday life and reach out to a larger existence."[5] That "larger existence," that something greater than ourselves, is what we refer to when we discuss that which is transcendent or sacred. To the extent that anything has religious value, it has it through its relation with the transcendent or sacred. "Objects or acts," Eliade writes, "acquire a value, and in so doing become real, because they participate, after one fashion or another, in a reality that transcends them."[6] What the transcendent is varies religiously and culturally. It can be Brahman, God, nirvana, or, as we will see in the next chapter, society itself.

Another important characteristic of the sacred or the transcendent is that it is associated with order—the cosmos—rather than chaos. In suggesting that sports have taken over for what religion used to do for us, Slusher notes that the former, like the latter, helps to "keep order and loyalty."[7] The sacred, in providing meaning and stability and a general orientation to the world, prevents a sense of chaos. It tells us what is important and what is not, and this helps to order the world for us.

This fundamental urge for order that is within human beings is one of the reasons why the sacred, in all its many forms, is an indispensable element of human life. Even among the most secular individuals and in the seemingly most unreligious societies, our relationship to the sacred, to that which separates the meaningful and valuable from the insignificant and profane, persists. For Eliade, "Even the most desacralized existence still preserves traces of a religious valorization of the world."[8] The ceremony to celebrate the opening of the new town hall, for instance, would re-create the very creation of the universe and mark that building and its location as a sacred place.

---

[5] Howard Slusher, "Sport and the Religious," in *Religion and Sport*, ed. Charles Prebish, 179.

[6] Mircea Eliade, *The Myth of the Eternal Return, or, Cosmos and History*, trans. Willard R. Trask (Princeton NJ: Princeton University Press, 1954) 4.

[7] Slusher, "Sport and the Religious," 183.

[8] Eliade, *The Sacred & Profane*, 23.

These considerations suggest to us that to understand what is sacred is to understand something critical about the way human beings *are* at the most basic level. Human beings have some fundamental characteristics. While individuals and cultures do differ, the differences remain within certain limits. Nobody and no culture is absolutely different from all others. Human beings and cultures all have a need for and relation to the sacred and thereby exhibit characteristically religious behavior. *We are homo religious.* The sacred may change and look very different from one epoch to another, from one culture to another. People may even fail to be fully conscious of the sacred and may fail to recognize their own religious behavior, but they remain inextricably drawn to what is sacred in the sense described—a desire to identify and associate with that which is "really real," an orientation towards the transcendent, and a need for some sense of order—and thus are undeniably religious.

The kind of expansion of our thinking about the sacred and religion that Eliade initiates can be seen in the work of more contemporary scholars. David Chidester—especially in *Authentic Fakes: Religion and American Popular Culture*—is a good example. Chidester writes, "Religious ways of being human engage the transcendent—that which rises above and beyond the ordinary. They engage the sacred—that which is set apart from the ordinary. And they engage the ultimate—that which defines the final, unavoidable limit of all our ordinary concerns."[9] This approach to religion does not focus on the existence or character of the transcendent or sacred or ultimate (all very much synonymous), but the ways that these concepts or realities are "engaged" by human beings and how such engagement responds to and shapes our existential circumstances. The key is not to narrowly define these concepts, but to understand how they, defined broadly, function in human life. Thus, "something is doing religious work if it is engaged in negotiating what it is to be human."[10] In other words, religious work is being done if it helps to tell us who we are, what we

---

[9] David Chidester, *Authentic Fakes: Religion and American Popular Culture* (Berkeley: University of California Press, 2005) 1.

[10] Ibid., 18.

should seek, how we should conduct ourselves, and more. That said, we can see that many ideas, activities, objects, or institutions might contribute to "negotiating what it is to be human." Certainly, there are stereotypically religious ideas, activities, objects, and institutions that help us negotiate what it is to be human. But many things may do this, including elements of popular culture. Chidester investigates such elements of popular culture throughout *Authentic Fakes*. He concludes: "Traces of religion, as transcendence, as the sacred, as the ultimate, can be discerned in the play of popular culture. As a result, we can conclude that popular culture is doing a kind of religious work, even if we cannot predict how that ongoing religious work of American popular culture, now diffused all over the globe, will actually work for the United States of America."[11]

Seeing popular culture not only as a place where religions express themselves but as religious itself is one of the more compelling theoretical moves in religious studies in recent years. Sport, of course, is one example of this trend. In this vein, Bonnie J. Miller-McLemore writes that football "embodies the ongoing power and survival of myth and ritual in popular culture" and that games provide "encounters with the sacred."[12] It should be somewhat clear how this could be the case. But now we must turn to greater details, to evidence, that will make the case that college football in the South has religious elements to it and functions religiously for many people. We begin with myths and legends.

Myths and Legends

Myths and legends can mean many things. Often there is a pejorative connotation with the terms "myths" and "legends" as defining things that are false or imaginary, as in "That's just a myth" or "That's merely a legend." More positively, though, myths and legends can be stories or

---

[11] Ibid., 231.

[12] Bonnie J. Miller-McLemore, "Through the Eyes of Mircea Eliade: United States Football as a Religious 'Rite de Passage,'" in *From Season to Season: Sports as American Religion*, ed. Joseph Price (Macon GA: Mercer University Press, 2001) 132.

narratives about great heroes, heroines, gods, or goddesses that tell us something important about human existence—how it ought to be lived or what its purpose is. Of course, most myths and legends are about people who lived a long time ago, or, in the case of gods and goddesses, about things they did a long time ago. But through the process of mythicization, more recent or even contemporary figures can take on qualities typically associated with great heroes, heroines, gods, and goddesses.

The "metamorphosis of a historical figure into a mythical hero" may involve the assimilation of the historical personage to a pre-existing mythical model.[13] For example, stories of the superior strength of an athlete may entail comparison to Hercules. But direct comparison to a mythic or legendary figure is not necessary for mythicization. When a historical figure demonstrates certain human excellences (as determined by the community in which he or she lives), accomplishes great tasks, or demonstrates a superior way to live (thus revealing something about the very meaning or purpose of human life), stories about that person are circulated and often embellished. This developmental process does not mean that the stories lack any historical validity. It simply means that *what* they did and *how* they did it are so valued by a particular community that stories about them are told and retold as a way for a group of people to affirm their own identity and community values.

Eli Gold tells the story of the Alabama player W.T. "Bully" Vandegraaf, who "is an absolute legend in Alabama football."[14] In a 1913 game against Tennessee, Vandegraaf's ear was badly mutilated. "His ear had a real nasty cut, and it was dangling from his head, bleeding badly," a Tennessee player described. "He grabbed his own ear and tried to yank it from his head. His teammates stopped him and the managers bandaged him. Man, was that guy a tough one. He wanted to tear off his own ear so he could keep playing."[15] Vandegraaf thus becomes an exemplary model of

---

[13] Eliade, *Eternal Return*, 42, 43.

[14] Eli Gold, *Crimson Nation: The Shaping of the South's Most Dominant Football Team* (Nashville TN: Rutledge Hill Press, 2005) 25.

[15] Ibid., 25.

the kind of toughness and perseverance expected of Alabama players and, in a sense, of all those fans who identify with Alabama football.

In 1897, Georgia football player Richard Vonalbade Gammon was injured badly during a game against Virginia. As he was being taken off the field, a teammate asked him whether or not the injury would keep him out of the game. Gammon supposedly responded, "No...I've got too much Georgia grit for that."[16] By the time he reached the sideline, he had slipped into unconsciousness and died later that night. The legislature of the state of Georgia, in response to the player's death, passed a bill banning football. But Gammon's mother urged the governor *not* to sign the bill, asking him not to ban the sport that killed her son. The governor did not sign the bill, and football was never banned in the state of Georgia. A simple story with basic historical facts, this account is legendary not because it includes superhuman elements or events that defy the laws of nature but because it affirms ideals that were held in the past that are still valued today. The story valorizes the sacrifice of a young man who gave his life in competition for his university and his state, affirming the importance of college football in the history of both.

In 1988, Auburn was playing Louisiana State in LSU's stadium, referred to as Death Valley. When LSU scored a late touchdown to take the lead, the roar of the crowd was so great that the earth shook—confirmed by a seismograph reading in the university's geology department. Here, the myth or legend is about a collectivity rather than an individual person. What are the values related by this story? Again, we see an affirmation of the role of football in the culture of the university and larger community, and the loyalty and exuberance of the fans of LSU are demonstrated. But we also need to keep in mind the immediate experience of the fans at the game. At that moment of primal roar, nothing was more significant, nothing had more value, and nothing was more meaningful than the event—the ritual—that was being played out on the field; an event that transcended

---

[16] Russ Bebb, *The Big Orange: A Story of Tennessee Football* (Huntsville AL: Strode Publishers, 1974) 46.

the fans as well as the individual players. The experience was a manifestation of the sacred: Something powerfully meaningful and qualitatively different occurred.

Football coaches, like players and fans, have often been sources of mythicization. Robert Neyland, coach of some of the greatest Tennessee teams, "was without a doubt a savior figure, an epic hero of the gridiron."[17] Almost any major college football program in the South (and elsewhere for that matter) has this kind of pivotal figure in its past. But perhaps the most mythological or legendary figure in the history of Southern college football is Paul "Bear" Bryant.

Born into abject poverty in a small Arkansas village in 1913, Bryant rose to become one of the greatest cultural icons of the South—perhaps second only to Elvis. His nickname came from accepting a challenge as an adolescent to wrestle a bear. Though the bear eventually got the better of him (it even drew blood by biting his ear), Bryant earned a nickname. As a member of the University of Alabama football team, Bryant may not have been the best player (the great receiver Don Hutson was a teammate), but he certainly was one of the toughest. In a 1935 game against Tennessee, Bryant played with a broken leg, which was confirmed by a reporter at the time who insisted on seeing the x-ray.

Bryant became a coach after his playing days were over, garnering success at every step of the way. George Blanda, the quarterback for his first Kentucky teams, remarked upon seeing him, "This must be what God looks like."[18] Another player, Harry Jones, said, "In those days, the coach was like God," adding that Bryant "was the most impressive human being I have ever been around.... He was just everything you wanted to be."[19] In his first year as head coach at Texas A&M, Bryant took his new team to the dusty town of Junction for a pre-season training camp that became famous

---

[17] Robert J. Higgs, *God in the Stadium: Sports & Religion in America* (Lexington: University Press of Kentucky, 1995) 273.

[18] Keith Dunnavant, *Coach: The Life of Paul "Bear" Bryant* (New York: Thomas Dunne Books, 2005) 71.

[19] Ibid., 71, 73.

(infamous?) for how grueling it was. Many players simply left. Those who remained became the nucleus of successful teams in the coming years. Later, a book and then a movie were made about the "Junction Boys." In a television special on ESPN, several of the players noted how the book and movie misrepresented or embellished some of the stories about those difficult weeks in the Texas heat—an exemplary case of mythicization.

Then Bryant's beloved Alabama called, a call he likened to "Mama calling." Bryant answered the call and returned to his alma mater in 1958. It was at Alabama that he became larger than life. By the time his career was over, Bryant had won more games than any other coach in the history of the game, leading Alabama to 13 conference titles and six national championships. While Joe Paterno at Penn State and Bobby Bowden at Florida State have surpassed Bryant in victories, nobody has matched his level of championship success.

Bryant was a cultural hero. Andrew Doyle argues that Southerners viewed Bryant as "an affirmation of their own values and virtues."[20] As such, Bryant reflected "the perennial societal need for heroes who give form to cherished dominant values."[21] But "hero" might not be a strong enough appellation. One poll indicates that approximately a quarter of Crimson Tide fans "associated the Bear with 'godlike qualities.'"[22]

Charles Reagan Wilson, the renowned scholar of Southern culture, writes that in "his last years, and especially after his death in 1983, Bear Bryant was as close to a southern saint as the modern South has produced, with frequent comparisons to General Lee."[23] In short, "Southerners made

---

[20] Andrew Doyle, "An Atheist in Alabama Is Someone Who Doesn't Believe in Bear Bryant: A Symbol for an Embattled South," in *The Sporting World of the Modern South*, ed. Patrick B. Miller (Chicago: University of Illinois Press, 2002) 253.

[21] Ibid., 271.

[22] Warren St. John, *Rammer Jammer Yellow Hammer: A Journey into the Heart of Fan Mania* (New York: Crown Publishers, 2004) 124.

[23] Charles Reagan Wilson, *Judgment & Grace in Dixie: Southern Faiths from Faulkner to Elvis* (Athens: University of Georgia Press, 1995) 28.

him into a modern saint of the civil religion."[24] Bryant's funeral was one of the most elaborate in the history of the Southern states. The motorcade from Tuscaloosa, home of the University of Alabama, to Birmingham, the burial site, a distance of about 55 miles, was lined with admirers paying tribute to a fallen hero. Still today, visitors to Elmwood Cemetery need simply follow the crimson painted line on the driveway in order to pay their respects at Bryant's gravesite.

Wilson writes that the "rhetoric of the Bryant myth expressed during the death ceremonies suggested that he was most admired in the South because he was a winning leader. For a people whose heroes sometimes symbolized lost causes, Bryant was a change."[25] Bryant was a symbol for any Southerner's aspiration to rise above the kind of poverty that typified much of the region. He was a symbol of what hard work and dedication could achieve, a symbol of victory. It is little wonder, then, that the Bryant image appears on a wide range of material artifacts (postcards of him walking on water, for instance) in the popular culture of the South and that so many people continue to make pilgrimages to his gravesite.[26] Dunnavant, one of his biographers, writes, "He always seemed larger than life, and in death, he seems larger still."[27] As Robert J. Higgs and Michael C. Braswell conclude, Bryant "has entered into apotheosis, and it is questionable whether or not there are any other gods before him, especially in football."[28]

The virtues attributed to Bryant may have been found in other cultural heroes such as Robert E. Lee, but mythicization elevated his life to the level of an archetype. Eliade used the term archetype to describe those models of behavior (heroes or heroines, gods or goddesses) that we should try to emulate. Indeed, it is to the degree that we can emulate those lives

---

[24] Wilson, *Judgment*, 39.

[25] Wilson, *Judgment*, 46.

[26] Ibid., 41, 43.

[27] Dunnavant, *Coach*, 327.

[28] Robert J. Higgs and Michael C. Braswell, *An Unholy Alliance: The Sacred and Modern Sports* (Macon GA: Mercer University Press, 2004) 345.

that our own become meaningful, become more sacred. Bryant's "mythologized career"[29] and life certainly became an archetype not only for future coaches at Alabama and throughout the South at all levels, but for many Southern men and boys. Michael Novak writes, "What we mean by 'legend' is what we mean by 'art': the reaching of a form, a perfection, which ordinarily the flesh masks, a form eternal in its beauty. It is as though muscle and nerves and spirit and comrades were working together as flawlessly as God once imagined human beings might."[30] Bryant may not have been perfect: He drank and smoked too much, there are suggestions of infidelity,[31] and he sometimes engaged in questionable recruiting practices.[32] But, obviously, none of the game's legendary players

---

[29] Dunnavant, *Coach*, 324.

[30] Michael Novak, *The Joy of Sports: Endzones, Bases, Baskets, Balls, and the Consecration of the American Spirit*, rev. ed. (Lanham MD: Madison Books, 1994) 16–17.

[31] On the drinking and infidelity, see Dunnavant, *Coach*, 192, 196, and 197. Dunnavant writes,

> In Alabama, the heart of the Bible Belt, where more than half the counties forbid the sale of alcoholic beverages, and where many consider drinking a sin, a large segment of the population saw the man as a saint. They wanted him to be more than he was; they loved him so much that they wanted him to be perfect, but as great a man as he was, he was a man prone to ordinary human weaknesses. His tendency to drink to excess was well known among his friends and among the news media, yet no one ever reported a word about this glaring flaw. (*Coach*, 196)

[32] Oriard discusses how Bryant's ethical lapses were ignored beginning early in his career:

> Paul "Bear" Bryant, left a trail of reprimands and probations as he moved from Maryland to Kentucky, Texas A&M, and then finally Alabama, but he was celebrated in *Collier's* for his recruiting prowess as "Dixie's No. 1 Gridnaper" and in the *Post* as "Football's Jittery Genius." The story of Bryant's first football team at Maryland—he arrived the week of the opening game with fourteen just-discharged servicemen, whom he paraded through the admissions office on the way to the football field—was told not as a case of academic

or coaches has ever been perfect. Still, Bryant and others occasionally did attain perfection, in a certain sense; Bryant had undefeated and untied teams in 1961, 1966, and 1979. In the eyes of their admirers, these men became archetypes for the attaining of perfection;[33] not only as reflections of sacrality but as guides to it.

In addition to presenting us with archetypes that express the values of the community, myths and legends often explain why certain symbols are important; why some objects, spaces, and times are sacred; and what the origins and meanings of rituals are. It is to these many other elements of the sacred that we now turn.

Symbols and Sacred Objects

Symbols and signs point us in the direction of something else. Whereas signs are merely "pointers" to something else, symbols somehow embody what they point toward. For example, a road sign that says that the University of Georgia is 12 miles in a particular direction is simply a sign. But if the sign has a depiction of a Bulldog on it (the mascot of the university's sports teams), then the sign also has a symbol, since the Bulldog embodies something about the university and its teams. Symbols, then, are richer and more meaningful than mere signs. While signs may have a religious function, symbols are what contain religious meaning, which is why, for example, the Christian cross is not just a sign but a symbol as well.

For Eliade, symbols of the sacred are hierophanies; that is, manifestations, appearances, or expressions of gods and goddesses.[34] A symbol, or hierophany, "effects a permanent solidarity between man and the

---

laxity but as an amusing anecdote about an enterprising young man who already knew where he was going. (Oriard, *King Football,* 153)

[33] Dunnavant notes, "On talk shows and in living rooms across the state, every decision related to the program he left behind is held up to the light of his well-chronicled, mythologized career" (*Coach*, 324).

[34] Eliade, *Patterns in Comparative Religion,* trans. Rosemary Sheed (New York: Sheed & Ward, 1958) xiv, 13.

sacred."[35] Symbols bring us into contact with the sacred. While there are certain things that may be more predisposed than others to be hierophanies—the sun and the moon have been popularly perceived as these types of symbols in the history of humankind—hierophanies really can be anywhere and anything. It is unlikely that any Jew or Roman before the life and death of Jesus would have imagined that a simple wooden cross used to punish criminals would become a sacred symbol or hierophany. Therefore, as Eliade states, "We must get used to the idea of recognizing hierophanies absolutely everywhere, in every area of psychological, economic, spiritual and social life. Indeed, we cannot be sure that there is *anything*—object, movement, psychological function, being or even game—that has not at some time in human history been somewhere transformed into a hierophany."[36] If sport is religious and if college football in the South is sacred in some way, are there symbols or hierophanies surrounding its fans? There certainly are.

While letters of the alphabet almost always are signs rather than symbols, the distinctive lettering associated with some college football teams are symbols as well. For example, the "T" that represents the University of Tennessee is referred to as a "Power T." Thus, that particular letter not only serves as a sign of the university and its athletic teams, it also embodies certain characteristics of those teams—power or strength.

By far the most obvious symbols of college football in the South, or anywhere else for that matter, are mascots. Sometimes the mascots are humans, such as the Vanderbilt Commodores, the Ole Miss Rebels, or the Tennessee Volunteers, but most often they are animals. In the Southeastern Conference there are the Tigers (twice), Gamecocks, Gators, Bulldogs (twice), Wildcats, Razorbacks, an elephant representing the Alabama Crimson Tide, and a blue-tick hound dog representing the Tennessee Volunteers. In all these cases, the characteristics of the mascots—strength,

---

[35] Ibid., 447.
[36] Ibid., 11.

ferocity, determination—represent some quality deemed important about and even essential to those teams.

When images or depictions of these symbols appear on objects, those objects become sacred—they are infused with meaning and value that they otherwise would not have. A t-shirt or sweatshirt is merely a garment until it bears the image of the symbol. It may then be treated differently or worn only on special occasions, as on the day of a game, for example.

These symbols also may appear in the form of statues. In Athens, Georgia, statues of the Georgia Bulldog can be found throughout the downtown area adjacent to the university. As one enters Sanford Stadium at the lower level, there is a pillar upon which sits the statue of a bulldog. The statue is adjacent to an area in which all the departed mascot bulldogs, each named Uga, an acronym for the University of Georgia, are buried. On game day, fans visit the cemetery and read the plaques describing the achievements of the teams during the years that each of the dogs served as mascot. In addition, fans take pictures of themselves next to the cemetery and especially standing beside the statue. The statue's symbolic power—its sacredness—is demonstrated not only in this picture taking, but in the constant rubbing or patting that its head receives. A steady stream of fans pays homage not to the statue, but to the animals that served the teams. Ultimately, they are paying homage to the teams, the university, and the state that the animals represented.

Many objects associated with college football games are sacred or take on sacredness for some people. Team uniforms certainly are sacred, especially jerseys worn in games. The exorbitant price of these souvenirs or replica jerseys is evidence of their special value and the importance that fans place on having them. Items related to the field of play are also sacred. Fans who rush the field after "the big win" often head for the goalposts. Once torn down, these sometimes end up in private homes (at least pieces do) or in local establishments like restaurants or bars. Fans on the field also sometimes take handfuls of grass with them as souvenirs. More traditional souvenirs, such as programs, ticket stubs, and caps, also can attain sacred status—whether purchased inside the stadium or in the many stores around the university that cater to fans.

Artifacts or relics from the past, such as game balls, cleats, jerseys, and more—especially if associated with pivotal games or periods in the history of the university's football team—are considered to be of high value and are preserved for posterity. Statues, monuments, or plaques to famous coaches and players take on a degree of sacrality. At many universities throughout the South, these objects can be found around the campus at various sporting venues or even in non-sporting public areas.

In many cases, the sacred objects or artifacts possessed by fans are thought to have special powers. For example, one Alabama fan writes to Paul Bryant in 1968:

> Every time Alabama plays on TV, our machine is draped with mementoes received from Coach Thomas [an Alabama coach]—a sweat shirt with hood, No. 42—and from Coach Drew [another Alabama coach]—a track sweater—plus common pictures of you, normally flanking the three metal elephants [the Alabama mascot] given to me by Uncle Hugo.... At game time, I am always prepared to put on my personal game shirt, but only if we get in a tight.... Your new picture—which I now call The Big Medicine— I centered atop the TV with smaller ones sort of trickling off on each side. Every other totem I own was out [for a recent game], in service, supposedly producing as they always have before.[37]

Here we have not only a description of various sacred objects that serve as symbols of Alabama football, but an expression of belief in their sacred powers.

---

[37] Doug Bailey to Paul Bryant, 2 January 1968, Bryant Correspondence, Paul W. Bryant Museum Library, Tuscaloosa AL.

Sacred Space

The discussion of sacred objects leads us to a consideration of sacred space. Artifacts or relics are not just left around anywhere. They end up in Halls of Fame or museums or their equivalents at major universities throughout the South. These buildings or spaces are sacred, and fans make a special point of visiting them either on game day or throughout the year. We see that the sacred object, the hierophany, "transforms the place where it occurs: hitherto profane, it is thenceforward a sacred area."[38] As Eliade notes, the sacred object disrupts the homogeneity of space and creates something sacred instead.[39] It is better, more meaningful, to be in some places rather than others.

When one enters the rotunda of the Butts-Mehre Heritage Hall on the University of Georgia campus, the building named after two of the school's most renowned coaches, one is encircled by the names of the greatest Georgia athletes—athletes immortalized by having their names included in the Circle of Honor. On the floor and encased in glass for protection and preservation are a wealth of artifacts and relics from Georgia athletic history. Equally, if not more impressive, is the Paul W. Bryant Museum on the campus of the University of Alabama. The Bryant museum is a celebration of Alabama football, with a vast array of artifacts and relics as well as original artwork, video and audio displays, a research library, and gift shop. An impressive bust of the "Bear" marks the entrance to the exhibit area, behind which is a wall with photographs of each of the coach's teams and a listing of all the players' names. The dim background lighting, pierced by the brighter lights of the exhibits, signals to the patron (devotee? pilgrim?) that one should conduct oneself with appropriate solemnity.

Of course, the most sacred structure for the college football fan is the stadium in which one's team plays. Novak describes these as our

---

[38] Eliade, *Patterns in Comparative Religion,* 367.
[39] Eliade, *The Sacred & Profane,* 21, 26.

"cathedrals."[40] The stadium is not only a place for competition; it takes on a sacred value itself. Particularly with regard to the great structures that pepper the landscape in the South, people develop a fondness and attachment to the space both inside and outside the stadium. Walking through the tunnels or archways to the seating areas, one sees the vast expanse of green on the field amid the, in some cases, 100,000 seats. It is not unusual to experience a sense of awe—just as one might feel when entering any great cathedral, such as my first experience of St Patrick's Cathedral in New York City.

Of particular sacrality is the field itself, the very place where teams meet in weekly combat. It not only is set apart (is sacred) by virtue of the design of the stadium itself, but it is set apart by rule as well. Only certain individuals are allowed on the field. It is taboo, or prohibited, for others. Any fan who has ever run onto the field after an important victory, abandoning oneself in the surge of collective exuberance, understands the adrenaline rush of breaking this taboo. "Fans who have rushed into this special territory in the excitement of the crowd in the last seconds of a victory," Miller-McLemore observes, "know the awesome quality of the space which only minutes earlier excluded them from its playing surface."[41] But like many taboos, rushing onto the field is not always strictly prohibited. Rushing the field has become a college football ritual, and thus accepted to some extent and under special circumstances. Some universities maintain token security presence, but the authorities clearly recognize that they will be unable to prevent tens of thousands of fans—charged with the spirit of the conquest—from entering the sacred space. They even prepare for it by installing "break away" goal posts (lighter and easier to bring down) in an effort to prevent fans from incurring major injuries or even dying, though these tragedies still occur with disturbing regularity.

Even fields no longer used for competition can maintain sacrality. Herty Field is a somewhat small plot of land in the middle of academic

---

[40] Novak, *Joy of Sports*, 134.

[41] Miller-McLemore, "Through the Eyes of Mircea Eliade," 129.

buildings on the University of Georgia campus. Shrubbery and flowers surround it, and at one end, there is a fountain. At the other end is a plaque that tells the story of the first football game played at and by Georgia. The 1892 game, billed as the first football game ever in the deep South, was a 50–0 victory for the home team. Whether or not that 1892 game in Georgia represents the true first game ever played in the South (Transylvania College and Centre College in Kentucky apparently competed in 1880), the plaque nevertheless communicates a mythic tradition that stands against any competing facts.

While stadia, museums, and places like Herty Field are particularly infused with sacrality, the university campus itself often has an aura of the sacred as well. It is a special place, especially for alumni. For alumni, the university is the place where an important rite of passage (or several) occurred in their lives. They often can be found wandering the campus on game day, visiting important places from their past.

The game may be played in the stadium, which is frequently located at a prominent place on campus, but game day festivities often involve most of the open space on the campus. Sometimes even the locations of various buildings or structures can have symbolic import. For example, on the University of Alabama campus, there is a central axis that connects the president's mansion (positioned in the shadows of Bryant-Denny Stadium, named after the coach and a past president), Denny Chimes (a bell tower named for the same past president, and around which are the hand and cleat prints of Alabama football captains), a Civil War memorial honoring those Alabama students who defended the campus (unsuccessfully) against encroaching Yankee forces, and the library. These are all spaces with great meaning, with sacrality, and the axis that connects them affirms important values and the harmony of those values: leadership, devotion, sacrifice, and education. "Fans love to walk by and place their hands into the prints of past gridiron stars," Gold writes. "They love to gather at the base of Denny Chimes to get a better view of their Crimson and White [Alabama colors] world."[42]

Rituals and Sacred Time

Novak writes that when one is in a stadium, "one feels present at a liturgy, at a kind of worship service where delight and fun are proper decorum."[43] This idea of liturgy and decorum, the idea of prescribed action, indicates the role of ritual in the experience of college football in the South. The activities and customs that make up game day, and often even the week beforehand, are part of a process that Catherine Bell calls "ritualization." Bell writes:

> ...[R]itualization is a way of acting that is designed and orchestrated to distinguish and privilege what is being done in comparison to other, usually more quotidian, activities. As such, ritualization is a matter of various culturally specific strategies for setting some activities off from others, for creating and privileging a qualitative distinction between the "sacred" and the "profane," and for ascribing such distinctions to realities thought to transcend the powers of human actors.[44]

Some things we do are more charged with meaning and significance than others. Some things we do are sacred and some are profane. On any given Saturday in the South, hundreds of thousands of people will engage in loosely to strictly prescribed activities and customs that make up the ritual context of college football in that region. In doing so, they participate in that which has become sacred, which infuses meaning and significance into their lives.

---

[42] Gold, *Crimson Nation*, 21.

[43] Novak, *Joy of Sports*, 258.

[44] Catherine Bell, *Ritual Theory, Ritual Practice* (New York: Oxford University Press, 1992) 74.

Pep rallies on Friday nights or before games on Saturday are standard at major college campuses in the South and elsewhere. Cheerleaders, the band, players, coaches, and fans (students, alumni, and others) gather to denounce the opposition, show support for the team, join in call-and-response cheers, sing along with or listen to traditional school songs, and much more. At the University of Mississippi, a band shell in the middle of campus is used by the cheerleaders, with the marching band adjacent, to rally the crowd before the game.

"Tailgating" gets its name from the tailgate of a station wagon or truck that was used as an impromptu seat or table as fans prepare meals and enjoy one another's company during the time before the game. While still used to describe what happens on a football Saturday in the South, the term tailgating hardly does justice to the extravagance of what actually takes place. It would be more apt to describe the scene on many college campuses as extended and elaborate communal festivals.

Perhaps no campus has perfected this ritual more than the fans at the University of Mississippi. Famous for "The Grove," an expanse of tree-lined property in the middle of the campus, Rebel supporters have taken tailgating to new heights. On game day, "The Grove" is covered with canopies, one next to the other. Tables are topped with foods from the ordinary to the extravagant and are accentuated by elaborate centerpieces. Beer and mixed drinks flow liberally. Sound systems play a variety of music, while many people relax and watch other games on televisions that are hooked up to satellite dishes. But the action is not limited to "The Grove." While it certainly is the most famous piece of property on the campus, at least on football Saturdays, what takes place there also occurs all across the campus. This pre-game ritual is central to what it means to participate in game day at Ole Miss, and for older fans it is a ritual that they have engaged in for decades. For some families, participation crosses multiple generations. The practice of the ritual across time accentuates its transcendent character by extending beyond any particular person or generation, thereby adding to and/or signifying its sacrality.

Marching bands are integral to the many rituals of college football. As mentioned above, marching bands are an important part of pep rallies before the games. Many bands have prescribed marches through the campus, with fans lined along the streets in anticipation, prepared to listen, clap, and sing along as the band marches by. "The Pride of the Southland Marching Band" at Tennessee culminates its march through campus at an intersection near the stadium and at the foot of "The Hill," the oldest part of the campus. In this large, bowl-shaped area surrounded by tens of thousands of fans, the band delights the crowd with the Tennessee fight song and several renditions of "Rocky Top."

Bands are part of the ritualized walks that the teams make to the stadium. At Ole Miss, the team walks from the student union to the stadium via "The Grove," a stroll known as the "Walk of Champions." The band plays while along the sidewalk fans reach out to touch the players and coaches and offer their support. At Tennessee, the "Vol Walk" is the procession of the team from the athletic center to the stadium, several blocks away, led by cheerleaders and a portion of the band. The other portion of the band is stationed near the stadium, entertaining the fans waiting for the team's arrival.

Of course, the bands also play in the stadium before the game begins, during the game, at halftime in an elaborate performance on the field, and often after the game. There is a special seating section for the band. An important moment occurs when the home team rushes onto the field before the game. Many schools have ritualized activities (band performances, video retrospectives on the "Jumbotron," and others) in preparation for this moment. At Tennessee, the music and cheering before the game culminate with the team running through a 50-yard-sized "T" formed by the band, always accompanied by the roar of the Volunteer faithful. An Alabama fan describes his first game at Bryant-Denny Stadium this way:

> As the crowd inside got larger, the band got louder and the energy in the stadium intensified. I had never seen so many people, heard so much noise, or felt so much excitement. When

the team finally burst out of the tunnel, I started cheering with everything I had and didn't stop until the Tide had beaten the Hokies [Virginia Tech] 31–7. My indoctrination was complete. I had been baptized into Alabama football—washed in the Crimson Tide.[45]

Even after the game, there can be important rituals. After a win at Auburn, fans head to Toomer's Corner in the middle of town and stream toilet paper rolls through the trees and street lamps. After victories at Georgia, many fans, including a great number of children, line up to ring the Chapel Bell.

One important consequence of all rituals, including these, is to demarcate sacred time from profane time. Just as objects and spaces can be charged with meaning and value and thus made different (greater) than other objects and spaces, so it is with periods of time as well. Some time is simply more meaningful and valuable than other time, and such sacred time is initiated and sustained by rituals. The sacrality of a church service, for example, may begin when the minister calls the congregants to prayer or when the choir leads them in the opening hymn—rituals to mark the beginning of a sacred time.

Eliade recognized that human beings seek periods of heightened states of experience; they desire sacred time. Indeed, profane time—that time spent struggling for survival and performing all the mundane yet necessary tasks that we must do as human beings—only is bearable because human beings break it up with periods of sacred time. Sacred time makes life worth living.[46]

The desire for sacred time has not abated simply because many people no longer find traditional religion attractive or compelling. As Eliade notes, we "find in man at every level, the same longing to destroy profane time

---

[45] *Tales of the Tide: A Book by Alabama Fans…For Alabama Fans,* ed. Clint Lovette and Jarrod Bazemore (Birmingham AL: FANtastic Memories, 2004) 68.

[46] See Eliade, *The Sacred & Profane,* 88–89.

and live in sacred time."[47] Living in sacred time is not the creation of some new time but is achieved through the repetition of rituals, like archetypes or models, that have proven capable of giving rise to sacred time. Indeed, part of what we think of when we think about rituals is repetition— something done over and over again. This common-sense understanding is fundamentally correct. Rituals, established, for example, by custom or scripture, are repetitive, and each time we engage in them we repeat the actions of those (sometimes divine beings, sometimes heroes or ancestors) who established the rituals as effective means of bringing us into contact with the sacred, of initiating sacred time.[48] Thus, it is more appropriate to speak here not of the creation of a new time but of a regeneration of sacred time.[49]

As we have seen, the college football experience not only contains rituals, but the experience is structured by rituals. Rituals very much *are the experience.* The game may begin at noon, but the pep rallies, tailgating, band performances, and other game day-oriented rituals initiate the sacred time in which the game (yet another ritual) is played. As Alabama fans prepare for another game, they realize at some level that the rituals in which they engage are part of a tradition, that their team is part of a tradition, and that these are important and valuable. Participating in these rituals gives rise to sacred time.

Of course, sacred time cannot be conjured simply whenever we want. Sacred time often is communal and prescribed as to when and where it can occur. Setting up a tailgating site in June in the supermarket parking lot will probably not give rise to a heightened experience of the sacred. In sport, just as in traditional religions, a liturgical calendar tells us when sacred time is appropriate or even possible. As Joseph Price writes,

---

[47] Eliade, *Patterns in Comparative Religion,* 407.

[48] For Eliade, "any human act whatever acquires effectiveness to the extent to which it exactly *repeats* an act performed at the beginning of time by a god, a hero, or an ancestor" (Eliade, *Eternal Return,* 22).

[49] Eliade, *Eternal Return,* 52.

[I]t is to the seasons of the games on grass, the hardwood, and the ice that Americans turn for ordering their quotidian interests and attention, for seeking escape from the boredom of work routines, and for thrilling with the vicarious conquest over stress. For with the games and in their fanatic observation, tension is created and resolved; and with the cycle of the seasons, resolution and renewal can be effectively anticipated and realized.[50]

He adds, "The primary function of the American sports calendar is to provide some kind of ritual transition from the chaos of secularity to the cosmos of sports, from cultural malaise to corporate hope."[51] The cosmos, as opposed to chaos, is order. It represents the sacred; it *is* the sacred. The calendar orders our time and helps to create a cosmos, providing the structure of sacred and profane time.

Just as sport in general has a liturgical calendar, so does college football. While the topic is a subject of ongoing debate throughout the year, especially in the South, particular times clearly fall into the category of the sacred. To the truly devoted fan, the year begins with spring practice and the concluding intrasquad game, often attended by tens of thousands of fans with accompanying rituals of its own. The long summer is endured in high anticipation for the beginning of the football season, preceded, of course, by fall practice, which is really late summer. The first game and the "home opener" (often one and the same) are moments of great hope and excitement. Expressions of eager expectations, anxiety, anticipation, and nervousness fill the week leading up to a game as fans analyze their team's chances. It also is filled, especially if it is a home game, with specific rituals, such as huge parties and pep rallies. Game day and the game itself are the most sacred of times, structured by the many rituals previously detailed. Certain games—such as key rivalries and homecoming—are of especially

---

[50] Joseph Price, "From Season to Season: The Rhythm and Significance of America's Sporting Calendar," in *From Season to Season: Sports as American Religion*, ed. Joseph Price, (Macon GA: Mercer University Press, 2001) 54.

[51] Ibid., 57.

heightened significance. The sacrality of all these times is apparent in fans' remarks, such as when you hear people expressing that this is "the most exciting time of the year" and that they think this is "the best time of life."

The rhythm of the college football calendar in the American South also helps to orient other events in one's life. As Tony Barnhart observes, "For Southerners, the passing college football seasons are not just a series of games played. Oh, no. They are the markers that serve to connect the important events of our lives."[52] For example, in order to remember the birth year of my daughter, Hannah, I often recall that she was born the same year that Tennessee won its last national championship in football (1998).

Conclusion

So it appears that college football in the American South has many of the elements that we associate with traditional religion: myths, symbols, rituals, and a sense of sacrality. But does this complex combination of rituals and beliefs function religiously? Do people get out of these elements what they get out of traditional religion? Does college football in the American South provide people with the social and psychological "goods" of traditional religion? These are the guiding questions in subsequent chapters.

---

[52] Tony Barnhart, *Southern Fried Football: The History, Passion, and Glory of the Great Southern Game* (Chicago: Triumph Books, 2000) 227.

2

You and 100,000 of Your Closest Friends:
The Social Function of College Football

While the experience of myths, symbols, and rituals and the experience of the sacred certainly can be described from the perspective of the individual, religion is very much a social phenomenon. Myths or legends are the possessions of communities and cultures, not individuals. To the extent that they have any unity in their meanings, symbols acquire significance only through communities and cultures that define those meanings. While habits can be personal, rituals and symbols have shared meanings. Certainly, individuals perform rituals, but rituals usually (only?) make sense in the context of the community or culture that affirms and sustains them. Individuals, then, may encounter the sacred, but it is only through a social structure of myths, symbols, and rituals that any particular individual is able to understand it and gain access to it. Even the most individualistic of spiritual experiences (e.g., prayer) is shaped by its social context.

The relationship between the individual religious experience and its social context can be stated much more emphatically. This greater understanding of that relationship entails the extent to which the social context is dependent upon religion for its very existence. As David Chidester notes, "Religious symbols, myths, and rituals are resources for merging the first person singular into a first person plural, for transforming any particular 'I' into a collective 'Us.'"[1] In other words, religion is not simply dependent on society, but society exists in part through the functioning of religion. Religion—not any particular religion or kind of religion, but religion as a dimension of human existence—is the

---

[1] David Chidester, *Authentic Fakes: Religion and American Popular Culture* (Berkeley: University of California Press, 2005) 24.

way the particular individual is transformed into the whole of the community or culture. Chidester's observations echo the work of Emile Durkheim, the noted sociologist of the early twentieth century. His *The Elementary Forms of Religious Life* is one of the defining texts of the sociology of religion.[2] Though much of the evidence he presents as well as some of his arguments have received significant and justified criticism, Durkheim's work remains a powerful and compelling account of the relationship of religion to society. It is with his work that this chapter will begin, with the goal of gaining clarity on how college football, as part of what we will identify as Southern civil religion, functions socially for many fans in the American South.

Durkheim's Sociology of Religion

Emile Durkheim (1858–1917) was a French scholar of sociology and one of the founding fathers of the discipline. His work covered a range of institutions and issues in society, from the division of labor to the social causes of suicide. He also wrote on religion, and much that he wrote on that subject continues to carry weight today.

Durkheim divides religious phenomena into two categories: beliefs and rites (rituals or practices).[3] All religious beliefs, he notes, presuppose the dichotomy between the sacred and the profane. He argues that the sacred and profane are radical opposites and that running through the religious life is the continual separation of the sacred from the profane. Additionally, religious beliefs and rites are not held simply by individuals but by individuals who are part of a group that holds the beliefs and rites in common. Indeed, it is this holding of beliefs and rites in common that helps to form the group itself. "Religious beliefs proper are always shared by a definite group that professes them and that practices the corresponding rites. Not only are they individually accepted by all

---

[2] Emile Durkheim, *The Elementary Forms of Religious Life*, trans. Karen E. Fields (New York: The Free Press, 1995).

[3] Ibid., 34.

members of that group, but they also belong to the group and unify it. The individuals who comprise the group feel joined to one another by the fact of common faith."[4] Durkheim calls such a group a "Church." Though predominantly a Christian term, Durkheim simply means any religious community when he speaks of Church. Durkheim defines religion in this way: *"A religion is a unified system of beliefs and practices relative to sacred things, that is to say, things set apart and forbidden—beliefs and practices which unite into one single moral community called a Church, all those who adhere to them."*[5]

While Durkheim believes that his definition of religion holds universally, his particular interest in *The Elementary Forms of Religious Life* is totemic religion in aboriginal Australia. In a sustained argument, Durkheim makes the case that the totem (for example, a particular animal, such as a kangaroo) of a tribe or clan is what is most sacred. The totem also represents the tribe or clan. For Durkheim, these are one and the same. Take a hypothetical example of a tribe with a kangaroo as its totem. What is most sacred may be the kangaroo, but the kangaroo simply represents the tribe. Thus, it is the tribe or clan that is most sacred and is the object of religious devotion—only not directly but via the totem.

Now the totemic principle is that which comes to organize all people, animals, and things. It helps to designate the relative importance of everything by virtue of any particular thing's affinity or relatedness to the totem. For example, a particular field where kangaroos tend to congregate would be especially sacred, as would be the water in the stream that runs through the field. Stones from the field might be used in certain rituals, as would, of course, the kangaroos themselves, particularly in sacrifices. The result is a coherent system of beliefs organized around the totem, about the world, and including a set of rituals that affirm and sustain those beliefs.

Of particular interest to Durkheim is how the totemic principle comes to organize human beings and other human-like beings, such as great

---

[4] Ibid., 41.
[5] Ibid., 44 (emphasis original).

ancestors, gods, and goddesses. Gods and goddesses (culminating, eventually, in the idea of one god) developed from the idea of ancestors. The idea of ancestors living on after the death of the body was implied by the empirical evidence of the survival of the tribe or clan, even as individuals pass away. The idea of ancestors comes from the sense that there is something eternal and objective in us, separate from our bodies and idiosyncratic thoughts. This eternal and objective thing is the soul.

The soul is what is sacred about human beings, as opposed to the body, which is profane. The soul is the spark or fragment of the divine (the totem) that connects human beings to ancestors, gods, and goddesses. It is our moral conscience, that which guides our thoughts and actions and somehow seems other than ourselves. This is why Durkheim writes of our "double nature." Any person is both an individual and something else— this something else which is denoted by the idea of the soul. But this "something else" is not unique to the individual; it is what is shared in common with everyone else, or at least everyone else in the tribe or clan. Our soul, then, is really a spark or fragment of the collective soul, as represented in the totem. Durkheim writes, "There truly is a parcel of divinity in us, because there is in us a parcel of the grand ideals that are the soul of collectivity."[6] In short, we are both individual and social beings, and the soul simply is the idea of the social side of us. Thus, Durkheim concludes that "man is double. In him are two beings: an individual being that has its basis in the body and whose sphere of action is strictly limited by this fact, and a social being that represents within us the highest reality in the intellectual and moral realm that is knowable through observation: I mean society."[7]

The soul, then, represents what is transcendent. It is immortal, greater than any individual life. Durkheim observes:

---

[6] Ibid., 267.
[7] Ibid., 16.

In sum, belief in the immortality of souls is the only way man is able to comprehend a fact that cannot fail to attract his attention: the perpetuity of the group's life. The individuals die, but the clan survives, so the forces that constitute his life must have the same perpetuity. These forces are the souls that animate the individual bodies, because it is in and by them that the group realizes itself. For that reason, they must endure. Indeed, while enduring, they also must remain the same. Since the clan always keeps its characteristic form, the spiritual substance of which it is made must be conceived of as qualitatively invariable.[8]

The soul is the same as what makes the ancestors, gods, and goddesses sacred and what connects us to them. Yet the soul is nothing more nor less than society itself. The soul is our social nature, experienced by us as something other and greater than ourselves. Ultimately, our soul is identified with God, the ultimate, most powerful totem. Thus, according to Durkheim, God is society.

This idea of transcendence, represented by the concept of the soul as the psychological experience of the power of the collectivity within us, is central to understanding what rituals achieve. Rituals entail our participation in something greater than ourselves, with that something greater being society itself. This collective enrichment is true for Muslims who gather for prayer, for Christians joining for communion, but also for people engaged in a wide variety of ritual activities, including, for our purposes, sports. Those who participate in sporting events, whether as athletes or spectators, are joining in something that transcends their individual egos and connects them with a greater reality. As Lee Roy Jordan, the great Alabama and then NFL player, said, the lives of Alabama fans "form part of something much larger than themselves."[9]

---

[8] Ibid., 271.

[9] *Tales of the Tide: A Book by Alabama Fans...For Alabama Fans,* ed. Clint Lovette and Jarrod Bazemore (Birmingham AL: FANtastic Memories, 2004) vii.

Though critical of the notion that we should celebrate sport as religion, Robert J. Higgs and Michael C. Braswell get it right when they claim that the "individual is called upon to surrender the ego, individual consciousness that is, to the group. He or she is asked to become a 'fan' and to take up all the totemic practices fandom entails, such as getting 'the spirit' or 'fever' and painting one's face."[10] The comparison to totemic practices should not be taken lightly here. What Higgs and Braswell note about the contemporary sports fan echoes what Durkheim sees in totemism in Australia: "Those who conduct them [totemic rites], playing the role of celebrants—and sometimes even those who are present as spectators—always wear designs on their bodies that represent the totem. One of the principal rites of initiation, the one that initiates the young man into the religious life of the tribe, is the painting of the totemic symbol upon his body."[11] Anyone who has been to a major college football game (or even a minor one), may be struck by how well Durkheim's account fits with what fans often do to themselves as part of their participation in the game-day experience. Whether it is wearing the totem (team mascot) on apparel or painting it on their faces or chests, fans seem to engage in the same kind of totemic representation that Durkheim found among totemic tribes and clans. Anthropologist Victor Turner also writes about the following characteristics of the rites or rituals that he studied: "[S]inging, dancing, feasting, wearing of bizarre dress, body painting, use of alcohol or hallucinogens."[12] All of these, for good or ill, also are characteristic of the game-day experience at any major college football program in the South.

Durkheim divides rituals into "negative cult" and "positive cult." The negative cult has to do with that which is prohibited, often those things that are associated with the totem. These prohibited items constitute the idea of taboo. Certain things associated with the totem, certain powerfully

---

[10] Robert J. Higgs and Michael C. Braswell, *An Unholy Alliance: The Sacred and Modern Sports* (Macon GA: Mercer University Press, 2004) 211.

[11] Durkheim, *Elementary Forms*, 116.

[12] Victor Turner, *Dramas, Fields, and Metaphors: Symbolic Action in Human Society* (Ithaca NY: Cornel University Press, 1974) 55.

sacred things, are too great to be handled at will. They are taboo for most people. That is, most people are prohibited from touching them. Priests or others who conduct rituals may be allowed to handle taboo elements, but even they may have to go through rites of purification to do so.

There are few elements of the college football experience that are taboo, in this sense, that people are prohibited from touching. There are, however, elements that *some* people, at least, are excluded from touching. For example, fans generally are excluded from touching or handling the football. They also are prohibited from being on the field. But what is more relevant for our purposes is what Durkheim describes as the positive cult. The positive cult is not about avoiding the sometimes dangerous power of sacred elements, but bringing the participants of the ritual into communion with the sacred. Thus, it is a system of ritual practices that "regulate and organize" our bilateral relationship with the sacred.[13] Remember, however, that the sacred is society itself. So it is through the collective enactment of ritual that people are brought into contact with the sacred—the sacred being, ultimately, that very collective enactment itself when properly performed and engaging the appropriate emotions.

A great example of the positive cult is the sacrificial feast. Here, the power of the totem is released and incorporated by the tribe or clan through, as one example, the killing (sacrifice) and eating of a representative totemic animal. Remember, however, that the totem is a symbol for the society itself, and in this instance, any particular totemic animal is like an individual. Even as a particular totemic animal may be sacrificed—and through its consumption, its power is distributed throughout the members of the tribe or clan—so, too, any individual in a society must be prepared to sacrifice himself or herself for the good of the whole.

The sacrificial feast is not simply about consumption, however; it also entails renunciation; that is, a giving up of some of the totemic animal and/or other goods to the gods. Sacrifice "always presupposes that the worshipper relinquishes to the gods some part of his substance or his

---

[13] Durkheim, *Elementary Forms*, 330.

goods."[14] But what is even more important as an offering in the sacrificial feast is the thought of the participants.[15] The ritual is performed to strengthen the society as a whole, albeit through the strengthening of individual members, through an act of communion. And while it is believed that this strength comes from oblation to the gods and/or the ingesting of the totemic animal, it really comes from the active participation of the community's members in the ritual. So while it is believed that the ritual strengthens members of the tribe or clan, and through the offering strengthens the totem and/or the gods, according to Durkheim's analysis, it is society itself that is preserved and revived by the ritual.

What happens to the participants in the sacrificial feast or other rituals of the positive cult is what Durkheim describes as "collective effervescence." He notes that the "state of effervescence in which the assembled faithful find themselves is translated outwardly by exuberant emotions that are not easily subordinated to ends that are defined too strictly."[16] In other words, the effervescence is not about achieving some other practical end. It is an end in itself. It is an end because it represents the social and psychological unity of the community itself, and the community is the highest good, not a means to some other good.[17]

What Durkheim refers to as collective effervescence is similar to what Turner and others describe as "communitas." Communitas refers to the direct confrontation of concrete, particular individuals with one another. This confrontation is not between, for example, a teacher and a student or a clerk and a customer; it is between two human beings stripped of their roles and statuses in society.[18] Such a confrontation between human beings, though

---

[14] Ibid., 347.

[15] Ibid., 350.

[16] Ibid., 385)

[17] The experience of "collective effervescence" may be similar to what Mihaly Csikszentmihalyi describes as the experience of "flow." I will leave that discussion, however, for chapter four.

[18] Victor Turner, *The Ritual Process: Structure and Anti-Structure* (New York: Aldine de Gruyter, 1995) 131–32.

the most fortuitous and beneficial of encounters, cannot be maintained indefinitely. All human societies need or, at least, seem to need some kind of division of labor, clearly understood power relations and duties/obligations for their citizens, and orderly and effective social institutions with accompanying hierarchies. All of this together is what Turner calls "structure." Structure is "a more or less distinctive arrangement of mutually dependent institutions and the institutional organization of social position and/or actors which they imply."[19] Structure allows societies to function effectively. The "spontaneity and immediacy" of communitas inevitably gives way to structure.[20] But it is communitas that provides the powerful emotional bond to one another that human beings need as social creatures. As Turner relates, it is through communitas that "*anomie* [the psychological distress caused by chaos in the social order] is prevented or avoided and a milieu is created in which a society's members cannot see any fundamental conflict between themselves as individuals and society. There is set up, in their minds, a symbiotic interpenetration of individual and society."[21] What we have then is a continual tension, a dialectic, between communitas (also called anti-structure) and structure. Both are necessary for human life, and our objective should be finding the appropriate balance between the two. Turner concludes:

> Spontaneous communitas is richly charged with affects, mainly pleasurable ones. Life in "structure" is filled with objective difficulties: decisions have to be made, inclinations sacrificed to the wishes and needs of the group, and physical and social obstacles overcome at some personal cost. Spontaneous communitas has something "magical" about it. Subjectively there is in it the feeling of endless power. But this power untransformed cannot readily be applied to the organizational details of social existence. It is no substitute for lucid thought and sustained will. On the other

---

[19] Turner, *Dramas*, 272.

[20] Turner, *Ritual Process*, 132.

[21] Turner, *Dramas*, 56.

hand, structural action swiftly becomes arid and mechanical if those involved in it are not periodically immersed in the regenerative abyss of communitas. Wisdom is always to find the appropriate relationship between structure and communitas under the *given* circumstances of time and place, to accept each modality when it is paramount without rejecting the other, and not to cling to one when its present impetus is spent.[22]

The rituals of the game-day experience, like religious rituals, contribute to the establishment of communitas. Durkheim notes that the concept of games originated in a religious context, and that recreation "is one form of the moral remaking [society itself] that is the primary object of the positive cult."[23] Games or recreation help to create communitas, for the players encounter one another directly, not mediated by the structures of the social order. In the end, there are numerous rituals—religious and apparently non-religious—that allow communitas to occur. What Durkheim's work clearly indicates is the great need we have for all collective rituals. "There can be no society," he writes, "that does not experience the need at regular intervals to maintain and strengthen the collective feelings and ideas that provide its coherence and its distinct individuality."[24] There can be no society that does not engage in rituals to achieve "collective effervescence" or communitas. The question is whether or not college football in the South includes the kind of rituals that lead to collective effervescence or communitas.

Durkheim in the South

While many books have focused on the "religious" experiences of athletes in competition, this work has focused on the fans. Research and writings on explicitly religious institutions can focus on those who perform the

---

[22] Turner, *Ritual Process*, 139.

[23] Durkheim, *Elementary Forms*, 386.

[24] Ibid., 429.

rituals and have positions of power in the institutions, such as priests and deacons, or on those who witness the performances and are under the charge of those in authority (the congregation). This work has been about the congregation.

But congregants are not passive bystanders in either a church service or at a major sporting event. In both instances, the congregants or fans are active participants in the rituals and the unfolding events. "The mode of observation proper to a sports event is *to participate*," Michael Novak writes, "that is, to extend one's own identification to one side, and to absorb with it the blows of fortune, to join with that team in testing the favors of the Fates."[25] It is more than merely the fact that the fans identify with the team and its accomplishment or failures. The participation of fans is part of the spectacle of the sporting event, part of what makes it the sacred event that it is. Patrick B. Miller, writing about intercollegiate sporting events in the South, concludes that:

> [A] myriad of rituals and symbols reinforced for many southerners the intensity of the intercollegiate sporting experience. The anthems and totems of college athletic culture in the South took a variety of forms and projected a range of images.... The iconography of college sport, manifest in the waving of flags, the orchestration of chants and cheers, and the singing of inspirational songs, formed circles of significance around the actual sites of races or games, actively involving fans as well as participants in the intercollegiate sporting spectacle. The sights and sounds of boisterous athletics went beyond competitive exchange on the diamond or gridiron; those who watched became immersed in something like a sacrament against which a book, a lecture, or a

[25] Michael Novak, *The Joy of Sports: Endzones, Bases, Baskets, Balls, and the Consecration of the American Spirit*, rev. ed. (Lanham MD: Madison Books, 1994) 152.

laboratory experiment—among other academic offerings—often seemed to pale in comparison.[26]

In the previous chapter, many of the rituals of the college football game-day experience in the South were described. These included pep rallies, tailgating, the team walk, activities in the stands, and more. Even well before the game or even on the game day, there is an important ritual that fans participate in: the pilgrimage to the campus.

Turner's work on pilgrimages seems particularly relevant. For example, he tells the story of the Dark Virgin of Guadalupe, an image of the Virgin Mary mysteriously imprinted on a rough cloak. According to Turner, thousands of people came each day to see the image, as of 1974 when Turner's account was published.[27] While the individuals who make the pilgrimage to Guadalupe come from a vast variety of occupations and social strata, on the pilgrimage they simply are pilgrims. The structure of daily life is set aside and communitas among the pilgrims is achieved. Joined in pilgrimage together, the pilgrims are affirmed in their beliefs and are nourished by the support of one another.[28] Because pilgrimages, religious in this case, are to sites in specific countries, they also "are, in a way, both instruments and indicators of a sort of mystical regionalism as well as of a mystical nationalism."[29] In other words, pilgrimages affirm the sacrality of the places to which the pilgrims go, be they a city, state, region, or nation.

Anyone who has made their way to a major college football game in the South, or just about anywhere for that matter, understands the connection between Turner's account of pilgrimages and what fans do on the way to the game. Going down the road, the pilgrims to the game

---

[26] Patrick B. Miller, "The Manly, the Moral, and the Proficient: College Sports in the New South," in *The Sporting World of the Modern South*, ed. Patrick B. Miller (Urbana: University of Illinois Press, 2002) 29–30.

[27] Turner, *Dramas*, 189.

[28] Ibid., 198.

[29] Ibid., 212.

encounter one another, their cars decorated with the symbols (totems) of their team. They are not doctors or lawyers or teachers or plumbers: They are fans, and they experience communitas as such. Their devotion and loyalty to the team, as we saw in chapter one, is bound with their pride in their state or region. As they join together in their pilgrimage to the sacred sites—primarily the stadium, but also sometimes to halls of fame or museums, where they look at famous "cloaks" worn by their heroes—to participate in the game-day rituals, they affirm one another in their beliefs, in particular, a belief that their team will win, or at least that their team is the one that should win. When reflecting on the sight of thousands of Crimson Tide fans on a game day making their way through the Paul W. Bryant Museum on the University of Alabama campus, Keith Dunnavant concludes that "the procession of fathers and sons often resembles a sacred pilgrimage."[30]

The sharing of a common meal is another way in which community is formed and the values and beliefs of the community are affirmed. On game day, this affirmation happens through tailgating. Food and the sharing of meals, especially in the context of picnics or other outdoor activities, are a large part of Southern culture and a central part of the game-day experience for many fans. Meals often are started early in the morning, with smoked meats being prepared all day. People at a tailgating site spend the day in communion and often join with others at adjacent sites.

Every tailgating site has a story, a narrative about how people came to tailgate together or near one another. At Louisiana State University, larger tailgating sites and even some small ones have special names chosen by their members. One particularly interesting tailgating group was founded in 2000. Several of the founding members of the group regularly sat in the third row of the student section at the Tigers' home games, a row that apparently was a bit loose and in disrepair. After one particularly momentous win by the home team, a few of the occupants of the third row

---

[30] Keith Dunnavant, *Coach: The Life of Paul "Bear" Bryant* (New York: Thomas Dunne Books, 1996) 323.

ripped the bench from the stadium and left with it. Note that this all occurred while the authorities were busy trying to maintain order on the field as fans spilled out of the seating sections. Since that time, the group has called itself the "Third Row Tailgaters." The group even has a slogan ("Run Like You Stole Something"), a logo (a Tiger carrying a section of stadium bleacher seating), and a website (www.thirdrow.org). Of course, nobody at the tailgating site will admit on record to taking the seating or that they know of its whereabouts, but the myth of the group is well known and certainly contributes to the strong identification that its members have for the group.

Through their participation in pilgrimages, tailgating, and all the other rituals of the college football game day, fans create a distinctive community. They generate, as Turner notes, communitas. Many people have recognized that sports function in this way. Michael Mandelbaum writes about sports as a source of integration and solidarity.[31] Daniel Wann and his collaborators conclude, "For better or worse, the integrative powers of national sport teams and heroes far exceed those of the most exceptional militarists, politicians, explorers, entertainers, educators, scientists, and clergy men."[32] With regard to the latter (clergy), they conclude that "one of the key functions of the religious institution from a sociological perspective is to help maintain social cohesion, a critical imperative facing any society. To put it more simply, what the religious institution does for society is bind people together through ritual and belief by offering common values and goals toward which they may strive.... Cannot a similar case be made for the binding, integrating, and organizing functions of sport fandom?"[33] Novak, on this point, notes the contrast between the universal claims yet

---

[31] Michael Mandelbaum, *The Meaning of Sports: Why Americans Watch Baseball, Football, and Basketball and What They See When They Do* (New York: PublicAffairs, 2004) 32, 34, 35–36, 37.

[32] Daniel L. Wann, Merrill J. Melnick, Gordon W. Russell, Dale G. Pease, *Sports Fans: The Psychology and Social Impact of Spectators* (New York: Routledge, 2001) 194.

[33] Ibid., 199.

sectarian realities of organized religion and the way that the "symbols and liturgies" of sports truly unite Americans.[34] Of course, he realizes that within the larger community of sporting America are more localized communities. Yet this very tension is intrinsic to the human condition. He writes:

> Intense group loyalties are part of being human. They are important to the survival of the race. They teach forms of fairness, justice, and fellow feeling on which other moral forms are based. In every sport, these local loyalties are transcended by the rules of play. The game is larger than the local passion. Sports help to show how one can be particular and universal at the same time; partisan, yet not self-enclosed; loyal, yet rule-abiding; attached to one's own, yet capable of recognizing worth in others.[35]

The ability of sport to create communities and to foster communal feelings certainly can be seen on any game day in places like Athens, Georgia, Tuscaloosa, Alabama, and Oxford, Mississippi.[36] Sometimes college football even becomes a means to affirm communities that transcend or encompass the more localized communities. For example, soon after Hurricane Katrina in 2005, I was in Athens, Georgia. During the week before a home football game, t-shirts were being sold by the Red Cross that expressed a popular sentiment at the time. Printed on the back of the shirts was the promise that the people of Alabama, Mississippi, and Louisiana could count on Georgia fans, that Georgia fans "got your back."

In the survey data that I collected in a variety of locales, Southern college football fans ranked their game-day experience as one where they experienced a significant sense of community. College football ranked behind family and friends with regard to where those surveyed experienced

---

[34] Novak, *Joy of Sports*, 292.

[35] Ibid., 276.

[36] In today's more technologically savvy fan groups, community also is being created through online discussion groups and/or team websites.

the greatest sense of community. College football ranked *ahead* of church as well as job or career.[37]

But is the community that is formed simply one based on the support of a common team against common enemies (the opposing teams)? Not really. Remember, in totemic tribes or clans the attention or devotion directed toward the totem is not merely because the totem is considered valuable, but because the totem represents the society itself, including, most importantly, its values. Similarly, the community formed through the team is one that inculcates and affirms certain values. When considering the place of sport in American society, Wann and his colleagues write,

> Sport has the potential to model several values regarded as crucial to a democratic and humane society, such as legitimization of authority, honesty, justice, equality, respect for the rule of law, respect for the rights of others, cooperation, competition, and fair play, to name just a few.... However imperfect, sport typically offers spectators and fans demonstrable evidence of the ideological elements that constitute the dominant value structure in American society.[38]

Recalling the previous example from the Georgia fans in the aftermath of Hurricane Katrina, we can see that sport became a vehicle by which compassion and charity could be expressed.

Harry Edwards agrees that "sport is a social institution which has primary functions in disseminating and reinforcing the values regulating behavior and goal attainment and determining acceptable solutions to problems in the secular sphere of life."[39] Among these values, Edwards includes character development, discipline, competition, physical and

---

[37] See survey card in appendix.

[38] Wann et al., *Sports Fans*, 190.

[39] Harry Edwards, *Sociology of Sport* (Homewood IL: Dorsey Press, 1973), 90.

mental fitness, religiosity, and nationalism.[40] Whether or not sport effectively achieves these values for its participants or fans is a debatable issue, and Edwards, himself, is not always convinced,[41] but the values nevertheless are there, and at least one clearly is dominant. Edwards concludes that the "overriding value orientation salient throughout the institution of sport and the dominant sports creed is that of the 'individual achievement through competition.'"[42]

Certainly, the kind of individualism Edwards identifies fits well with the ethos of the South, even as expressed through a team sport. Cultural icons like Paul "Bear" Bryant affirmed the kind of fierce, tough individualism that would have been respected in the Southern frontier period during the Civil War and Reconstruction and well into the twentieth century in the context of the South's persistent poverty and racial strife. Another important value is loyalty. College football in the South may have a nationalistic element to it, but perhaps its most dominant call for loyalty is to one's school or state or, in cases of intersectional battles, one's region and the values associated with it; that is, devotion, pride, and the value of hard work.

Clearly, it is not simply that college football among other institutions inculcates these values out of the blue. College football also is a reflection of these values that are dominant in the culture. No simple cause-and-effect is legitimate. Following Durkheim, we can conclude that institutions like college football are shaped by the traditions of the cultures in which they exist, thereby reflecting what is most important to those cultures. Edwards also notes that "the values currently dominant within sport reflect the value emphases of the society at large."[43] In sum, sport both reflects and shapes our society, and the claim of this work is that it reflects and shapes Southern culture in a particular way that is worth considering.

---

[40] Ibid., 103–25.

[41] Ibid., 329.

[42] Ibid., 334.

[43] Ibid., 341.

Fan Identification

General investigations of fan culture (sports, music, television, movies, et cetera) reveal the close connection between the fan object—a celebrity or a team—and how the fan thinks of himself or herself. Cornel Sandvoss concludes that "the object of fandom, whether it is a sports team, a television programme, a film or pop star, is intrinsically interwoven with our sense of self, with who we are, would like to be, and think we are."[44] Sandvoss claims that the fan's relation to the fan object is less a matter of possession ("mine") as many would argue, but more a matter of identification ("me"). He writes that "the relationship between fans and their objects of fandom is based on fans' self-reflective reading and hence narcissistic pleasures, as fans are fascinated by extensions of themselves, which they do not recognize as such. The notion of fandom as self-reflection describes the intensely emotional involvement between fans and their object of fandom portrayed in a wide range of fan studies."[45] The fan object is not simply a mirror for the fan, it also works to shape the fan's self-image. Sandvoss argues:

> [I]t is not just the fan who appropriates the fan texts, but that the text assumes the power to appropriate the fan. While the object of fandom is subject to a radical reworking and appropriation into a reflection of the fan him- or herself, the fan text gains structuring influence over the fan. The burden of maintaining the self-reflective relationship between fan and object of fandom falls not on the mirror image alone, but equally on the fan him- or herself. Through fans' self-reflective reading, the object of fandom, the fan text, becomes a narrative focal point in the construction of life narratives and identities.[46]

---

[44] Cornel Sandvoss, *Fans: The Mirror of Consumption* (Malden MA: Polity Press, 2005) 96.

[45] Ibid., 121.

[46] Ibid., 110–11.

In this sense, we can see fan objects as doing "religious work," as Chidester would call it, in the way they help fans form an understanding of themselves and their place in the world.

So far, we generally have assumed a strong sense of identification between the fan and his or her team. We will see in later chapters that, in the South, it perhaps has something to do with how universities and their teams are viewed in light of Southern history and culture. In this chapter, we have seen how college football contributes to the constitution of a community and is an expression of it. But can we go deeper into the nature of this identification? Two works that already have been utilized, *Sociology of Sport* by Harry Edwards and *Sports Fans: The Psychology and Social Impact of Spectators* by Daniel L. Wann et al., may help.

Edwards observes, "Sport, whether by deliberate design or social happenstance, has achieved a stature not wholly unlike that enjoyed by traditional religions."[47] He adds that "[s]port involves 'feeling,' ritual, and the celebration of human achievement. It provides fans with a set of organized principles which give meaning to their secular strivings and sufferings. And beliefs about sport support social values and norms."[48] These social values and norms have their roots in more typical religious institutions and traditions that become infused in sport. Thus, Edwards notes that the values and norms of sport rarely are in contradiction to those of the relevant religious traditions because the values and norms originated from those traditions.[49] By virtue of its affirmation and support of these key social values and norms—values and norms that can be understood in both secular as well as religious terms—the institution of sport has achieved a "sacrosanct status."[50]

---

[47] Edwards, *Sociology of Sport*, 260.

[48] Ibid., 262.

[49] Ibid., 90.

[50] Ibid., 250.

Edwards details the ways in which the basic elements of religious institutions can be found in sport as an institution.[51] These include beliefs, male domination of the most significant positions (football is almost exclusively male), saints (great players and coaches), patriarchs (founding fathers of the sport), gods (for example, think of the apotheosis of Paul Bryant), high councils (the governing bodies), scribes (reporters), seekers of the kingdom (athletes or fans), shrines (Halls of Fame), houses of worship (stadia and arenas), and symbols of faith (totems). For all these reasons, Edwards calls sport a "quasi-religion."

While I agree with Edwards that there are many common elements between religious institutions and sport as an institution—commonalities identified and addressed in the previous chapter—I think we legitimately can call sports (at least some) religions. Edwards claims that despite the fact that sports look a lot like religion, they are not an alternative or substitute for "formal sacred religious involvement."[52] But unless his objection to the identification of sport with religion is based on a religious commitment itself, it is hard to understand why he would object. Sport functions the way religion functions, in a way that Edwards also recognizes.

Edwards argues that "involvement through the fan role does give rise to both a feeling of identification or belonging and to the opportunity to express suppressed emotions via a socially approved outlet."[53] This identification or belonging is a function of the shared values or norms found in the fan's everyday or secular life, in sports, and even in religious institutions. These values are the guidelines by which the fan must live. Thus, the institution of sport "reaffirms the viability of the values or rules under which the fan must operate in his day-to-day instrumental pursuits—and may thereby sustain the individual's faith in and willingness to abide by those rules."[54] Consequently, the fan's "chosen team or athlete represents himself in his own struggles in the greater society

---

[51] Ibid., 260ff.
[52] Ibid., 90.
[53] Ibid., 242.
[54] Ibid., 243.

Game Day and God

within the context of prescribed societal values. Opponents in sports events represent the forces and obstacles confronting the fan and hindering achievement in his own life's struggles."[55] Despite the "forces and obstacles" that work against the fan's objectives, it is important for the fan to realize the fundamental legitimacy of the social order, including all its values and norms, in which he must pursue his aims.

Edwards claims that "when he [the fan] is cheering for his team, he is really cheering for himself as well. When he screams insults and abuse upon the opposition sports unit, he is verbally assaulting those forces he has confronted and that so often have combined to frustrate his own personal goal achievement efforts and his own social and psychological security."[56] This argument parallels Durkheim's analyses. The team in this case is the totem. It represents the fan and all the people (from his university or college, state, region, or nation) like him or her. In particular, a successful team represents the people more comprehensively and affirms the larger social order and its values and norms. Edwards concludes, "A winning team reinforces the societal values upon hard work, discipline, good character, mental alertness, hard but honest competition, the 'American way of life,' and so forth. Its performance is evidence that the system is still capable and viable, despite occasional or even frequent contradictions."[57] Given the history of the South and that college football has been connected to it in the last century or so, it is easy to see how this strong sense of identification between fans and their schools has been so important. The university's football team has come to represent the fans— their aspirations, their pride in their state or regions, and their commitment to excelling within the parameters of rules and regulations affirmed to be legitimate.

Wann and his collaborators also note the important ways in which the fan identifies with his or her team. While recognizing a variety of reasons

---

[55] Ibid., 271.
[56] Ibid., 243.
[57] Ibid., 245.

for why fans are motivated to be fans,[58] they recognize that those fans who are particularly devoted to their team have a very high level of identification.

> For fans with a low level of team identification, the role of team follower is merely a peripheral component of their self-concept. As a result, these persons tend to exhibit only mild reactions to the team's performances. However, for fans with a high level of team identification, the role of team follower is a central component of their identity.... Because of their close association with a team, highly identified fans often view it as a reflection of themselves. That is, the team becomes an extension of the individual.[59]

It is for these highly identified fans that sports most function as a religion.

In their review of the relevant research, Wann's group concludes that being a sports fan can be part of one's overall psychological health. Research shows correlations between being a fan and a host of mental health indicators, including self-esteem, infrequency of depression, having positive emotions, avoiding negative emotions and alienation, and collective self-esteem.[60] Contrary to the popular image of the couch potato husband who neglects his wife and children, there is little evidence that marital relations are harmed as a consequence of sports fanaticism.[61]

What is even more interesting and directly applicable to the concerns of this work is the research that looks at the geographical proximity of the fan's team as a variable. Wann and his colleagues write that "one can conclude that psychological connections with a geographically close sport team are related to psychological well-being, while simply being a sport fan or being a 'displaced' fan with a high level of identification with a distant

---

[58] Wann et al., *Sports Fans*, 31, 45.

[59] Ibid., 4.

[60] Ibid., 164.

[61] Ibid.

team is not."[62] While fans of geographically close sports teams may experience negative emotions when those teams lose, "research indicates that highly identified fans (at least those identified with a local team) have a more healthy psychological profile than lowly identified persons."[63] In sum, "recent evidence suggests that strong attachments to a geographically close sport team is positively (albeit modestly) related to a number of indexes of psychological stability, including personal and collective self-esteem, affective expression, alienation, and vigor."[64]

Most Southern college football fans identify with a team in their state. The teams become an "extension" of themselves as well as their fellow citizens. One Tennessee Volunteers fan writes:

> I grew up in Knoxville [home of The University of Tennessee] and graduated from UT. After graduating I married a girl not from Knoxville (but a UT grad) and moved away and haven't lived there since. However, Knoxville is still my home and I have very fond memories of my time there—and I'm proud of being from that part of the country. I met my wife there and some of my best friends and my parents still live there. As such, I have a deep connection with Knoxville and the VOLS, and a big part of my identity is with the VOLS. You could say that it is in my blood and I take great pride in the wins and losses; my devotion to Knoxville and the VOLS is as if both are family. I invest a great deal of time, money and emotional energy because of these reasons. My one or two annual game weekend trips back home are among the highlights of any year for me. Having the opportunity to experience the game day environment, seeing the sea of orange, feeling the fall air, seeing the Tennessee River and Smokey

---

[62] Ibid., 165.
[63] Ibid., 168.
[64] Ibid., 178.

Mountains from Neyland Stadium and partying with my fellow Tennessee fans is a purely joyous experience for me.[65]

Given the evidence of psychological well-being that comes from such identification with a local team, we now may have some additional insight into why fans identify with such teams, why they continue to maintain that identification even through tough losses or losing seasons, and why fans feel so strongly about their identifications with teams. The reason in all these cases is that identification with a team brings psychological "good"— psychological well-being—to the fan. In the case of the specific fan just quoted, it brings "pride" and "a purely joyous experience." Why would he *not* want to be a fan? As we have seen, this sense of well-being is achieved in part through the ritual participation of the individual in something transcendent or greater than him- or herself: the collective fandom of their team.

Wann's group suggests that sports fanaticism is good not only for the individual but for society in general. They argue that "spectator sports produce necessary and important affects as well as encourage considerable social interaction.... Judged from a functionalist perspective, sport fandom can provide an antidote to feelings of apathy, marginalization, and neglect—serious threats to a society's well-being."[66] Such an antidote, in the form of the large university football team, would have been just what the doctor ordered in the late nineteenth and early twentieth centuries, when the South continued to struggle from the trauma of the Civil War and Reconstruction. It would be helpful, too, in the mid-twentieth century, when the region remained the impoverished stepchild of the nation, when footage from the Civil Rights era broadcasted across the country a picture of bigotry and brutality. While perhaps not as *necessary* today, the positive effect of sport in the South is easily seen on game day throughout the autumn months.

---

[65] Tennessee Volunteers fan, e-mail message to author, 30 August 2006.

[66] Wann et al., *Sports Fans*, 182.

Summary

The arguments and research conclusions of Edwards and Wann's group would not have surprised Durkheim. His argument for the social-psychological function of religion in communal life provides an excellent blueprint for understanding the ways in which sport, and college football in the South as one example, functions religiously. In my survey of Southern college football fans conducted in the fall of 2005 and 2006, a little more than 11 percent of respondents claimed that college football was the place where they experienced the greatest sense of community. Out of a choice of seven options, college football ranked, on average, just behind family, friends, and just ahead of church. This evaluation is consistent with Durkheim's argument that religion functions to create community and express its values and norms, with Turner's understanding of communitas, with Edwards and Wann's groups' understanding of the identification of the fan with the team, and with the latter's insistence that "sport locales are venues alive with communal, Gemeinschaft [community] possibilities."[67]

Durkheim, like many social scientists of his time, imagined a future in which religion no longer would have such a hold on the general population. He even thought he saw a societal move in that direction in his own time. He writes:

> If today we have some difficulty imagining what the feasts and ceremonies of the future will be, it is because we are going through a period of transition and moral mediocrity. The great things of the past that excited our fathers no longer arouse the same zeal among us, either because they have passed so completely into common custom that we lose awareness of them or because they no longer suit our aspirations. Meanwhile, no replacement for them has yet been created.... A day will come when our societies once again will know hours of creative effervescence during which new

---

[67] Ibid., 188.

ideals will again spring forth and new formulas emerge to guide humanity for a time.[68]

Perhaps in the South that time already was arriving as Durkheim wrote these words. Perhaps for many the advent of Southern college football already was becoming that institution that "excited" them, where they shared in a "creative effervescence," and where "new ideals" and "new formulas" emerged. Wann and his researchers indicate that no longer "do traditional institutions such as the family, workplace, and neighborhood fully satisfy our need for social interaction and engagement."[69] Clearly sport, and in the South college football for many, has come to take on the important functions that predominantly were performed by religious institutions.

Edwards argues that "for the price of a ticket, the sociologist who has done his homework and knows what to look for, can gain access to a mirror reflecting the past traditions, the present turmoil, and to a great extent, the future destiny of society."[70] This chapter has tried to make the case that sport, like religion, very much reflects the past and the present of the society in which they function. It has tried to make the case that this perspective on college football in the South helps us to see the ways in which it functions religiously. As for the "future destiny of society," that discussion is best left for the conclusion.

---

[68] Durkheim, *Elementary Forms*, 429.

[69] Wann et al., *Sports Fans*, 188.

[70] Edwards, *Sociology of Sport*, 364.

3

Ritualized Violence:
From Religion to Sport to Football

While the ritual of football is enacted in dramatic style—with powerful personal stories of tragedy and glory, thrilling last-second victories with the accompanying heartbreak for the losers, and moral lessons that shape not only the participants and spectators, but sometimes entire communities—it is ritual drama with recurring (about every minute) explosions of brutal physical contact that literally threaten both the lives and limbs of the participants. To neglect the violence of football in a consideration of its meaning in the South or elsewhere would be like doing an investigation of politics and neglecting the exercise of power. This chapter will take up the question of violence, first by placing it in the context of religion, then considering its prominence in sports in general, and finally by looking more specifically at football. A more extensive analysis of violence, religion, and football in the South is reserved for chapter five.

Religion and Violence

Robert J. Higgs and Michael C. Braswell, who are not sympathetic to the comparison of sports to religion, argue that religion around the world has become a "blood sport."[1] They bemoan this development, but it really is nothing new. Violence by people in religious communities on the basis of and in the service of religious beliefs or institutions often has been seen as something that happened only in primitive or tribal religions and cultures. But even the major religious traditions in more "civilized" areas of the world have been bound with violence. Krishna encourages the warrior Arjuna to enter the battle in the Hindu *Bhagavad Gita* because it is

---

[1] Robert J. Higgs and Michael C. Braswell, *An Unholy Alliance: The Sacred and Modern Sports* (Macon GA: Mercer University Press, 2004) 27.

Arjuna's sacred duty. The Abrahamic traditions are punctuated with acts of violence, often by God. Whether it is Yahweh's wrath against the Egyptians (the story of the Exodus) or his own people in Hebrew scripture (Exodus 32:25–35), God's brutal sacrifice of his own son in the Christian New Testament, or Allah's legitimation of military force and conquest against unbelievers (see Surah 9:73 in the Qur'an), violence is central to the history and narratives of the Abrahamic traditions. This embrace of violence, of course, carries right up to today, as Jews, Christians, and Muslims often turn to violence as a means of protecting or forwarding explicitly or implicitly religious objectives. Mark Juergensmeyer details this persisting mode of expression in his book *Terror in the Mind of God: The Global Rise of Religious Violence.*[2]

Violence in religion is more than simply the monumental acts of God or divinely ordained warfare. Violence in religion includes that which we do to ourselves—self-imposed privations or sacrifices done for religious reasons. Durkheim, whose work was based on accounts of aboriginal totemic religions in Australia, provides good examples. He notes the role of sacrifice and even pain in totemic religions. This is what he describes as the "negative cult":

> [T]he grandeur of a man is made manifest by the way he braves the pain. Never does he rise above himself more spectacularly than when he subdues his nature to the point of making it follow a path contrary to the one it would take on its own. In that way, he makes himself unique among all the other creatures, which go blindly where pleasure leads them. In that way, he takes a special place in the world. Pain is the sign that certain of the ties that bind him to the profane world are broken. Because pain attests that he is partially emancipated from that world, it is rightly considered the tool of his deliverance, so he

---

[2] Mark Juergensmeyer, *Terror in the Mind of God: The Global Rise of Religious Violence* (Berkeley: University of California Press, 2000).

who is delivered in this way is not the victim of mere illusion when he believes he is endowed with a kind of mastery over things.[3]

While such sacrifice is performed in the name of the totem, ancestor, or god, remember that these ultimately are expressions of the collectivity for Durkheim. Thus, the sacrifices made symbolically for the totem, ancestor, or god reflect the real sacrifices that must be made by the individual for the good of the collectivity. Durkheim concludes:

> Precisely because society lifts us above ourselves, it does constant violence to our natural appetites.... There is an inherent asceticism in all social life that is destined to outlive all mythologies and all dogmas; it is an integral part of all human culture. And, fundamentally, that asceticism is the rationale and justification of the asceticism that religions have taught since the beginning of time.... We cannot be devoted entirely to the ideals to which the cult is addressed, and entirely to ourselves and our sensuous interests also; entirely to the collectivity and entirely to our egoism as well.[4]

Thus, the sacrifices made by "primitives" may not seem so strange to us when we consider the sacrifices, for example, in war, that we are willing to make for the good of the collectivity.

A more contemporary scholar like Rene Girard also tries to make connections between the violence we find in religion, particularly ancient, and events and structures in the world today. Girard is interested especially in the role of sacrifice in religion, whether of animal or human. His hypothesis is that "society is seeking to deflect upon a relatively indifferent victim, a 'sacrificeable' victim, the violence that would otherwise be vented

---

[3] Emile Durkheim, *The Elementary Forms of Religious Life*, trans. Karen E. Fields (New York: The Free Press, 1995) 320.
[4] Ibid., 321.

on its own members, the people it most desires to protect."[5] How does sacrifice do this? "The sacrifice serves to protect the entire community from *its own* violence," Girard writes, "it prompts the entire community to choose victims outside itself. The elements of dissension scattered throughout the community are drawn to the person of the sacrificial victim and eliminated, at least temporarily, by its sacrifice."[6] Any community necessarily will have tensions among its members. By directing negative emotions and energy onto the shoulders of the sacrificial victim, the "scapegoat," members of the community are able to overcome those negative emotions and energy through the ritualized killing of the victim.

Girard's conclusions clearly have roots in religious life. Indeed, for Girard, violence and the sacred are "inseparable."[7] Put more strongly, "the operations of violence and the sacred are ultimately the same process."[8] The purpose of religion is to prevent "reciprocal violence."[9] This continuous retaliation is the never-ending cycle of violence, which eventually will destroy a society. Thus, instead of providing an unending cycle of real victims of violence, societies develop sacrificial rituals in which surrogate victims suffer the violence of the community. Since these rituals are grounded in religious institutions and settings, it is clear that religion is central to the development and preservation of social life. Girard concludes:

> It should now be apparent that humanity's very existence is due primarily to the operation of the surrogate victim. We know that animals possess individual braking mechanisms against violence; animals of the same species never fight to the death, but the victor spares the life of the vanquished. Mankind lacks this protection. Our substitution for the biological mechanism of the

---

[5] Rene Girard, *Violence and the Sacred*, trans. Patrick Gregory (Baltimore MD: Johns Hopkins University Press, 1977) 4.

[6] Ibid., 8.

[7] Ibid., 19.

[8] Ibid., 258.

[9] Ibid., 55.

animals is the collective, cultural mechanism of the surrogate victim. There is no society without religion because without religion society cannot exist.[10]

Ritual, clearly, is central to Girard's theorizing. The function of ritual, as we may have surmised by now, is "to 'purify' violence; that is, to 'trick' violence into spending itself on victims whose death will provoke no reprisals."[11] In other words, "the objective of ritual is the proper reenactment of the surrogate-victim mechanism; its function is to perpetuate or renew the effects of this mechanism; that is, to keep violence *outside* the community."[12] Girard looks across time and cultures to find ritualized behavior that supports his thesis. One of the most common rituals in which the surrogate-victim mechanism is operative is the festival. The festival will include a variety of behaviors that affirm the social norms via the ritualized practice of breaking those norms. In other words, by permitting *only through ritual practice* what is otherwise prohibited, the norms of the society during everyday or profane times are affirmed for the members of the community. Girard writes, "Almost every society has festivals that have retained a ritualistic character over the centuries. Of particular interest to the modern inquirer are observances involving the deliberate violation of established laws; for example, celebrations in which sexual promiscuity is not only tolerated but prescribed or in which incest becomes the required practice."[13] Festivals also are the events in which the surrogate-victim mechanism is operative. While killing is normally prohibited, during the festival it is permitted—either literally or symbolically.

While most of the examples that Girard uses are from ancient times, he nevertheless affirms the role of sacrificial rituals in the formation of all societies and the continuing need for them. While Girard may insist that

---

[10] Ibid., 221.
[11] Ibid., 36.
[12] Ibid., 92.
[13] Ibid., 119.

Christianity is an exception to the rule, it is not hard to imagine how it might fit the model. One could argue that Christian churches regularly celebrate the sacrifice of a surrogate victim (Jesus) and engage in the ritual eating and drinking of his corporeal body (symbolically or, in the case of transubstantiation, literally). However, Girard believes that we more often than not are in a state of "sacrificial crisis." This crisis is a consequence of the disappearance of sacrificial rituals, preventing the society's ability to find or create a surrogate-victim and perpetrate its violence against that victim. Girard argues that "the disappearance of the sacrificial rites, coincides with the disappearance of the difference between impure violence and purifying violence. When this difference has been effaced, purification is no longer possible and impure, contagious, reciprocal violence spreads throughout the community."[14] When all violence is condemned, then we are incapable of ritually affirming violence through the surrogate-victim mechanism. The consequence, ironically, is an increase in non-ritualized violence (including vendetta) throughout the society. This is why, Girard writes, "[s]acrifice is the boon worthy above all others of being preserved, celebrated and memorialized, reiterated and reenacted in a thousand different forms, for it alone can prevent transcendental violence from turning back into reciprocal violence, the violence that really hurts, setting man against man and threatening the total destruction of the community."[15] Thus, sacrificial rituals are an effective way to prevent sacrificial crises and thus guard societies against excessive violence.

While sacrifice and promiscuity may be stereotypical aspects of festivals, so too is play. Durkheim argues that games originated in a religious context.[16] Games or play also give rise to collective effervescence.[17] Play, for Girard, is an expression of the sacred. It is another means by which genuine violence is avoided by virtue of the ritualized nature of the play itself. Girard states, "We must subordinate play to religion, and in

---

[14] Ibid., 49.

[15] Ibid., 124–25.

[16] Durkheim, *Elementary Forms*, 385.

[17] Ibid.

particular to the sacrificial crisis. Play has a religious origin, to be sure, insofar as it reproduces certain aspects of the sacrificial crisis. The arbitrary nature of the prize makes it clear that the contest has no other objective than itself, but this contest is regulated in such a manner that, in principle at least, it can never degenerate into a brutal fight to the finish."[18] The play may be rough and even violent at times. There even is a victim in the form of the losers. But play never gives itself over to unwarranted violence or reciprocal violence. The rules of the ritual prohibit this possibility.

With this consideration of play, the directions we might go in interpreting football in light of this theory should be clear. Religion has an element of violence in it. Play originates in or at least is related to religion. Football is play, but also ritualized violence. In many locales, including major and not-so-major universities throughout the South, this ritual is performed in the context of a festival, one characterized by the violation of norms that indeed affirms those norms for more profane times. For example, while many people on game day drink alcoholic beverages publicly on the grounds of the university (sometimes to great excess), they would be escorted off campus or even arrested if they consumed alcohol in the same place at other times. In this case, the exception (being allowed to drink publicly on campus) affirms the rule (no public consumption of alcohol on campus).

The game itself entails violent confrontations between players but controlled violence nonetheless. Michael Novak argues that the controlled conflict "ventilates" our rage.[19] "The human animal suffers enormous daily violence," he adds. "Football is an attempt to harness violence, to formalize it, to confine it within certain canonical limits, and then to release it in order to wrest from it a measure of wit, beauty, and redemption."[20]

---

[18] Girard, *Violence*, 154.

[19] Michael Novak, *The Joy of Sports: Endzones, Bases, Baskets, Balls, and the Consecration of the American Spirit*, rev. ed. (Lanham MD: Madison Books, 1994) 84.

[20] Ibid., 94.

There also is sacrifice in football. This sacrifice is not only the "surrogate" or loser of the contest, but the players themselves. As Novak notes:

> Once an athlete accepts the uniform, he is in effect donning priestly vestments. It is the function of priests to offer sacrifices. As at the Christian Mass, in athletics the priest is also the victim: he who offers and he who is offered are one and the same. Often the sacrifice is literal: smashed knees, torn muscles, injury-abbreviated careers. Always the sacrifice is ritual: the athlete bears the burden of identification. He is no longer living his own life only.[21]

Examples of sacrifices abound. In 2004, Tyrone Prothro, a star receiver for Alabama, suffered a catastrophic career-threatening compound fracture in his leg. Multiple surgeries later, it still is unclear whether or not he will ever play again. In 2006, Tennessee was hit hard by a number of devastating injuries. Defensive back Inquoris Johnson suffered a shoulder injury, including extensive nerve damage. Even after multiple surgeries, including one at the famous Mayo Clinic, there is doubt about a return to football. Defensive lineman Justin Harrell suffered a torn bicep and then delayed surgery so he could play in one more home game. Many Tennessee players had post-season surgeries performed, including seven players on a single day. As Novak concludes, "Football dramatizes the sacrifice, discipline, and inner rage of collective behavior"[22]—sacrifice, discipline, and rage that Girard would find to be fundamentally religious. As Howard Slusher insists, "Sacrifice is of great import to the sport scene and let no one be naïve in believing it does not appeal to the 'religious in man.'"[23]

---

[21] Ibid., 141.

[22] Ibid., 207.

[23] Howard Slusher, "Sport and the Religious," in *Religion and Sport: The Meeting of Sacred and Profane*, ed. Charles Prebish (Westport CT: Greenwood Press, 1993) 184.

Higgs and Braswell are critical of the linking of religion and that which is sacred with violence—and especially critical of Girard. While there indeed may be a link, they argue that the relation between religion and violence is only one part of religion and certainly not the most important part. They conclude that "there are only these two types of religion—(1) the religion of the sacred, with rituals built around stories of sacrifice and preparation for engagement in war or sports and (2) the religion of the holy, emphasizing prayer, meditation, cultivation of the land, caring for the sick, and observance of shepherd principles."[24] It is this latter form of religion that, for Higgs and Braswell, is religion at its best. However, while acknowledging that in modern times we generally do not kill the losers in our athletic contests, Higgs and Braswell concede that "we still require sacrifices of all kinds for our tribal teams, asking athletes in effect to waive or at least delay an education and to play while hurt, and firing losing coaches when they don't 'produce' as if they were farmers under contract."[25] Girard, indeed, may be on to something, something that is relevant to our investigation of the meaning of football.

The Appeal of Sports Violence

"Since the earliest times," Michael Mandelbaum writes, "from gladiatorial contests in ancient Rome to public hangings in early modern England to boxing in the nineteenth and twentieth centuries—not to mention Hollywood movies of the twenty-first—staged events with violence at their core have commanded public attention."[26] Several questions emerge in our recognition of this historical fact of life. What does this trend tell us about college football? Is it its "staged violence" that gives it its vast appeal? And what is it, precisely, that the spectator gets out of witnessing such a violent spectacle?

---

[24] Higgs and Braswell, *Unholy Alliance*, 139.

[25] Ibid., 164.

[26] Michael Mandelbaum, *The Meaning of Sports: Why Americans Watch Baseball, Football, and Basketball and What They See When They Do* (New York: PublicAffairs, 2004) 176–77.

Everyone seems to be in agreement that the catharsis theory of sports violence is not sufficient. The catharsis theory suggests that the violence we engage in or watch in sports relieves us of our excessive violent urges and thus allows us to function better psychologically and certainly socially. Higgs argues that explanations like the catharsis theory may help to explain the "ubiquity" of sports, but they do not explain "the reverence paid to them."[27] Michael Oriard insists that the catharsis theory may not be wrong, but it at least is "oversimplified."[28] Higgs and Oriard are neither social scientists nor psychologists, but their conclusions are supported by researchers who are. Wann and his colleagues note that "there is virtually no empirical evidence validating the existence of catharsis in sport.... The 'blowing off steam' theory of sport spectating may be attractive, but it is quite inaccurate."[29] John H. Kerr likewise is suspicious of a catharsis theory of sports violence, insisting that there is little experimental evidence to support it.[30]

These perspectives (especially those from Wann et al. and Kerr) would seem to contradict Girard and the application of this theory either to religion or sport. Girard's work seems to rely upon some notion of a catharsis theory in which the sacrificial victim relieves us of the violence we otherwise would commit against one another. But note that the catharsis theory is not completely and conclusively discredited. In fact, Kerr urges a reconceptualization of the theory. With regard to sport, he asks, "Might it not be better to think of catharsis in a wider sense, not limited to just aggression and hostility, but as a form of emotional or psychological

---

[27] Robert J. Higgs, *God in the Stadium: Sports & Religion in America* (Lexington KY: University of Kentucky Press, 1995) 97.

[28] Michael Oriard, *Reading Football: How the Popular Press Created an American Spectacle* (Chapel Hill: University of North Carolina Press, 1993) 6.

[29] Daniel L. Wann, Merrill J. Melnick, Gordon W. Russell, Dale G. Pease, *Sports Fans: The Psychology and Social Impact of Spectators* (New York: Routledge, 2001) 198.

[30] John H. Kerr, *Rethinking Aggression and Violence in Sport* (New York: Routledge, 2005) 124.

purging, which might include a more complete palette of emotions within the whole experience of being a spectator or fan?"[31]

Kerr argues for a more comprehensive psychological understanding of sports violence than simply a catharsis theory, though his understanding certainly can accommodate that theory as well. Kerr notes that contemporary life, at least in Europe and the United States, is not very exciting. In other words, the range of emotions, especially at the highest or most pleasant end, is fairly narrow. Consequently, "People have to actively seek out thrills and vicarious risk-taking through, for example, watching sports."[32] Anyone watching a crowd at a major sporting event can witness the intensity of the emotions that many fans experience. Fans attain high levels of arousal, and this intense experience is a "pleasant excitement,"[33] which is particularly true with violent sports. Kerr concludes that "watching violent sports produces increases in levels of arousal, and…people deliberately watch to achieve elevated arousal."[34]

The question remains, is such arousal good or bad for us? The flip side of the catharsis theory—that participating in or watching violence prevents violence in other contexts—is that participating in or watching violent sports spurs people to act violently in other contexts. This argument is similar to ones made about violence on television or in the movies; that is, that such violence encourages others, especially children, to act violently. Higgs, for example, tries to connect violence in sports with aggression or violence towards women in America.[35] Along with Braswell, they argue that sports initiate a cycle of violence or aggression. "[I]nstead of ventilating aggression," they claim, sports "refuel it so that a loss or setback in sports as in war is a call for stronger retaliation. In the Church of Sports, there is no answer to this that we can see, only rivalry, revenge, and

---

[31] Ibid., 129.
[32] Ibid., 118.
[33] Ibid., 98.
[34] Ibid., 118.
[35] Higgs, *God in the Stadium*, 320–22.

redemption from season to season."[36] While such retaliation usually is contained within the context of the rules of the game, there are instances in which the violence of a sport spills into the stands, leading to physical confrontations between players and fans or between rival fans. Kerr's work recounts many of these instances, including some, such as soccer hooliganism in Europe, that have led to the deaths of non-participants.

However, it may not be that the violence between players and fans or among fans is a consequence of the violence on the field. A possible alternative explanation may have to do with the very nature of group formations, an explanation explored in chapter six. For now, it is worth noting, as Kerr does, that the research is split on the issue of the connection between violence in various forms of entertainment (sports may be included) and among those who participate in or view them. Thus, Kerr concludes that the "popular wisdom which suggests media violence and media sports violence has harmful effects on people, especially where those viewers are young children, may not be correct."[37] So if sports violence perhaps does us no harm, does it do any good? The answer for Kerr is affirmative. The "pleasant excitement" of violent sports can be an important part of our overall psychological health. Thus, he concludes that "there are situations where certain types of aggressive and violent acts are central to people's enjoyment of activities. These activities range from athletic contests to viewing violent sports as a spectator, or watching violent sports movies. Being a part of these activities does no psychological harm to the vast majority of those who participate and may actually benefit their psychological health."[38] The argument that participating in or watching violence produces a psychological good may go a long way to explaining why violence has been such an integral part of our games, sports, and religion through the centuries.

---

[36] Higgs and Braswell, *Unholy Alliance*, 107.

[37] Kerr, *Rethinking Aggression*, 130.

[38] Ibid., 148.

Higgs argues that violence in sports has long been a part of American history. The American frontier, for example, was a place where violence was simply a part of life—including sports and games.[39] But long after the frontier was conquered and closed, violence in sports has continued to be integral to American history, and this persistence can be seen in the close relationship between sports and American militarism. Higgs traces the ways in which military training, physical education, and combative sports coalesced in American higher education in the twentieth century.[40] He and Braswell note that we also see the strong connection between sports and militarism in the fact that so many stadia are named in honor of American soldiers.[41] They conclude that the model for the American athlete has never been the shepherd, that is, the religious (nurturing, pacific, loving) model, but the knight, representing the military (conquering, violent, triumphant) model.

Other observers and commentators on sports in American life also have noted how violence serves as a common thread in the American experience. William Dean argues that violence in football is "the *sine qua non* of the game."[42] Like Higgs, Dean sees sports and football in particular as intimately bound with American history and culture. "Violence came to play this central role in the history of football," Dean writes, "because America's own story made the game a ritual of conquest, undertaken by people who lacked an ancient culture and who saw themselves as improvising a civilization in a dangerous wilderness."[43] Michael Mandelbaum not only ties football into American military culture and the Cold War, a period during which, for example, professional football came

---

[39] Higgs, *God in the Stadium*, 60.

[40] Ibid., 212.

[41] Higgs and Braswell, *Unholy Alliance*, 47.

[42] William Dean, *The American Spiritual Culture: And the Invention of Jazz, Football and the Movies* (New York: Continuum, 2003) 148.

[43] Ibid., 153.

to particular prominence,[44] but also to the process of industrialization. "Football is the sport of the machine age because football teams are like machines," he writes, "with specialized moving parts that must function simultaneously. Players are like workers in a factory."[45]

In short, the United States has become, over the course of the twentieth century, the most militarized and, some might say, militant nation. This development has gone hand-in-hand with rapid and unprecedented industrialization. Americans have been driven by a desire to be first in everything—economy, industry, technology, and military power. Mandelbaum even argues that contemporary Americans are "the most competitive people since the ancient Greeks."[46] It is little wonder that football, an intensely competitive and violent, militaristic game, would become so immensely popular.

Oriard, one of the most insightful scholars writing on the cultural history of American football, recognizes the integral role that violence plays in the sport:

> [Football is] the dramatic confrontation of artistry with violence, both equally necessary. The receiver's balletic moves and catch would not impress us nearly as much if the possibility of annihilation were not real; the violence of the collision would be gratuitous, pointless, if it did not threaten something valuable and important. The violence, in fact, partially creates the artistry: the simple act of catching a thrown ball becomes a marvelous achievement only in defiance of the brutal blow. Football becomes contact ballet.[47]

It is the violence and aggression of football that makes it a "manly sport." The ruggedness and aggressiveness of football was critical to its

---

[44] Mandelbaum, *Meaning of Sports*, 128, 141, 184–85.
[45] Ibid., 120.
[46] Ibid., 30.
[47] Oriard, *Reading Football*, 1–2.

adoption and success in the American context. In the late nineteenth century, mechanization and industrialization, the closing of the frontier, and a general increase in leisure time made "physical prowess" less and less relevant.[48] Football became the medium through which physical prowess could be inculcated and displayed. Of course, violent excesses were a concern, especially given a set of rules, or lack thereof, that promoted uncontrolled brute force. "The outcry against football brutality was great," Oriard writes, "but concern over the possibility of an emasculated American manhood greater; football was saved not by eliminating violence but by compromising on an acceptable degree of physical danger."[49] Violence in this case would not be a matter of catharsis or even sacrifice, but a rite of passage designed to usher young men into the rough-and-tumble world of adulthood.

Of course, not everyone can "make the team" or is "cut out" for even the controlled violence of football today, but everyone—participant or spectator—can share in the expression of that violence. "Contemporary life is…not very exciting," Kerr reminds us, "and people have to actively seek out thrills and vicarious risk-taking through, for example, watching sports."[50] The preeminent sport in the United States for thrills and risk-taking, even to the point of endangering life and limb, is football.

Conclusion

In later chapters, we will consider the potentially unique role that violence and aggression in football play in the context of the American South, but for now, we can see that violence and aggression have been expressed through human cultures, beginning perhaps with religion and continuing through today in a cultural form like sport, for millennia. This predilection toward violence does not simply mean that individuals always have been violent. Of course they have. The point is that violence always

---

[48] Ibid., 190.
[49] Ibid., 191.
[50] Kerr, *Rethinking Aggression*, 118.

has been embraced and controlled socially, and that this acceptance has served certain purposes, whether those be the scapegoating of the surrogate victim or the euphoria of vicarious "risk taking."

Novak reminds us that football "makes conscious to me part of what I am."[51] Whether I like it or not, part of what I am (perhaps more so as a male) is a creature who uses physical prowess, who uses violence, and whose existence is defined in part by an uncomfortable relationship and compromise with violence and aggression. Football is a "revelatory liturgy," Novak explains. "It externalizes the warfare in our hearts and offers us a means of knowing ourselves and wresting some grace from our true natures."[52] We might not always want to know of our violent and aggressive selves, but at least some cultural creations can turn that violence and aggression into something that has some merit and some beauty. Football, perhaps, is such a thing. It is, as Oriard describes it, "contact ballet."

---

[51] Novak, *Joy of Sports*, xx.
[52] Ibid., 96.

4

Ecstasy, Joy, and Sorrow:
The Experience of Southern College Football

It should be clear by now that sports, especially college football in the South, elicit powerful emotions among fans. With regard to college football in the South, renowned college football analyst Tony Barnhart writes that Southerners have formed an "emotional bond with college football that I have not seen in any other part of the country or with any other sport."[1] But what are these emotions? Are they similar to those of a religious experience? How is the experience of the fan comparable to the experience of the religious adherent? Or can we talk about some kind of identity between the two?

Michael Novak claims that "sports are at their heart a spiritual activity, a natural religion, a tribute to grace, beauty, and excellence."[2] Football, for example, can "touch you deeply, and to probe further and further in the depths of your psyche, you will find that it can go far more deeply than you ever had imagined."[3] But what do Novak and others mean when they say that sports are a "spiritual activity"? What are these emotions to which Barnhart and others refer? In my survey of college football fans in the South, conducted during the 2005 and 2006 seasons, I asked participants to provide words that described the game-day experience for them. Some of the words may or may not have religious connotations. For example, participants described the experience as fun, great, entertaining, drunk,

---

[1] Tony Barnhart, *Southern Fried Football: The History, Passion, and Glory of the Great Southern Game* (Chicago: Triumph Books, 2000) xiii.

[2] Michael Novak, *The Joy of Sports: Endzones, Bases, Baskets, Balls, and the Consecration of the American Spirit*, rev. ed. (Lanham MD: Madison Books, 1994) 346.

[3] Ibid., 87.

utter chaos, and "better than sex." Whether or not these make any sense in a religious context probably depends on what kind of religion one practices. But other terms were provided that easily could be used, and, in fact, stereotypically have been used, to describe religious experience. Friendship, fellowship, and community were used forty times out of a total of 225 surveys completed. These certainly are positive terms used to describe religious organizations, rituals, or institutions. The following words were also used frequently: excitement or exciting (forty-six times), tradition (seventeen times), awe-inspiring or awesome (fifteen times), and passion or intensity (eleven times). Even terms like spirit (three times), love (four times), hope (once), godliness (once), heaven (once), and energy (twice) were used. Interestingly, the concept of ineffability was expressed on eight surveys. In other words, some fans found that no words could adequately describe the experience they have on game days. Ineffability is a common (non-)descriptor of mystical religious experiences. Indeed, ineffability is considered by some to be constitutive of a genuine religious experience. In other words, if one is able to describe a religious experience then what one is describing is not it. The religious experience, according to this characteristic, is necessarily of a transcendent content, beyond what our senses can tell us, beyond our cognition, and beyond anything we can imagine and thus describe.

More than half of the respondents used at least one religious or possibly religious descriptor to explain the game-day experience. While the use of these descriptors may be simply a matter of their ready availability, their use seems particularly significant given the deeply religious context of the fans. No region of the United States is more religious than the South, which often is equated with the "Bible Belt." Any number of surveys and polls indicate that Southerners are more likely to attend church on a regular basis than other Americans and hold stereotypically religious beliefs (see the next chapter for more details). Given this context, it is reasonable to imagine that many Southerners would be hesitant to use any potentially religious expressions to describe the game-day experience. To do so would be blasphemy. Indeed, in numerous interviews with fans, I noticed this hesitancy. After explaining the hypothesis driving my research—that is, that college football functions religiously for many people in the South—fans expressed their agreement with the hypothesis "in theory" but refused to really embrace it. They seemed to understand the argument but psychologically could not assent to it.

In sum, Southern fans identified their game-day experience as emotionally positive and powerful. They often used religious or possibly religious descriptors to express how they experienced college football. When asked to rank a number of aspects of their lives (family, friends, church, work, hobbies, et cetera), fans ranked football immediately behind church as the place where they have "the deepest and most positive emotional experiences." Given the importance of religion in the lives of many Southerners, the survey information at a minimum is suggestive of the power and importance of college football in the lives of these fans. Certainly, religion is more than emotional experiences, and not all religious experiences are "deep or positive." But religious emotions are significant in the lives of many people, and to make the case that college football in the South or any sport functions religiously, one would need to show that the emotions of the fans are the same as or at least akin to what typically are considered to be religious emotions. Such emotions (for example, joy and fellow feeling) and the intensity of these emotions often are found in religious contexts, and they differ from everyday emotional experiences.

More extensive descriptions of the game-day experience confirm that the emotional experience associated with being a college football fan in the South is not like any other experience. In fact, one might even say that it is qualitatively greater than our everyday experiences. For instance, one Alabama fan writes, "Put simply, Alabama football has not, is not, and never will be just a game. It's much, much more. It's a way of life. You are born with it, you die with it, and your happiness during those moments in between greatly depends on it."[4] Another Alabama fan observes, "I guess

---

[4] Kevin Turner, "Some Things Never Change," in *Tales of the Tide: A Book by Alabama Fans...For Alabama Fans*, ed. Clint Lovette and Jarrod Bazemore (Birmingham AL: FANtastic Memories, 2004) 81.

it's similar to church—sometimes you don't really choose who to be for—you just are. For me, there was no moment of conversion. I was born into an Alabama family, and for that I'm thankful to this day."[5] For this fan, being an Alabama fan became intricately bound with his other more common religious beliefs (for example, in God) and practices (specifically, prayer). In the weeks leading up to the national championship game between Alabama and Miami at the conclusion of the 1992 season, he began to pray each night for five Alabama players. Each night it was a different group of five players, and by the day of the game, he had been able to pray for all the players on the team. Alabama won the national championship. The fan concludes, "After the game, I thanked God for allowing us to beat Miami. I was overjoyed when we brought the national championship back to Alabama. In some way, I felt like I had helped. I felt like I was a part of the Alabama family, and felt like God had smiled upon us."[6]

Of course, seasons do not always end in championships. In fact, sometimes entire seasons can be great disappointments to fans. The 2005 season was particularly disastrous for the University of Tennessee. Not only did they finish the season with a losing record, including a shocking home loss to Vanderbilt, a perennial doormat in the conference, it also was the first time since 1989 that the team failed to make it to a bowl game. One Tennessee fan writes:

> During [the 2005] season…it literally put me in a mild state of depression for the entire fall—and I wasn't totally aware of it until my wife brought it up. I realized at that point that I probably take it a little seriously. However, given the fact I have such a deep connection to Knoxville and the VOLS, there really is no other way, and I'd gladly trade the occasional anguish I feel for the good

---

[5] Al Davis Blanton, "A Prayer for the Tide," in *Tales of the Tide*, 121.
[6] Ibid., 123.

times. Moreover, the really good times are euphoric to say the least.[7]

This sense of euphoria is central to my effort to show how the emotional intensity associated with college football in the South can be compared to—even identified as—a religious experience. Warren St. John, in his wonderful account of Alabama fans, particularly those who travel and tailgate in their RVs, describes well this euphoria. After a game-winning touchdown, he writes that "joy engulfs us like a wave. That chamber of the psyche that houses our ancient tribal instincts is torn open, compelling thousands of strangers to embrace in a frenetic tumble. The glee is pure and uncomplicated."[8] He writes of the power and "mystery" of the experience. The euphoria and the way it brings people together in a common ecstatic state are described well in this passage about the hours after Alabama won a conference championship:

> Outside the stadium, I'm swept into a crowd of revelers, and we sing our way to a bar called Jocks & Jills; the name, like every thing we encounter, is also hilarious, but so is that stop sign, so is that drunk person, so is that nondescript office building over there. There's nothing that's not utterly wickedly wackily funny. A hip-hop mix throbs. The patio is now a dance floor. And we dance—hundreds of us, all with beer bottles in our hands, swaying and commingling like the tentacles of anemone in a brisk current. The air is cool and clean, a beautiful late-autumn night in the South so perfect as to seem custom ordered from heaven. The women, all their pretty Southern pretense having left them sometime in the middle of the third quarter, twirl and shout. Wild tangles of hair brush unexpectedly against my face.[9]

---

[7] Tennessee fan, e-mail message to author, 30 August 2006.

[8] Warren St. John, *Rammer Jammer Yellow Hammer: A Journey into the Heart of Fan Mania* (New York: Crown Publishers, 2004) 230.

[9] Ibid., 263.

St. John's account indicates the centrality of community in the experience of the Southern college football fan and reminds us of the importance of community in many religious experiences. In the survey data that I collected in a variety of locales, Southern college football fans ranked their game-day experience as one where they experienced a significant sense of community. College football ranked behind family and friends in regard to where those surveyed experienced the greatest sense of community. But forty-eight percent of the respondents ranked college football *ahead* of church with regard to where they experience the greatest sense of community. If a central function of the religious experience is the construction of community and a sense of belongingness, it would appear that college football in the South might be religious in the same way in which church is.

My point is not that the survey data prove that Southern college football fans have religious experiences. My point is that the survey data and the way fans describe the experience are such that one might assume that they are having religious experiences as a consequence of their participation in Southern college football rituals. Still, when St. John describes a certain euphoric moment as an Alabama fan as a "near-religious experience,"[10] we must ask: Is it a "near" religious experience or is it *in actuality* a religious experience?

Defining Religious Experience

Determining whether or not participation in sports, whether as an athlete or fan, can be a religious experience necessitates first defining what a religious experience is. This task is much easier said than done. Defining what religion is can be tough enough. Religion certainly is not merely a kind of emotional experience. Religion involves institutions, doctrines, material culture, actions (rituals, for instance), and much more. Religious experience is but one aspect of religion. But how can we define the

---

[10] Ibid., 185.

subjective characteristics of this experience? Is it an impossible task? Perhaps. Nevertheless, human beings do have experiences that they identify as religious or spiritual, and though the task is daunting, we should not be deterred from giving up on theorizing about these experiences.

In the nineteenth century, theologians and scholars of religion started to identify feeling or emotion as that which was most characteristic of religion. Wayne Proudfoot argues that this identification primarily occurred for two reasons. First, it was thought that feelings or emotions are more grounded in the lived experience of adherents than is doctrine. Feelings or emotions are more powerful than dogma. Second, the move to feeling or emotion helped to avoid a rationalist critique of religion. At least since the Enlightenment, religious doctrine had been subject to powerful philosophical criticism. Indeed, in the nineteenth century and continuing into the twentieth, many intellectuals predicted and still predict the demise of religion as individuals and whole societies become more rational. Religious doctrines, it is thought, will be seen as erroneous and/or superstitious, and no reasonable person will continue to affirm them. But reason often reaches a certain limitation when confronted with feeling or emotion. At the very least, feeling or emotion do not seem subject to the same level of rational critique as does doctrine.[11] A person's beliefs may be susceptible to being proven wrong, but we cannot say a person's feelings or emotions are wrong, at least not in the same sense.

Christian theologians like Friedrich Schleiermacher (late eighteenth and early nineteenth centuries) and Rudolf Otto (first half of the twentieth century), whose interests included the more general study of religion as well, were instrumental in moving the study of religion in this theoretical direction. Schleiermacher urges his educated readers to avoid the troubles found in conflicting doctrines and dogmas and instead "direct your attention solely toward the inner stirrings, moods, and dispositions to

---

[11] Wayne Proudfoot, *Religious Experience* (Berkeley: University of California Press, 1985) 75–78.

which the utterances of divinely inspired men and their deeds attest."[12] Schleiermacher argues, "The contemplation of pious men is only the *immediate consciousness* of the *universal being* of all finite things in and through the *infinite*, of all temporal things in and through the *eternal*. To seek and to find this *infinite* and *eternal* factor in all that lives and moves, in all growth and change, in all action and passion, and to have to know life itself only in *immediate feeling*—that is religion."[13] Otto likewise highlights feelings or emotions. He is critical of the "bias of rationalization" not only in theology but in comparative religion as well.[14] He describes religious feelings or emotions with concepts like awe, energy, and mystery as constitutive of religious experience. These terms already have come up in our review of Southerners' descriptions of their experience of college football. In the religious context, Otto argues that these feelings or emotions are "immediate" or arise "spontaneously" when the person encounters the divine, however conceived.[15]

William James, the early twentieth-century philosopher and psychologist, also emphasized the subjective experience of religious phenomena as central to the study of religion. His *Varieties of Religious Experience* is a seminal work in the typology of religious experience. In it, he describes religion not in terms of doctrines or institutions, but as "*the feelings, acts, and experiences of individual men in their solitude, so far as they apprehend themselves to stand in relation to whatever they may consider the divine.*"[16] Likewise, in works like *The Sacred & the Profane: The Nature of Religion*, the twentieth-century historian of religion Mircea Eliade very

---

[12] Friedrich Schleiermacher, *On Religion: Addresses in Response to Its Cultured Critics*, trans. Terence N. Tice (Richmond VA: John Knox Press, 1969) 58.

[13] Ibid., 79 (emphasis mine).

[14] Rudolf Otto, *The Idea of the Holy: An Inquiry into the Non-Rational Factor in the Idea of the Divine and Its Relation to the Rational*, trans. John W. Harvey (New York: Oxford University Press, 1958) 3.

[15] Ibid., 10, 11.

[16] William James, *The Varieties of Religious Experience* (New York: Collier Books, 1961) 42 (emphasis original).

much emphasizes subjective experience. In his phenomenology of religion, he argues for the qualitatively greater experience associated with the sacred as opposed to what is associated with the profane.

In our day, Proudfoot offers a compelling critique of this historical and theoretical development in the study of religion. He finds that many of the approaches to understanding religious experience simply protect that experience against rational investigation and criticism. They are "protective strategies" rather than coherent accounts of religious experience. Consequently, these approaches fail philosophically. Take, for example, Proudfoot's critique of Schleiermacher—one that can be (and is) extended to other theorists as well.

Schleiermacher describes religious experience as an immediate apprehension of the divine or religious object or being. By making the religious experience immediate, Schleiermacher preserves it against the argument that it is the "idea" or "thought" of the divine that causes the experience. If this experience is "immediate," that means that it is *not* "mediated" by concepts or ideas—by cognition. We then cannot say that the divine is *merely* an "idea" or "thought" and thus has no external reality, or, at least, following Kant, that we cannot know that reality. Religious consciousness, according to Proudfoot's reading of Schleiermacher, "is both intentional, in that it is directed toward the infinite as its object, and immediate. It is not dependent on concepts or beliefs, yet it can be specified only by reference to the concept of the whole or the infinite."[17] Such a move, however, is impossible. "If the feeling is intentional," Proudfoot writes, "it cannot be specified apart from reference to its object and thus it cannot be independent of thought."[18] In other words, Schleiermacher "defends the incoherent thesis that the religious consciousness is both independent of thought and can only be identified by reference to concepts and beliefs."[19] He cannot have it both ways. Either religious experience is truly immediate—that is, not mediated by

---

[17] Proudfoot, *Religious Experience*, 11.

[18] Ibid., 11.

[19] Ibid., 18.

thought—in which case it becomes hard to identify it vis-à-vis an intentional object, or it is indeed mediated by thought, in which case it is not immediate and thus open to philosophical critique.

There are at least two key points that come out of Proudfoot's critique of Schleiermacher—again, points that can be extended to subsequent theorists who attempt, either explicitly or implicitly, to protect religious experience from critical inquiry. First, Proudfoot makes the point that religious language is both expressive and formative of experience. Religious language may describe an experience but the words and ideas that we associate with religious language also cause or at least shape the experience itself. Thus, Proudfoot argues that religious language "is not only the expressive, receptive medium Schleiermacher takes it to be. It also plays a very active and formative role in religious experience."[20] The second, related point is that it is illegitimate to separate religious feeling or emotion (in short, religious experience) from thought. Proudfoot admits that Schleiermacher "is correct to view primary religious language as the expression of a deeply entrenched moment of consciousness," but he is "incorrect to portray that moment as independent of thought and belief. Schleiermacher has mistaken a felt sense of immediacy for a guarantee that piety is not formed or shaped by thought or inference."[21]

The question of the cognitive status of feelings or emotions is critical and deserves more of our attention here. Take the example of anger. Anger is not an immediate emotional experience, unmediated by thought. How do we know when someone is angry? It certainly is not because we empathically feel what the individual is feeling. We ascribe anger to a person based on the visible evidence, based on how he or she is reacting. Often, this evaluation will include our interpretation of the actions relative to our understanding of the entire context in which the person is acting. Frank seems agitated, and I interpret that as anger because I know his boss has just told him that he will not be receiving a raise this year. In short,

---

[20] Ibid., 40.
[21] Ibid., 36.

my ascription of anger to someone is a consequence of my reflection about all sorts of pieces of evidence provided to me. What is even more interesting is that our self-ascription of anger is very similar. As Proudfoot argues, "I don't appeal to private inner states in ascribing emotions to myself any more than I do in ascribing them to others. I often come to know what I am feeling by interpreting physiological changes or my behavior in exactly the same way in which another might interpret them if the data were available to him."[22] Coming out of a meeting with my boss, I may notice that my heart is racing and my teeth are clenched. These physiological changes alone are not enough for me to determine that I am angry. Certainly they can contribute to such a determination, but I will come to ascribe anger to myself by interpreting the situation, realizing that my boss is a jerk, and that I have been completely screwed by him. Indeed, I may not even realize that I am angry based just on increased heart rate and clenched teeth. I may not notice these physiological changes at all. To that extent, the physiological changes alone do not constitute anger. Only when interpreted and understood within a context of perceived sleight, injury, et cetera, can we connect these physiological changes to the feeling or emotion of anger. The word "anger" is not merely a description of our experience but is an interpretation of it. Proudfoot concludes that emotion words "are employed, not as simple descriptions of bodily changes, behavior, or dispositions to behave, but as interpretations and explanations of those phenomena."[23] Even more, the interpretation is constitutive of the very experience.

But what does this example of anger have to do with religious experience? The point here is not that religious experience has much to do with anger, but that religious experience gives rise to certain emotions and that, like anger, these emotions are experienced as religious in part because those who experience them interpret them that way. Those who experience these religious emotions also interpret and understand the situation in such

---

[22] Ibid., 92–93.
[23] Ibid., 93.

a way that one reasonably would ascribe religious content or character to the emotions being experienced. There is not some magical religious experience that is unconnected to thought and context. We have religious experiences because we are in situations where we expect to have them and/or we interpret and understand our emotional state through religious concepts and systems.

Proudfoot's turn to the psychological research of Stanley Schachter may further clarify the line of argument. Schachter's experiments confirm that physiological changes alone are not clear indicators of particular emotions or feelings. In other words, the same physiological changes may be interpreted in different ways depending on the person who is experiencing them and the context in which they occur. What is the relevance of Schachter's work for Proudfoot's interest in religious experience and for our own concerns here? "Given the results of Schachter's experiments," Proudfoot concludes, "it seems quite plausible that at least some religious experiences are due to physiological changes for which the subject adopts a religious explanation."[24] Thus, if understood in the same way that we should understand other emotions or feelings, the physiological changes (the felt experience) of the religious experience are, in fact, religious to the extent that they are interpreted religiously.

This understanding of what constitutes an experience is critical to Proudfoot's distinction between descriptive and explanatory reduction in the study of religious experience. Descriptive reduction is "the failure to identify an emotion, practice, or experience under the description by which the subject identifies it. This is indeed unacceptable."[25] Proudfoot uses the example of a hiker seeing a bear in the woods, thus leading to an experience of fear in the hiker. As it turns out, it really was not a bear but a tree stump instead. It would be a case of descriptive reduction to claim that the hiker was in fear of a tree stump. The tree stump indeed was the object he saw, but he thought it was a bear. To say that he was afraid of a tree stump

---

[24] Ibid., 102.
[25] Ibid., 196.

would be to fail to make sense of the story. Still, it would not be wrong to say that the cause of his fear was a tree stump that looked to him, perhaps at a distance, through some fog or mist, like a bear. This would be explanatory reduction, "offering an explanation of an experience in terms that are not those of the subject and that might not meet with his approval. This is perfectly justifiable and is, in fact, normal procedure."[26] It might be the hiker refuses to believe that there was no bear and that what he really saw was a tree stump. I certainly am not obligated simply to accept his account of the experience, though, especially if I have strong evidence supporting the claim that what he saw really was a tree stump. In other words, I have to take him seriously when he says that he saw a bear and that this is what made him afraid, but I need not accept that as the final explanation of the event. Proudfoot concludes:

> Where it is the subject's experience which is the object of study, that experience must be identified under a description that can plausibly be attributed to him.... The explanation the analyst offers of that same experience is another matter altogether. It need not be couched in terms familiar or acceptable to the subject. It must be an explanation of the experience as identified under the subject's description, but the subject's approval of the explanation is not required.[27]

Proudfoot's analysis can be applied to religious experience in the following way. If a religious adherent claims to have had a religious experience of God's love, then any investigation of this experience must begin with the adherent's description. But a complete explanation of the experience may entail an account of the full context in which the experience occurred in order to more accurately identify the factors or causes that gave rise to the experience. For example, perhaps it was an emotionally taxing

---

[26] Ibid., 197.
[27] Ibid., 195.

period in the adherent's life. Maybe she was part of a prayer group that emphasized the experience of God's love during its communal activity. Maybe even she was on medication that fostered such loving emotions. Naturally, she might reject these latter explanations, but while we must begin with her description, we need not end with it. As Proudfoot argues, "To require that any explanation of a religious experience be one that would be endorsed by the subject is to block inquiry into the character of that experience."[28] In other words, if all I can do is to accept her description of the experience, then there is no room for any other explanation or even for an investigation of her experience in the first place.

There seems to be two possible directions to go from here. First, we could say that the experiences of the religious and sports fanatics very much could be the same but differ only in the explanations or interpretations. Or, second, because the pre-existing explanations or interpretations for potential experiences are different (between religious ones and sports), then the actual experiences come to be qualitatively different. In other words, if we interpret and understand an experience by looking through a theological or religious prism then—surprise!—we probably will not only think the experience is religious but *experience it that way.*

Proudfoot concludes that the "distinguishing mark of a religious experience is not the subject matter but the kind of explanation the subject believes is appropriate."[29] Another way of putting this is that it is not the content of the experience that defines it—increased heart rate, feelings of elation, forms of ecstasy, et cetera—but the explanation we give to that content. In the case of experiences surrounding the participation in sporting events, either as athlete or spectator, it very well could be the case that the participants have similar physiological and psychological experiences that religious practitioners have, but that the former are not having "religious" experiences because they simply do not label them that way, as do the latter. If, for example, the participants in the sporting event had a

---

[28] Ibid., 200.
[29] Ibid., 231.

different understanding of what religion is or what a religious experience is, perhaps they would be more likely to use the term "religious" to describe their experiences, meaning that those experiences legitimately could be considered religious.

The approach Proudfoot represents certainly opens up the experience of the sporting event to a deeper and more thorough investigation. There are other theorists whose work supports or is supported by such an approach. Mihaly Csikszentmihalyi champions the psychological concept of "flow," which involves the immersion of the individual psyche in an activity that is productive, creative, and personally valuable. Flow is "the state in which people are so involved in an activity that nothing else seems to matter; the experience itself is so enjoyable that people will do it even at great cost, for the sheer sake of doing it."[30] Flow experiences can occur in all sorts of activities, ranging from painting a picture to dancing to making a cabinet. They can occur in religious settings. They also can occur in sports. "Play, art, pageantry, ritual, and sports are some examples [of flow]," Csikszentmihalyi writes. "Because of the way they are constructed, they help participants and spectators achieve an ordered state of mind that is highly enjoyable."[31] He adds that in the sporting event, "players and spectators cease to act in terms of common sense, and concentrate instead on the peculiar reality of the game."[32] Thus, the flow experience is a universal characteristic of human beings that can occur in the art studio, the church, or the stadium, with these differing contexts shaping how we label it.

Howard Slusher argues, "Something of faith, something of peace, a touch of power, a feeling of right, a sense of the precarious—all of these and more is what the *real spirit* of sport *is*."[33] He acknowledges the mystical

---

[30] Mihaly Csikszentmihalyi, *Flow: The Psychology of Optimal Experience* (New York: HarperCollins, 1990) 4.

[31] Ibid., 72.

[32] Ibid.

[33] Howard Slusher, "Sport and the Religious," in *Religion and Sport: The Meeting of Sacred and Profane*, ed. Charles Prebish (Westport CT: Greenwood Press, 1993) 191 (emphasis original).

dimension of sport and religion, concluding that both "open man towards the acceptance and actualization of being."[34] Sociologist Harry Edwards and anthropologist Victor Turner both remind us that while the religious experience, be it in a church or stadium, happens to individuals, it nevertheless takes place in a communal context. For Edwards, sports provide us with a sense of belonging and an opportunity to foster and express powerful emotions.[35] The sense of belonging, of face-to-face encounter with others in a community, is what Turner calls *communitas*. It is an experience of the sacred or holy.[36] Again, this religious experience of communitas can happen in a variety of locales, from the church pew to the bleacher seat. The experience of communitas is universal; it is the same in both cases (the pew or the bleacher); it simply is labeled differently.

If, then, the content of the experience is similar—ecstasy, "flow," et cetera—but we simply label it differently, then it should not surprise us when people decide that it is appropriate and perhaps necessary to use religious language to more accurately describe the experience of the sporting event. Such was the case with the Southern college football fans I surveyed. Perhaps they have come to believe that the content of the experience is similar to, if not identical with, those experiences described by religious practitioners, like mystics.

It is important to remember, however, that Proudfoot makes a convincing case that our labels of experiences do not merely describe them but help to constitute them. Religious language is formative of experiences as well as expressive of them. There still might be something different about the religious experience—because it in part is constituted by religious concepts and ideas—that separates it from the often equally powerful experiences at the sporting event. But here we are pushed to our reflective limits, to the recognition that we now are probing psychological and existential areas where we cannot have anything close to definitive answers.

---

[34] Ibid.

[35] Harry Edwards, *Sociology of Sport* (Homewood IL: Dorsey Press, 1973) 242.

[36] Victor Turner, *The Ritual Process: Structure and Anti-Structure* (New York: Aldine De Gruyter, 1995) 128.

We also are left with a most intriguing question: If we came to conclude that the content of the religious and sporting experience is similar, and if we started to adopt the language of the former to describe the latter, would the latter soon be indistinguishable from the former, since both the content *and* interpretation of the experiences would be the same?

Conclusion

If nothing else, this chapter has indicated how difficult it is to define religious experience. Such is the case with subjective experiences. If the religious experience can be measured physiologically, by increased heart rate, blood pressure, or other bodily change, then we certainly could see such experiences in a variety of settings, stereotypically religious or not. While such physiological changes are part of the experience, there also is a cognitive experience as well. Is the cognitive aspect of religious experiences found in other experiences? It might seem that the answer is no. If I say that I have had an experience of God, it is hard to imagine my saying the same thing while at the stadium, though, according to my survey responses, that might not be so farfetched as it sounds. But in saying this, we beg the question, what does "God" mean? Emile Durkheim, for example, argues that God simply is a symbol for society itself—society's projection of itself into the heavens. If the religious adherent worships God and the sports spectator worships society, and society *is* God, then their experiences may be very similar if not identical.

In sum, we are left with good reason to expand our understanding of what we mean by religious experience or, at the very least, to be suspicious of definitions too narrowly circumscribed. Recognizing the role of interpretation in the constitution of experience opens up some epistemological space that allows for broader and more flexible understandings or definitions of religious experience. We may not have proven that sports provide opportunities for religious experiences, but at least we can see that a reasonable case can be made for such a conclusion. Perhaps we have good reason to take more seriously claims by observers and fans that game days at universities throughout the South are occasions for religious experiences.

5

From Lost Cause to Third-and-Long: College Football and the Civil Religion of the South

It often is said that the South was born with Robert E. Lee's surrender at Appomattox Courthouse in 1865. Defeat and surrender gave birth to the *idea* of the South. Defeat and surrender gave birth to the "Lost Cause," that amalgamation of ideas and beliefs, history and legend, that would define what the South meant for the years immediately after the war, through the twentieth century, and even today. The "cause," of course, was the defense of the Confederacy. Southerners (and unless otherwise noted, this generally means *white* Southerners) understood that the war was lost, though still they honored and memorialized the valor of those who fought. They blamed the Yankee victory on the vicious and arbitrary machinations of fate or even laid it on God's hands. But the Lost Cause refers to much more than simply a military defeat. It refers to an idealistic image of the South and its way of life, a hearkening to a Golden Age before the "War of Northern Aggression," and an unshakable conviction that there is something grander about the South and about being a Southerner.

While the claim about Lee's surrender is hyperbole, like much hyperbole there is some truth to it. And it reminds us that any geographical location, whether the size of a nation or a state or even a town, is little more than an expanse of land until those living there have an idea of who they are and what that location means to them. This certainly is true of the South. While there obviously was a geographic south in the United States from its very formation, this area does not seem to have attained much of a regional identity until the mid-nineteenth century. As W. J. Cash, in his influential *The Mind of the South*, writes:

> [I]t was the conflict with the Yankee which really created the
> concept of the South as something more than a matter of

geography, as an object of patriotism, in the minds of the Southerners. Before that fateful engagement opened, they had been patriots, but only to their local communes and to their various states. So little had they been aware of any common bond of affection and pride, indeed, that often the hallmark of their patriotism had been an implacable antagonism toward the states which immediately adjoined their own, a notable example being the ancient feud of North Carolina with Virginia on the one side, and with South Carolina on the other. Nor was this feeling ever to die out. Merely, it would be rapidly balanced by rising loyalty to the new-conceived and greater entity—a loyalty that obviously had superior sanction in interest, and all the fierce vitality bred by resistance to open attack.[1]

Of course, these interstate rivalries in the South still exist today, though they more commonly are manifested in the heated gridiron battles between, for example, the Tennessee Volunteers and the Alabama Crimson Tide or between the Georgia Bulldogs and the Florida Gators. But so, too, do the identification with and the pride in the South still exist today, again played out in intersectional meetings between innumerable Southern teams and, really, any team not from the South.

In the South, the football team at the state university came to represent the people of the state, and, more broadly, one's interest in and devotion to that team came to be part of what it meant to be a Southerner. College football became part of the Southern way of life. "Save some Southerners' unshakable belief that the Civil War was in fact the War of Northern Aggression," football analyst Tony Barnhart writes, "nothing is more ingrained in the Southern psyche than the love of Southern college football—not as a game or a mere diversion, but as a way of life."[2]

---

[1] W. J. Cash, *The Mind of the South* (New York: Vintage Books, 1991) 65–66.

[2] Tony Barnhart, *Southern Fried Football: The History, Passion, and Glory of the Great Southern Game* (Chicago: Triumph Books, 2000) 1.

Tradition is very important in the South. It is what perpetuated and perpetuates the Lost Cause. It is central to college football. As Barnhart notes:

> Tradition more than anything else is the cornerstone of college football in the South.... These traditions are the glue that binds the generations of Southern college football fans to one another and keeps them coming back to their beloved campuses year after year. People in the South take these football traditions very, very seriously. To many fans, the renewal of these traditions each fall provides all the physical and emotional comfort of a warm blanket on a cold winter's night.[3]

In short, college football has become a tradition in the South alongside and integrated with the other traditions that constitute the Lost Cause and the self-identity of Southerners. Take, for example, former Tennessee governor Winfield Dunn's preface to a book about the history of the University of Tennessee football team. Dunn recounts the history of the state nickname, "The Volunteer State." He praises the military successes of which Tennesseans were a part. He writes that this "historical fact, plus the deeds of many of those names mentioned earlier, perhaps had as much as anything to do with the development of the attitude and tradition of the great people of Tennessee. That attitude and tradition are characteristic of Tennessee football."[4] Thus, he adds that a book about Tennessee football is not just a book about a game. It is "a reminder of tradition, of life, of competition, of struggle, of history. It is Tennessee."[5] Similar statements could be made about Alabama football, Georgia football, and many other schools.

---

[3] Ibid., 151.

[4] Russ Bebb, *The Big Orange: A Story of Tennessee Football* (Huntsville AL: Strode Publishers, 1974) 10.

[5] Ibid.

In this chapter, I will lay out the case that the Lost Cause initiated a Southern civil religion; that this civil religion entailed a kind of devotion and reverence for the South that permeated throughout the culture; and that college football came to be an integral part of this civil religion.

Let us turn our attention, then, more broadly to history—the history of the South and its culture and the history of the context in which college football in that region must be understood.

A Brief Look at Southern History:
From the Civil War to World War II
(and Football Too)

The focus of this historical review is the twentieth-century American South, but no such review can begin without looking back to the Civil War and the civil religion of the Lost Cause that came out of that war and defeat.

Perhaps no one has chronicled and dissected the Lost Cause more significantly than Charles Reagan Wilson. Wilson argues that "the history of the attitude known as the Lost Cause was the story of the use of the past as the basis for a Southern religious-moral identity, an identity as a chosen people."[6] This "religious-moral identity" was formed fundamentally in response to a religious question: Why would God have allowed the defeat of the South? After the Civil War, there was a problem of theodicy; that is, a problem in understanding God's rule over the world. The religious-minded often face this question. For example, there always are the vexing questions like "Why do bad things happen to good people?" and "Why are children allowed to suffer?" Such questions force people to reflect upon God's nature and the meaning of existence. Southerners faced such questions individually and collectively after the Civil War. "The South faced problems after the Civil War which were cultural but also religious," Wilson notes, "the problems of providing meaning to life and society amid the baffling failure of fundamental beliefs [that is, that the South was a

---

[6] Charles Reagan Wilson, *Baptized in Blood: The Religion of the Lost Cause, 1865–1920* (Athens: University of Georgia Press, 1980) 1.

region especially blessed by God], of extending comfort to those suffering poverty and disillusionment, and of encouraging a sense of belonging in the shattered Southern community."[7]

Though having lost the Civil War, Southerners refused to relinquish the belief that their region and its people were "chosen" by God. Incorporated back into a union with the North, for instance, Southerners still believed that they had a special, "prophetic" role to play for the nation. Indeed, they believed that the very survival of the nation would depend on the South playing that role.[8] More generally, they continued to believe in the sacrality of the South. Given that sacrality, the South as a region, an idea, and an identity was something worthy of devotion and worship. "The South" was the holy or the god of Southern civil religion, a concept that is developed further below. Similar to other religious movements, the religion of the Lost Cause developed myths, rituals, and other trappings of religion.

Myth, perhaps, was the most important element of the religion of the Lost Cause, for it was myth that held all the various elements together. Wilson writes:

> According to the mythmakers, a pantheon of Southern heroes, portrayed as the highest products of the Old South civilization, had emerged during the Civil War to battle the forces of evil, as symbolized by the Yankees. The myth enacted the Christian story of Christ's suffering and death, with the Confederacy at the sacred center. In the Southern myth the Christian drama of suffering and salvation was incomplete; the Confederacy lost a holy war, and there was no resurrection. But the clergy still insisted, even after defeat, that the Confederacy had been on a righteous crusade.[9]

---

[7] Ibid., 10.
[8] Ibid., 164.
[9] Ibid., 24.

Consequently, Wilson argues that the myth of the Lost Cause can be considered the myth of the Crusading Christian Confederates.[10] Though those killed in battle would never return, like Christ, they had made the ultimate sacrifice for the greater good, in this case, the Confederacy. And, as in the example of Christ, there would be a resurrection. Only in this case, it would be the collective resurrection—and what exactly this meant differed among the adherents—of the Confederacy. "The myth of the Crusading Christian Confederates had enacted the Christian drama," Wilson notes, "but without a resurrection and redemption to complete the myth. In the theology of the Lost Cause, one can see that Southerners still hoped the spirit of the suffering and dead Confederacy would one day have, in the words from a Confederate monument, 'a joyful resurrection.'"[11]

Clearly, those who fought, suffered, and died for the cause of the Confederacy were central to the religion of the Lost Cause. And there were many. It is estimated that by 1865, approximately one in three Confederate soldiers had died from battle injuries or disease.[12] These heroes became the focus of devotion and became exemplary models of conduct for many Southerners. They had demonstrated characteristics that defined what a *real* Southerner was/is. "In mythologies," Wilson writes, "a hierarchical pantheon of heroes usually exists, and at the apex of the Lost Cause pantheon was Robert E. Lee."[13] Among the pantheon also were Stonewall Jackson, Jefferson Davis, and Sam Davis. Existentially, "Lee at Appomattox, Jefferson Davis in his cell awaiting possible execution, Stonewall Jackson on his deathbed, and Sam Davis on the scaffold—all were moral lessons for Southerners on the acceptance of death and defeat."[14] David Goldfield argues that these Confederate giants "were elevated from heroes to saints. Their writings became holy writ; monuments became icons;

---

[10] Ibid., 37.

[11] Ibid., 58.

[12] Tony Horwitz, *Confederates in the Attic: Dispatches from the Unfinished Civil War* (New York: Vintage Books, 1999) 55.

[13] Wilson, *Baptized*, 48.

[14] Ibid., 57.

cemeteries became shrines; white southerners made 'pilgrimages' to Richmond's Monument Avenue and to Davis's home, Beauvoir, in Biloxi, Mississippi."[15]

The churches regarded the Confederates as Christian crusaders. Thus, it was difficult if not impossible to separate the Confederates from their religious function. Wilson notes that Confederate heroes were popular choices as special guests at religious revivals in the late nineteenth century.[16] The mix of sacred and secular, religious and military, continued at Confederate soldiers' reunions. "The invitation to follow Christ, which was made during the memorial services, was also an invitation to follow once again Robert E. Lee, Stonewall Jackson, and Jefferson Davis. Some of these reunions thus resembled vast revivals, with tens of thousands of listeners hearing ministers reminding them of the imminence of death for the aged veterans, and of the need to insure everlasting life."[17]

Clergymen, of course, "compared the sacrificial, redemptive deaths of the Confederates to the passion of Christ."[18] Though a full understanding of God's purposes behind the Southern defeat could not be attained, some notion of divine punishment was not uncommon. In this regard, the blood shed by Southerners redeemed the region. The blood cleansed the South of its sins, which varied depending on the theological perspective, and thus prepared it for new life after the war. In addition, the sacrifices made by the living veterans as well as by those who died in the war were held up as examples of the kind of courage and selflessness needed by Southerners in order for them to preserve their way of life and cultural identity despite military defeat.

The identification of the South and the Lost Cause with the life, death, and resurrection of Jesus Christ was clear. "As Christ was sacrificed on the cross," Goldfield observes, "so the South was crucified. But, like Jesus, the

---

[15] David Goldfield, *Still Fighting the Civil War: The American South and Southern History* (Baton Rouge LA: Louisiana State University, 2002) 29.

[16] Wilson, *Baptized*, 34–35.

[17] Ibid., 35.

[18] Ibid., 44–45.

South would rise again. When the last federal troops left the region in 1877, southerners referred to the event as the Redemption, its leaders as Redeemers."[19] The Civil War and the Reconstruction "mirrored the death and resurrection of the Savior."[20]

Because of the sacred status of the war as well as those who fought in it, items or artifacts associated with them were charged with significance and power. Hymns were written and sung in praise of Southern heroes and the South. There was—and is—a Confederate Memorial Day. Funerals of Confederate veterans were occasions of (civil) religious observance. Battlefields became important pilgrimage sites.[21] The same can be said about particularly important cities in the South. Richmond, the first capital of the Confederacy, "was the Mecca of the Lost Cause, and Monument Boulevard [lined with monuments of Confederate heroes] was the sacred road to it."[22]

All these religious elements—the hymns, the sites, the heroes—all served to help Southerners to remember their history, to infuse it with sacrality, and to work through the trauma of the Confederacy's demise and the anxiety of their own impending deaths. Wilson observes:

> Each Lost Cause ritual and organization was tangible evidence that Southerners had made a religion out of their history. As with all ritualistic repetition of archetypal actions, Southerners in their institutionalized Lost Cause religion were trying symbolically to overcome history. By repeating ritual, they recreated the mythical time of their noble ancestors and paid tribute to them.... Every time a Confederate veteran died, every time flowers were placed on graves on Confederate Memorial Day, Southerners relived and confronted the death of the Confederacy.... Through the ritualistic and organizational activities of their civil religion, Southerners tried

---

[19] Goldfield, *Still Fighting*, 28.
[20] Ibid., 52–53.
[21] Wilson, *Baptized*, 26–29.
[22] Ibid., 29.

to overcome their existential worries and to live with their tragic sense of life.[23]

But the valorization of the past, of the South, and of Southerners also held out the hope of future resurrection and, to use a more secular term, revitalization. Southern defeat was not final. It did not entail the loss of the South's "chosenness" by God. Wilson concludes:

> Confederate defeat ultimately brought a renewal of faith for Southern Christians. The harsh lesson of evil triumphing—by God's command—strengthened an already present strain of fatalism. But Southerners learned a more important religious lesson from their defeat in a holy war: God's chosen people did not give up that chosen status when defeated.... Southerners thus retained their pride. They believed that God would bring good out of triumphant evil: a new good would be a purer, more holy chosen people prepared to face a special destiny.[24]

In short, what occurred in the minds of many Southerners was an inversion of reality and illusion. As Goldfield writes, "White southerners elevated defeat into a heroic Lost Cause, their fallen comrades and faltering leaders into saintly figures, their crumbled society into the best place on earth, and their struggle to regain control over their lives and region into a victorious redemption."[25]

The various Christian denominations in the South, almost exclusively Protestant, embraced the burgeoning civil religion of the Lost Cause. "After the war," Wilson writes, "ministers became the priests and prophets of a religion of the Lost Cause, which saw spiritual significance in the

---

[23] Ibid., 36.

[24] Ibid., 77.

[25] Goldfield, *Still Fighting*, 20.

Confederacy as the focus of a new civil religion."[26] The churches taught parishioners that they were special, that as Southerners they "were different and that difference had spiritual significance."[27]

In sum, Wilson argues that the "religious dimension of the Lost Cause all along had addressed the issues of who the southern people were, what their distinctive identity was, and whether they had a destiny under God."[28] These were issues that reasonably could be expected to be addressed in a religious service but also could be found at the center of a number of seemingly secular community activities. The rituals of a community came to bring religion and Southern history together. These rituals—from social gatherings to public holidays, such as Confederate Memorial Day or General Lee's birthday, to those in educational settings—helped to ensure that future generations always remembered Southern myths and heroes and showed them the reverence they deserved. In the end, Goldfield notes, the "links between God and the Confederacy, God and the South became so powerful that young children occasionally confused the two."[29]

While Southern whites avoided the link of the Lost Cause simply to slavery, there was a significant degree of racism that was part of the mythology, and its intensity depended on who you were talking to, where you were having the conversation, and when it was. While only a quarter or fewer white families actually owned slaves in the nineteenth century, whites nevertheless supported the institution and were willing to die to help maintain it. Why? Because "[r]egardless of their social or economic status, whites in the Old South shared one characteristic spread equally across their race: they were not black. In a society where slavery was racial, blackness meant servitude; whiteness, independence. Being white automatically conferred superior status. And whites, regardless of station,

---

[26] Charles Reagan Wilson, *Judgment & Grace in Dixie: Southern Faiths from Faulkner to Elvis* (Athens: University of Georgia Press, 1995) 5.

[27] Wilson, *Judgment*, 21.

[28] Ibid., 29.

[29] Goldfield, *Still Fighting*, 55.

guarded their independence fiercely; to lose independence was to slip toward slavery." Thus, the Lost Cause longing for a Golden Age (the antebellum South) was bound with whites' desire to maintain a superior status in the post-Civil War South. This desire for superior status goes a long way toward explaining not only the advent of Jim Crow but also the intensity of emotion that many whites had about it. As Goldfield concludes, whites "spent much of the next century attempting to restore the racial and gender hierarchy that existed in the South before 1861."[30]

Religious institutions were accomplices in the continuing racism of the Lost Cause, Jim Crow, and the violence that issued from it. Ministers used the Lost Cause as a means of reinforcing white supremacy.[31] Many whites believed that the liberation of blacks after the Civil War would result in their sinking back down into barbarism. In this sense, slavery was seen as a civilizing endeavor that actually raised up blacks. Segregation, then, was understood as an attempt to restore order among blacks and between blacks and whites. Wilson concludes:

> The ministers of the Lost Cause accepted segregation as a substitute for the discipline of slavery, but their vision of the Southern identity did not hinge only on race. Although racial superiority was assumed, the religion of the Lost Cause taught that the two fundamentals of the Southern identity were religion and regional history.... Nevertheless, the white supremacist outlook was so pervasive in Southern society and was perceived as being so synonymous with Southern tradition that most Southerners must have seen the caste system as visible evidence that the Lost Cause still lived.[32]

According to Goldfield, the "Lost Cause had elevated the fight for independence and the preservation of slavery to a holy endeavor,

---

[30] Ibid., 191.

[31] Wilson, *Baptized*, 100.

[32] Ibid., 118.

enshrining the Old South as a halcyon era of grace, order, and righteousness. Reconstruction threatened to disgrace, discredit, and disrupt this vision. Redemption offered the hope of setting things right again, of putting Yankees and blacks in their proper places: in the North and under the whites, respectively."[33]

Goldfield indicates here an important aspect of the Lost Cause perspective: The South identified itself as a place that was *not* like the North. One was a Southerner in part because one was *not* a Yankee.[34] "Southerners interpreted the Civil War as demonstrating the height of Southern virtue," Wilson notes, "as a moral-religious crusade against the atheistic North."[35] After the Civil War, many Southerners (whites particularly) understood themselves as distinct from Yankees and feared what the undue influence of Yankees would do to the Southern way of life. "Southerners brooded that the Civil War had unleashed powerful forces that would descend from the North, or perhaps even emerge indigenously," Wilson writes, "and destroy the Southern Zion they were building."[36] Consequently, Cash argues, the "need to justify itself in the eyes of the world and in its own and to assert its pride as against the Yankee was more imperative now than it had ever been before."[37] Part of this justifying entailed asserting the superiority of the South in religious fervor and moral rectitude[38] but also, as we will see, in secular activities like college football.

---

[33] Goldfield, *Still Fighting*, 222.

[34] It is worth noting that Northerners also distinguished themselves in juxtaposition to the South. As Goldfield writes, "Throughout our nation's history, the South has functioned, for good or ill, as a national mirror, an object of hate, love, and fantasy that rarely approached reality but nonetheless satisfied certain basic national needs" (Goldfield, *Still Fighting*, 7).

[35] Wilson, *Baptized*, 7–8.

[36] Ibid., 10.

[37] Cash, *Mind of the South*, 124.

[38] Goldfield, *Still Fighting*, 22.

Many historians and observers of the region identified certain characteristics that were emphasized in the South, such as honor, individualism, a willingness to be guided by feeling or intuition in contrast to reason, and a general feeling of inferiority vis-à-vis other regions of the country.

Perhaps no single characteristic is more prominent—or stereotypical—about the South than the idea of Southern honor. Of course, honor was not something easy to maintain, given the defeat of the Civil War and the humiliation of the Reconstruction. As Goldfield notes, "Southern white men could not live with failure and dishonor, so they manufactured a past that obviated both and returned their pride, dignity, and above all their control."[39] Thus, we end up with the Lost Cause, its myths and legends, the romanticizing of the antebellum South, Jim Crow, and even the violent reaction by many whites to the Civil Rights movement.

Cash defines honor as "something inviolable and precious in the ego, to be protected against stain at every cost, and imposing definite standards of conduct."[40] Every man must be prepared to uphold his honor. And every woman must have a man or men to uphold her honor. The upholding of honor should be accomplished by any means necessary, assuming the means itself is not dishonorable. Such means certainly could include acts of violence. As Cash explains, "One of the notable results of the spread of the idea of honor, indeed, was an increase in the tendency to violence throughout the social scale."[41] Violence, then, "has always been a part of the pattern of the South."[42] While Cash was writing in the mid-twentieth century, the pattern of violence has continued through the end of the century. Goldfield notes that the "South...remains the most violent section of the country, a legacy of the cult of honor in the Old South, where men derived status from their relationship to others and especially to the black slaves in their midst, and any question of that status turned an insult

---

[39] Ibid., 39.
[40] Cash, *Mind of the South*, 73.
[41] Ibid.
[42] Ibid., 414.

into a tragedy."[43] Thus, homicide rates in the South are higher than in other regions of the country (sometimes twice as high), and other violent crime rates also are higher.[44] Of course, higher crime rates are also consistent with greater poverty, and, as a region, the South always has stood out in this regard. Yet even here, we cannot set aside the role of honor: When one is destitute, one's honor may be all one has left.

The Lost Cause and the near obsession with the Civil War as well as the emphasis on the concept of honor led to a distinct militarism in the region. Cash argues that "the Civil War and the sentimental cult of the Confederate soldier reacted on the Southern hero-ideal to leave it definitely military, in the grand style."[45] It should not be a surprise, then, to see that football would become such a prominent sport in the South, given its military character, such as the comparison of the players to "warriors," the willingness to make physical sacrifices, the conquest of territory, et cetera.

In the South, the idea of honor was bound with a strong individualism and an emphasis on self-determination, both individually and in terms of individual states or the region. Cash, for example, notes the belief that "every man was, in economics at any rate, absolutely responsible for himself, and that whatever he got in this world was exactly what he deserved."[46] This belief is related to the South's inclination to encourage people to "pull themselves up by the bootstraps" and the consequent rejection of governmental assistance or meddling in people's lives. Thus, the current domination of the Republican Party in the South and its traditional call for shrinking the size and scope of government should be of no surprise. As John Shelton Reed notes, Southern individualism also may be related to the region's high homicide rate as

---

[43] Goldfield, *Still Fighting*, 10.

[44] For example, see United States Department of Justice statistics at www.ojp.usdoj.gov/bjs/homicide/region.htm.

[45] Cash, *Mind of the South*, 121.

[46] Ibid., 156.

people decide to take the law into their own hands rather than work through appropriate channels.[47]

In addition, an individual's feelings or "gut reaction" often is taken to be as meaningful and significant as a rational account of a situation. The Southerner, Cash writes, "did not (typically speaking) think; he felt; and discharging his feelings immediately, he developed no need or desire for intellectual culture in its own right."[48] Southerners emphasized and continue to emphasize feeling in country music lyrics, in their religious practices, and even in the rituals of college football. This sentimental orientation does not mean that Southerners completely rejected or reject the reasoning process. The point simply is that there are other ways of "knowing" and "being" than through rational discourse exclusively.

These particular characteristics of the South made the region and its people different. Combined with the loss of the Civil War, high illiteracy and infant mortality rates, significant poverty, and low life expectancy, though, the South was different in an inferior or substandard way. Thus, the people of the South felt inferior, and one reasonably can say that this feeling of inferiority shaped Southern self-perception throughout the twentieth century and perhaps even today. As renowned historian C. Vann Woodward observes, "Southern history, unlike American, includes large components of frustration, failure, and defeat."[49] He adds:

[The South] had learned what it was to be faced with economic, social, and political problems that refused to yield to all the ingenuity, patience, and intelligence that a people could bring to bear upon them. It had learned to accommodate itself to conditions that it swore it would never accept, and it had learned the taste left in the mouth by the swallowing of one's own words.

---

[47] John Shelton Reed, *My Tears Spoiled My Aim…and Other Reflections on Southern Culture* (Orlando FL: Harvest Book, 1993) 59.

[48] Cash, *Mind of the South*, 99.

[49] C. Vann Woodward, *The Burden of Southern History* (Baton Rouge LA: Louisiana State University Press, 1993) 19.

It had learned to live for long decades in quite un-American poverty, and it had learned the equally un-American lesson of submission. For the South had undergone an experience that it could share with no other part of America—though it is shared by nearly all the peoples of Europe and Asia—the experience of military defeat, occupation, and reconstruction.[50]

Poverty in the South was so persistent, Woodward argues, that "[g]enerations of scarcity and want constitute one of the distinctive historical experiences of the Southern people."[51]

This unique history shaped the way that Southerners viewed themselves, and particularly how they viewed themselves with respect to the North. In the 1920s and 1930s, the Southern Agrarian movement epitomized antagonism toward the North and fear of what its worldview could do to the South. This intellectual, social, and political movement was given its defining voice through the publication of *I'll Take My Stand*. The authors of that volume were responding, in part, to the rise of what was called the New South. Their criticism was that the New South "was rapidly acquiring all the worst characteristics of the urban industrial North—scientism, materialism, endless economic expansion, dissolving communities, and social fluidity."[52] While "the architects of the New South not only emphasized the magnificence of the antebellum regime and the heroism of the Confederate 'Lost Cause' but insisted on an umbilical connection between the New South and the Old,"[53] others viewed the increasing urbanization, commercialization, and industrialization of the New South as a blatant adoption of Yankee ways and a betrayal of the Southern way of life. The process might even lead to the destruction of the

---

[50] Ibid., 190.

[51] Ibid., 17.

[52] Susan V. Donaldson, "Introduction," *I'll Take My Stand: The South and the Agrarian Tradition* (Baton Rouge LA: Louisiana State University, 2006) xx.

[53] James C. Cobb, *Redefining Southern Culture: Mind & Identity in the Modern South* (Athens: University of Georgia Press, 1999) 153.

South on par with the defeat of the Civil War. This almost apocalyptic vision was taken up by ministers throughout the South. Wilson calls them "prophets of the Lost Cause," who contrasted the industrialism and capitalism of the New South movement "with the spirituality of the Confederacy and concluded that the South had declined since the Civil War."[54] He adds that the "North was a continual reminder of what Southerners must not become. The Lost Cause jeremiad thus touched deep emotions of the Southern people. The hope was that a cultural identity based on religion and regional tradition could be the answer to Southern fears of decline."[55] Many conservatives in the South—those opposed to the New South, religious or otherwise—believed that "[i]ntegration, unionization, progressive taxation, and government regulation could all be lumped together as a part of a massive Yankee plot to undermine the South's traditions and derail its progress."[56]

The Southern Agrarians sought to preserve the distinctiveness of the South's way of life and to espouse its virtues. John Crowe Ransom, one of the leading voices from the Southern Agrarians, argued that the Southerner's "fierce devotion is to a lost cause—though it grieves me that his contemporaries are so sure it is lost."[57] The "war of Northern aggression" may have been lost, but the cause was not, as long as Southerners preserved their distinctiveness against the onslaught of Northern social, economic, political, moral, and religious values. In this sense, the influence of the Yankees was likened to the very invasion of the North onto Southern soil. This animosity toward Yankees is reflected in the dichotomy between Northern industrialism and Southern agrarianism, the latter being the form of life that best preserved Southern values. Ransom concluded, then, that Southerners would be able to hold off the North "if industrialism is represented to the Southern people as—what it undoubtedly is for the most part—a foreign invasion of Southern soil,

---

[54] Wilson, *Baptized,* 79.

[55] Ibid.

[56] Cobb, *Redefining,* 18.

[57] John Crowe Ransom, *I'll Take My Stand,* 2.

which is capable of doing more devastation than was wrought when Sherman marched to the sea."[58]

The Southern Agrarians, however, did not believe that holding off the Yankees would be any easier in the twentieth century than it was in the nineteenth when, of course, the South experienced failure in this regard. The war, Reconstruction, and all that followed devastated the South economically and politically but also spiritually. Like Ransom, Frank Lawrence Owsley argued that "the North defeated the South in war, crushed and humiliated it in peace, and waged against it a war of intellectual and spiritual conquest. In this conquest the North fixed upon the South the stigma of war guilt, of slave guilt, of treason, and thereby shook the faith of its people in their way of living and in their philosophy of life."[59] As a consequence, the Southerner was left weak and demoralized because of the North's desire for domination. And continuing with the tone struck by Ransom and Owsley, Andrew Nelson Lytle wrote, the Southerner "has been turned into the runt pig in the sow's litter. Squeezed and tricked out of the best places at the side, he is forced to take the little hind tit for nourishment; and here, struggling between the sow's back legs, he has to work with every bit of his strength to keep it from being a dry hind one, and all because the suck of the others is so unreservedly gluttonous."[60]

Despite the hopes and efforts of Southern Agrarians and others, change was inevitable. In the early twentieth century, there were considerable changes in the population, including a significant migration of Southerners to the North and West, including large numbers from the African American population. There was a major development of industry and commerce coupled with the start of a movement away from a predominantly agrarian culture. In this time of dramatic change, it is little wonder that people found solace in their religious traditions and even started new ones. As Cash notes, "new churches were building in Dixie

---

[58] Ibid., 23.

[59] Frank Lawrence Owsley, *I'll Take My Stand,* 66.

[60] Andrew Nelson Lytle, *I'll Take My Stand,* 245.

almost as fast as factories."[61] It was during this period that "orgiastic" religions like the Holy Rollers, Church of God, and others rose to prominence.[62] It was the time of the rise of fundamentalism in the South. As more attention and money was directed to education, it also was a time in which many young Southerners began to critically examine their history and culture. It was a time of what Cash describes as the arising of the "modern mind" in the South, when there were "men who deliberately chose to know and think rather than merely to *feel* in terms fixed finally by Southern patriotism and the prejudices associated with it; men capable of detachment and actively engaged in analysis and criticism of the South itself."[63]

It is within this complicated history and the complicated attitudes of the South that we must view the rise and development of college football in the region. College football began in the Northeast—the land of Yankees— dating back, perhaps, to an 1869 match between Princeton and Rutgers that vaguely resembled what we now call the game of football. By the end of the nineteenth century, college football was a great success in the Northeast, dominated by what we now call the Ivy League schools (Harvard, Yale, Princeton, et cetera). By the end of the nineteenth century in the South, however, college football was just beginning to catch on. While Southerners came to college football later than their fellow citizens in the North, they did so for many of the same reasons.

Michael Oriard has detailed the cultural significance of football, particularly college football, better, perhaps, than anyone. He argues that college football attained a special status because of its differences from any professional sports teams or high school teams. Professional teams provided national exposure, but generally were made up of men from many different parts of the country. High school teams were composed of local boys but brought little attention to a town or city beyond the county or perhaps region. "[W]hat college football offered fans that professional

---

[61] Cash, *Mind of the South*, 222.
[62] Ibid., 289.
[63] Ibid., 327.

and high school football could not," Oriard writes, "was a local team competing in a national arena."[64] This national competition was critical to the development of college football in the South. Teams came to represent not only their states but also the region itself. This identification became more significant as college football came to prominence in the national media; that is, outside the media-rich Northeast. College football and other sports increasingly made up a large portion of newsreel footage, and sports became frequent contexts for full-length films.[65]

"As football teams became public symbols of universities, communities, and entire regions in a hugely publicized national drama," Oriard notes, "intersectional games and postseason bowl games proliferated in the 1920s and 1930s."[66] Nowhere were these intersectional games more important than in the South. The longstanding desire of Southerners to prove their worth in comparison with the North naturally carried over into gridiron contests. We cannot say that Southerners played any harder than players from Ohio or Massachusetts (though they might have). We can never know the comparable intensity that the players from different regions had or the comparable fervor of fans from different regions. But the history of the South and its particular condition—poor and illiterate beyond the national average—suggest that the sport very likely was experienced differently by Southerners than it was by fans and players from other regions.

Oriard notes that the "1920s and 1930s marked the age of intersectional football, when distinct football regions emerged, and competitions between their representatives each season mapped a shifting geographical balance of power."[67] This shift in power was from the Northeast to the Midwest and the South. While we are not concerned here

---

[64] Michael Oriard, *King Football: Sport & Spectacle in the Golden Age of Radio & Newsreels, Movies & Magazines, the Weekly & the Daily Press* (Chapel Hill: University of North Carolina Press, 2001) 7.

[65] Ibid., 11.

[66] Ibid., 7.

[67] Ibid., 65.

with the Midwestern shift in power, we already have touched upon the historical and cultural elements in the South that might explain its rise to prominence in the world of college football.

Keith Dunnavant notes that in "the South of the early twentieth century, the Civil War was still more of a closely held grudge than a page ripped from the history books."[68] The game of football, then, imported from the North, was played—especially in intersectional contests—with that grudge lurking somewhere in the minds of both players and spectators. Oriard argues that for a "broad cross-section of the entire South in the 1920s…triumphs of southern football teams validated the region against the scorn of outsiders."[69] In his account of Alabama football in the 1950s, Tom Stoddard writes that the "game was a powerful source of pride and self-esteem for individuals, families, towns, cities, and the entire state. The mythic connections to the Lost Cause of the Confederacy were part of the reason."[70] The degree of pride that Southerners took and still take with regard to their college football team is a function of how they saw themselves and see themselves through Northern (meaning now anywhere outside the South) eyes. Stoddard observes, "All they [Southerners] knew about the North was that people there looked down upon them and thought of them as bigoted, pellagra-ridden, and lazy. What better way to prove otherwise than to kick ass in a hard, physical game."[71]

In addition to the almost visceral reaction that Southern fans had or continue to have about their football programs, especially with regard to their games with non-Southern teams, it is important to remember that Southern college football teams are connected to actual universities. The universities themselves, as we saw in chapter one, are sources of identification and pride for many Southerners. As Southern universities

---

[68] Keith Dunnavant, *Coach: The Life of Paul "Bear" Bryant* (New York: Thomas Dunne Books, 2005) 34.

[69] Oriard, *King Football*, 85.

[70] Tom Stoddard, *Turnaround: Paul "Bear" Bryant's First Year at Alabama* (Montgomery AL: Black Belt Press, 2000) 49.

[71] Ibid., 49.

and education in general began to take on a more prominent role in the South in the twentieth century, the football team became a symbol of those efforts. In a strange reversal, however, the success of the football teams began to support, affirm, or validate the educational efforts of these institutions of higher education. "Certain college presidents," Oriard notes, "openly sought to build their institutions through the publicity won by a successful football team."[72]

It was not simply the fans who contributed to the growing zeal surrounding college football and its unique relationship with Southern history and culture: The media also played a significant role in affirming and exploiting the fervor of that relationship. Oriard's work perceptively details the media's role. "Southerners likely competed with no more intensity than players elsewhere," he writes, "but sportswriters both within and outside the region preferred to set them apart, and to attribute their fervor to the undying spirit of the Old South."[73] Sportswriters in both the North and the South used Southern history and the relationship of the South to the North to frame key intersectional matchups. "Every intersectional contest pitting the South against the East or Midwest became a small chapter in the developing narrative of southern football," Oriard argues. "Along the way, intersectional contests pitting the South against 'the East' and 'Midwest' came to an end, becoming instead the South versus the North in reenactments of the Civil War."[74] As Oriard adds, "The identification of Dixie running backs with DeForest's raiders or Pickett's cavalry at Gettysburg began with southern sportswriters but was embraced even more enthusiastically by their Yankee colleagues, as part of the entire nation's romance with the legendary Old South and Lost Cause."[75] Thus, "[l]inking southern football to the myths of the Old South and the Lost Cause began in Dixie…but it was taken up everywhere."[76]

---

[72] Oriard, *King Football*, 78.

[73] Ibid., 87.

[74] Ibid., 88.

[75] Ibid., 89.

[76] Ibid., 91.

Patrick B. Miller identifies several ways in which intercollegiate athletics, most especially football, became inextricably linked with Southern history and culture. We already have seen how militarism and the prominence of honor in Southern culture distinguish the region from others in the United States. Honor also played a role in the rise of intercollegiate athletics in the South in the late nineteenth and early twentieth centuries. Miller argues:

> A richly textured tradition of southern honor that had long animated the region also facilitated the rise of intercollegiate athletics.... Rough and romantic, like the martial valor representing the legend of the Lost Cause, athletic exploits thus could give young men a sense of exhilarating contest and conflict in battle. This was a shadow perhaps of what their fathers might have recalled from their exploits at Vicksburg and Gettysburg, but it was a deeper experience than marching on a parade ground might ever provide.[77]

The honor described here was not simply personal honor, though. The honor to be defended was that of the South or the Confederacy and—this was new—the honor of the institution for which the individual played. "The care and tending of an individual's honor many southerners had long understood," Miller claims, and "through athletics, some believed, the prestige of an entire institution might similarly need to be protected."[78] Cash writes, for example, that even into the 1930s there "were still plenty of Southern colleges whose only claim to respect was a football team."[79] The educational institution, of course, often represents the state, and the state

---

[77] Patrick B. Miller, "The Manly, the Moral, and the Proficient: College Sports in the New South," in *The Sporting World of the Modern South*, ed. Patrick B. Miller (Urbana: University of Illinois Press, 2002) 21.

[78] Ibid., 35.

[79] Cash, *Mind of the South*, 373.

represents the region to some extent, so all these powerful allegiances tended to be, and perhaps still are, bound together.

Football was a sport that naturally could draw upon the regional emphasis on honor. But how it did so may distinguish it from other sports. Football, Miller writes, "stood as a means of expressing or even inculcating the qualities of strength, endurance, and valor deemed highly honorable by generations of cultural commentators."[80] As such, the game "possessed enormous metaphorical value concerning the rites of passage toward southern manhood, and it clearly corresponded with the region's martial culture and tradition of blood sport."[81] On this latter point, Oriard agrees that for Southerners, "football is tied to long traditions of honor in blood sports."[82] Elsewhere in his work, Oriard argues that football was a general response by American society to living conditions that were less strenuous and included more leisure time. In such a situation, there arose the concern that boys would grow up to be "soft" or even "effeminate." This concern was overcome by their participation in the rough-and-tumble world of football. While fears of boys becoming "soft" or "effeminate" may have played some role in Southerners' participation in the sport, the region's history and cultural attitudes suggest there was more going on than that particular theory covers.

While the athletes in intercollegiate sports in the South had especially powerful reasons and motivations for playing—including playing to the point of serious injury or even death—spectators, especially students, also became participants in what Miller describes, consistent with the arguments made in chapters one and two, as sacrament. He writes:

> [A] myriad of rituals and symbols reinforced for many southerners the intensity of the intercollegiate sporting experience. The anthems and totems of college athletic culture in the South

---

[80] Miller, "Manly, Moral, Proficient," 24.

[81] Ibid.

[82] Michael Oriard, *Reading Football: How the Popular Press Created an American Spectacle* (Chapel Hill: University of North Carolina Press, 1993) 3.

took a variety of forms and projected a range of images.... The iconography of college sport, manifest in the waving of flags, the orchestration of chants and cheers, and the singing of inspirational songs, formed circles of significance around the actual sites of races or games, actively involving fans as well as participants in the intercollegiate sporting spectacle. The sights and sounds of boisterous athletics went beyond competitive exchange on the diamond or gridiron; those who watched became immersed in something like a sacrament against which a book, a lecture, or a laboratory experiment—among other academic offerings—often seemed to pale in comparison.[83]

As a sacrament, the intercollegiate sporting event became an important communal event. "Distinctive colors, nicknames, mascots, songs, and cheers intensified the experience of a Saturday afternoon," Miller observes.

Beyond the contest itself, even before the era when home-coming extravaganzas and precision marching bands added to the appeal of sporting events, other rituals contributed to an exciting atmosphere. From an early date, college baseball and football games in the South frequently became extended social occasions, offering to some a splendid opportunity for courtship, to others a fine setting for displays of prowess with a bottle.[84]

These social occasions built upon customs already existing in Southern culture. Loran Smith, a Southern writer with a long-time connection to the athletic department at the University of Georgia, remembers people coming into Athens for the day with picnic baskets to feast before the game. He notes that this activity likely drew upon the popular practice of "dinner on the green"—large communal feasts that often

---

[83] Miller, "Manly, Moral, Proficient," 29–30.
[84] Ibid., 33.

took place after church on a Sunday afternoon. The picnics that Smith witnessed now have become massive and complex tailgating scenes, with all of their feasting and courting and drinking accepted as a prominent part of the game-day experience. In other words, tailgating may very well represent an activity that stereotypically has been associated with a religious occasion being adapted to an increasingly popular "secular" event.

Ted Ownby, however, argues that sports were not central to the works of those identifying Southern manhood during most of the twentieth century. (Note that womanhood, of course, is not relevant to the issue here and will be touched on in the next chapter.) Given the importance of honor in the culture, definitions of manhood and guidelines about how to achieve it were and are prevalent. In contrast to Oriard's claims about football and ideas of manhood in American culture, especially during the late nineteenth and early twentieth centuries, Ownby claims that most Southerners did not conceive of football as important in relation to manhood and that they really did not identify manhood with any particular sport. He argues that "it becomes almost ridiculous to think about sports as playing a significant role in the works that analyzed southern identity at mid-century [1900s]."[85] While acknowledging that football might tap into traditional Southern attitudes about honor,[86] Ownby still insists that "it seems clear that modern sports offer white southern men a sense of regional identity that has little to do with southern history."[87]

Ownby's conclusion, at least as it applies to football, rightly cautions us to be wary of making broad generalizations about sport or football in Southern history and culture. The most significant Southern writers rarely, if ever, used football as a setting or plot element in their works. William

---

[85] Ted Ownby, "Manhood, Memory, and White Men's Sports in the American South," in *The Sporting World of the Modern South*, ed. Patrick B. Miller (Urbana: University of Illinois Press, 2002) 328.

[86] Ibid., 338.

[87] Ibid., 339.

Faulkner did not, although *The Hamlet* is perhaps an exception.[88] James Agee's literary ethnography *Let Us Now Praise Famous Men* is a powerful account of life in rural 1930s Alabama. This was one of the great decades for Crimson Tide football, yet the team is never mentioned in the approximately 400-page text. Football does play a more significant role in the plot development of Robert Penn Warren's *All the King's Men* (1946), in which Governor Willie Stark's son is a star on the state university's football team. Of course, the socio-economic status of the characters in Warren's novel are significantly different from many of the characters in Faulkner's tales of the decaying South as well as the poor sharecroppers that Agee encountered in the 1930s. Wayne Flynt argues that in the state of Alabama—and probably through most of the South—"[f]anaticism for the sport depended on high concentrations of alumni who were college football fans. Such concentrations presumed lots of white-collar jobs and college graduates."[89] Indeed, Ownby may very well be correct in his assessment that sports or football had little impact in the lives of many if not most Southern men. Yet Oriard and others may very well be correct that for some Southerners—particularly the increasing number of whites who were able to attend college during the twentieth century and who would have the wealth and leisure to support and enjoy contemporary sports—football became central to how they understood themselves, their history, and their culture.

---

[88] In his novel *The Hamlet* (set in the early twentieth century), William Faulkner creates a character who grows up in an isolated, rural area, but has the opportunity to attend the University of Mississippi. While at school, the young man discovers the game of football. Though he knew nothing of the game beforehand, it is clearly very important to those associated with the university. But the people back home know nothing of the game either. The story reminds us that, although college football was growing greatly in popularity in the 1920s and 1930s in the South, many Southerners would not have had much interest in it and, perhaps, did not even know about it.

[89] Wayne Flynt, *Alabama in the Twentieth Century* (Tuscaloosa AL: University of Alabama Press, 2004) 429.

Not everyone in the South was thrilled about the increasing popularity of college football in the region. Many religious institutions and their leaders railed against the game and the wild behavior of its fans. In particular, the violence of the game and the drinking of its spectators ran counter to the sensibilities of the devout. After World War I, however, much of the evangelical opposition to the game began to diminish.[90]

However broad or narrow the appeal of college football was to Southerners in the late nineteenth century and the first several decades of the twentieth century, there is no doubt that it became a regional obsession in the second half of the twentieth century, perhaps for many of the same reasons it had caught on in the first place. In explaining its rise to prominence in American culture, Oriard argues that football "stood not just for winning through sacrifice and physical toughness but also for youthful energy, for a social world in which 'everyone' had a role, for community cohesion, for unambiguous gender roles, and for the family."[91] Many of these themes—honor, sacrifice, family, and community—have been encountered already in this work.

The twentieth century in the South was one of significant anxiety. Entering that century, Southerners still felt the sting of the defeat from the Civil War and the humiliation of Reconstruction. Poverty, infant mortality, low life expectancy, illiteracy, and the way these phenomena were portrayed in the national media left Southerners with a distinct feeling of inferiority in comparison with other regions of the country. The encroachment of industrialization and commercialization from the North, embodied in part by the New South movement, was perceived as a threat to the Southern way of life and gave rise to the reactionary Southern Agrarian

---

[90] For a nice summary of this religious history, see chapter 5 ("When Dixie Took a Different Stand") of William J. Baker's *Playing with God: Religion and Modern Sport* (Cambridge MA: Harvard University Press, 2007). For an interesting case study that deals with some of these issues, see Andrew Doyle's "'Fighting Whiskey and Immorality' at Auburn: The Politics of Southern Football, 1919–1927" in *Southern Cultures* 10/3 (Fall 2004).

[91] Oriard, *King Football*, 198.

movement. By mid-century, the South's oppressed and largely silent and ignored segment of the population—African Americans—refused *en masse* to be oppressed, silent, and ignored any longer. Thus, the anxiety of whites increased exponentially as the stable, reassuring social order (hierarchy) of race began to crumble and white manhood challenged. For many if not most Southerners, both whites and blacks, the church provided a place of solace in these trying times. Indeed, religion is one of the most prominent institutions in Southern culture—past and present. And it is to that institution that we must now turn.

"Give Me That Old Time Religion": Religion, Race, and Southern Civil Religion

While it may not have always been the case, the South today is recognized as one of the more religious, if not the most religious, regions of the United States. The South is often equated with the "Bible Belt." Any number of surveys and polls indicate that Southerners are more likely to attend church on a regular basis than other Americans.[92] While church attendance data are renowned for their inaccuracies—people tend to say they go to church more than they really do—the regional differences still are significant. In the South, it is more often the case that church attendance is simply assumed, and learning what particular church a person attends is part of learning a good bit about him or her. "Belonging to a church, and being more or less active in it, is a taken-for-granted part of middle-class life in the South, in a way that it's not in many other parts of the country," Reed notes. "Nearly everybody, rich or poor, urban or rural or suburban, black or white, has a church to go to. Even those Southerners who don't go to

---

[92] A particularly useful resource is the website of The Pew Forum on Religion and Public Life (www.pewforum.org). There, one can find an interactive map of the United States that compares survey data about belief in God, church attendance, and other religious matters. Survey results from states in the South very consistently suggest greater religious belief and church attendance than states outside the region.

church at least know which one they're not going to."[93] Most likely, a Southerner will identify a Protestant church as his or her own, and among Protestant churches, Baptists are number one, followed by Methodists.[94] Goldfield reports on another survey that highlights the regional differences:

> Nearly one-half of southern respondents read the Bible at home during the week, compared with less than one-third of non-southerners. Nearly one-third of southerners admitted that their ministers offered advice and guidance on political matters, compared with 18 percent of non-southerners. Almost two-thirds of the southern respondents agreed that some people are possessed by the Devil; 44 percent of non-southerners expressed that belief. Nearly one-half of southerners claimed that prayer had cured an illness in their lives, compared with 28 percent of non-southerners.[95]

In short, religious beliefs and church activities are a more significant part of the worldviews of Southerners and a greater part of their daily or at least weekly lives.

Not only is religion of greater importance in the South, it also is distinct from that of other regions. In the late nineteenth and early twentieth centuries, one of the distinct aspects of Southern religion was the way in which it was still bound to the Confederacy with its strong antagonism towards the North. This antagonism, of course, was a carryover not only from the Civil War but also from the rhetoric that led up to it. Cash describes the "dark suggestion that the God of the Yankee was not God at all but Antichrist loosed at last from the pit. The coming [Civil] war would be no mere secular contest but Armageddon, with the South standing in the role of the defender of the ark, its people as the Chosen

---

[93] Reed, *My Tears*, 141.
[94] Ibid., 36.
[95] Goldfield, *Still Fighting*, 11.

People."[96] We will see that such a sentiment did not disappear wholly from the scene following the Civil War. Other characteristics of Southern religion have persisted more thoroughly through the region and the decades.

Wilson argues for five central characteristics of Southern religion.[97] First is the overwhelming prevalence of Protestant denominations. Baptists are the most prominent, followed by Methodists, and then others. The stereotypical characteristics of Southern religion, then, are those most associated with Protestants—Baptists and Methodists in particular.

The second characteristic of Southern religion is that it tends toward evangelicalism, in particular with an emphasis on personal experience and being "born again." As a result, there is a certain sense that Southern religion is individualistic. Although people identify strongly with their church communities, the individual's religious experience is paramount. One's salvation, for example, is one's own responsibility and is achieved, in a certain sense, alone. The individual is not dependent on an institution or ecclesiastical hierarchy or church doctrine to achieve the spiritual end. Such individualism parallels that of the general ethos of the South described earlier. Wilson concludes that the "predominant southern religion has been experiential, valuing spiritual experience over written, systematic theology."[98] This emphasis on personal religious experience obviously has a parallel on game day. The passion and fervor and even ecstasy of the college football fan takes place in a communal setting, but it is the personal experience that feeds the psyche or (dare I say) soul.

The evangelical character of Southern religion, though, goes beyond simply an emphasis on personal religious experience. Jon F. Sensbach writes:

> Evangelicalism embodies and has shaped so much that seems quintessentially southern—the preoccupation with sin and guilt,

---

[96] Cash, *Mind of the South*, 80.
[97] Wilson, *Judgment*, 7–11.
[98] Ibid., 114–15.

the emotional search for redemption, the plainspoken directness of the faith of ordinary folk, the Laocoon-like twining of race and religion.... Evangelicalism helped shape the emergence of the modern South. Fittingly, in a region awash in tragedy, pathos, and squandered opportunities, the triumph of evangelicalism reaped its share of those harvests; it also brought a message of hope and redemption to the South.[99]

In short, the existential or spiritual angst of the evangelical brand of Christianity fit well with the people of a region that has experienced the defeat of the Civil War, the humiliation of Reconstruction, the persistence of poverty and underdevelopment, and the condition of minimal education. The spiritual triumph of the individual was all the greater given a social context of defeat and a theological view of human beings as relatively hopeless sinners. In other words, long before college football tapped into a distinct Southern psyche that subsequently determined its appeal and encouraged its growth, religion already had done the same. In fact, in doing the same, religion can be seen as having prepared Southerners and the South for devotion to their college football team. Samuel S. Hill highlights these connections when he writes:

Since the end of Reconstruction, acquisition of power has been a particular temptation to a people beset by inferiority feelings and stung by criticisms from outside—a factor which may partially explain the southern infatuation with championship football teams and beauty contests, and Southerners' brashness in making claims for the superiority of regional social amenities. In tapping this aspect of southern consciousness we are probing the powerful

---

[99] Jon F. Sensbach, "Before the Bible Belt: Indians, Africans, and the New Synthesis of Eighteenth-Century Southern Religious History," in *Religion in the American South: Protestants and Others in History and Culture*, ed. Beth Barton Schweiger and Donald G. Mathews (Chapel Hill: University of North Carolina Press, 2004) 20.

appeal of a religious interpretation which exalts eternal spiritual victory.[100]

Spiritual victory is a matter of personal success and fulfillment, and victory on the gridiron bears spiritual significance. Whether it be in football contests, beauty pageants, or spiritual achievement, much of Southern life is a sport.

Related to this emphasis on personal experience is the third characteristic of expressiveness and emotion. Wayne Flynt, in his history of Alabama in the twentieth century, writes, "Southerners in general and Alabamians in particular believed they were uniquely and distinctly Christian. They believed they adhered to a stronger, purer, deeper, more personal, evangelical, Protestant faith than other Americans."[101] There is a certain fervor or passion to Southern religiosity and a desire to express to others their religion—again, evangelical in character. The emphasis on emotion parallels the general ethos of the region, where feeling is prioritized over reason or rational calculation. In addition, there is an important connection with college football. If one imagines the religious experience to be solemn, involving the believer in quiet reflection or prayer, then college football looks nothing like religion. But if one, instead, imagines religious services as loud and emotional, then one not only has a better idea of what much of Southern religiosity looks like but also opens the door for thinking about the game-day experience as a religious one. Certainly many of those who completed my survey (see chapter four) recognized the powerful emotional—religious?—experiences they had on game day. In writing about football in the South, Michael Novak notes that the "Baptist and Methodist churches are in the 'free church' tradition, and they cherish emotion, inspiration, charismatic speaking in tongues, the surges of

---

[100] Samuel S. Hill, *Religion and the Solid South* (Nashville TN: Abingdon Press, 1972) 41.

[101] Flynt, *Alabama*, 445.

personal conversion and sudden seizure."[102] Anyone who has observed fans at Tennessee, Alabama, Florida, or many other locales can understand the resemblance of what they see in the stands with what Novak asserts about Southern religiosity. The shaking and screaming and other ecstatic behaviors that one sees in the stands mirror the kind of scenes one can see in pews in many Southern churches.

A fourth characteristic of Southern religion, according to Wilson, is fundamentalism. Fundamentalism and evangelicalism are often equated, but they are not identical. While evangelicalism has to do with the power of personal experience and faith, fundamentalism has more to do with a commitment to certain "fundamental" doctrinal principles. Wilson argues:

> Although *evangelical* is sometimes used as a near synonym for fundamentalist, the two are very different impulses and concepts, albeit frequently found together in the South. Evangelical religion stresses the individual's experience of a life-transforming faith, a conversion that leads to the infusion of God's grace. Southern evangelicals downplay liturgies, sacraments, and creeds. Fundamentalists would, of course, passionately disagree with the denial of the importance of doctrinal creeds and enumerated moral agendas. The South has been more evangelical than fundamentalist.[103]

As Wilson suggests, many of the principles that fundamentalists insist upon have been moral in nature, and, certainly, the contemporary view of fundamentalists revolves around their moral as well as religious fervor. Thus, moralism is the fifth characteristic of Southern religiosity. Southern religion has sought to protect people against themselves, to steer them clear of the sins that will lead to eternal damnation, whether those sins be of the flesh, from the bottle, or from other vices. Southern

---

[102] Michael Novak, *The Joy of Sports: Endzones, Bases, Baskets, Balls, and the Consecration of the American Spirit*, rev. ed. (Lanham MD: Madison Books, 1994) 243.

[103] Wilson, *Judgment*, 81–82 (emphasis original).

moralism, as with all moralism, has tended to be stauncher in theory than in practice. For example, while many Southern counties remained "dry" long after Prohibition came to an end, and remain dry even today, Southerners seem to consume about as much alcohol as people from other regions.[104] In fact, there is a saying that goes, "As long as the people of Mississippi can stagger to the polls, they'll vote dry."[105]

Like so much that is Southern, religion in the region is bound with issues of race. Hill notes that "[w]herever the South exists as a specifiable culture, the pattern of white supremacy, whether aggressive or residual, stands as its primary component."[106] As a leading scholar in the study of religion in the South, he realizes that this "pattern" persists in religious life as well. Hill describes the South as having been dominated by two cultures: Southernness and religion.[107] But these were not two cultures that people alternated between, with racism being a part of the former and not the latter. The two cultures were woven together to form the fabric of Southern life. Goldfield argues that "[b]y 1900 white evangelical Protestantism had become so immersed in southern culture that few whites perceived the inherent contradiction between Christianity and white supremacy."[108] For much of the twentieth century and for many white Southerners, the contradiction remained unrecognized.

While some churches (black, of course, more than white) certainly resisted racism, especially through the Civil Rights Movement and into the latter half of the twentieth century, most white churches and their leaders either supported segregation—the social order based on racism—or at least accommodated themselves to the prevalent racism in the society. Even in the second half of the twentieth century, Hill argues that "religion has

---

[104] National Institute on Alcohol Abuse and Alcoholism (National Institutes of Health), "Surveillance Report #73" (Bethesda MD: National Institute on Alcohol Abuse and Alcoholism, 2005).

[105] Goldfield, *Still Fighting*, 59.

[106] Hill, *Religion*, 24.

[107] Ibid., 25.

[108] Goldfield, *Still Fighting*, 57.

further tightened the hold of racially discriminating convictions, at least that has been the net effect of the churches' influence."[109] In some cases, such institutional racism was accompanied by a kind of paternalism. Woodward writes that "the underlying assumption was that it was up to the white man to…lift up the black brother, to redeem the Negro."[110] This social advancement, however, rarely meant equality with whites.

If nothing else, it was easy for congregations simply to ignore the pernicious effects of racism and segregation not only for black communities but also for their own as well. In regard to churches in Alabama, Flynt argues that "[d]espite being enmeshed in the web of Lost Cause Christianity, glorifying its deeply flawed past, and proclaiming black inferiority, southern Christianity still found vindication in its spectacular rate of baptisms and church growth."[111] It also was easy to ignore social problems, such as racism and segregation, because the dominant form of Southern religiosity rarely emphasized social justice or actions to achieve it. As noted earlier, the emphasis was much more on individual experience and salvation, even if this transformation was experienced in the context of a strong communal bond. As Hill notes, "Theologically speaking, religious assumptions deflect moral earnestness because southern churchmen have been taught that the high God of heaven, who is life's ineluctable reference point, issues a single directive to each person: find forgiveness for your personal sins…. [W]hen religion is defined as status, that is, how one stands before a morally requiring God, it follows that racial concerns will not have more than proximate significance."[112] Hill adds that the "reduction of the faith to single emotional moments, trivial moralisms, and sanguine institutional loyalty" hampered an adherent's critical reflection.[113] They hampered it, however, not only with regard to the key elements of his

---

[109] Hill, *Religion*, 33.

[110] Woodward, *Burden*, 179.

[111] Flynt, *Alabama*, 447.

[112] Hill, *Religion*, 33.

[113] Samuel S. Hill, *Southern Churches in Crisis Revisited* (Tuscaloosa AL: University of Alabama Press, 1999) 186.

or her tradition, but also with regard to his or her ability to evaluate the shortcomings of the existing social order. Because religion for whites was so bound to the greater Southern "way of life," racism and segregation were no more questioned in a religious context than they were in others. In sum, "religion is [was?] dominantly a conservative or reinforcing agent for the traditional values held by white southern society"[114]—and those values included racial hierarchy and segregation.

Southern Civil Religion and Civil Rights: The Church and the Stadium

What we see with religion in the South is how an element of a culture is a part of a greater whole. In other words, there was and is a Southern culture of which religion is a part, in the same way that football and beauty pageants are a part of that culture. To the extent that various elements of a culture function to celebrate the "essence" of that culture, generate rituals that support that culture, and generally maintain the social order and beliefs of that culture, we have, then, a form of "civil religion."

Sociologist Robert Bellah popularized the use of the idea of civil religion in the 1960s. In "Civil Religion in America," Bellah writes, "The civil religion at its best is a genuine apprehension of universal and transcendent religious reality as seen in or, one could almost say, as revealed through the experience of the American people."[115] The idea is that the history and nature of the American people and their country become the means by which the "universal and transcendent religious reality" is known or understood. It is not a substitution of the secular or civil for the religious but a melding of the two. Consequently, we can talk of the doctrine of America—freedom, democracy—in religious terms; we can refer to American national holidays as analogous to a liturgical calendar; we can make note of important rituals that celebrate the nation and what it stands

---

[114] Hill, *Religion*, 36.

[115] Robert Bellah, "Civil Religion in America," in *American Civil Religion*, ed. Russell E. Richey and Donald G. Jones (New York: Harper & Row, 1974) 33.

for, such as the singing of the national anthem, before sporting events, no less; we can recognize certain prominent individuals as heroes or saints of the nation; and we can talk about central symbols, both in terms of what they mean and how they are treated as sacred objects (the flag, for instance).

While Bellah focuses on civil religion as the intersection of the civil and the religious, others have pushed further to argue that the civil (the state or nation) is not taken as an expression of the ultimate reality but is the ultimate reality itself. For example, Will Herberg argues that it is not "God" that is the object of devotion of American civil religion, it is the "American Way of Life."[116] The "American Way of Life" is the ultimate reality that brings unity to the nation, that is the referent of our rituals, symbols, and sacred narratives.

Although the South is not now a separate nation, it once was. And Southerners have long talked about, and often bragged about, the Southern way of life. Reed, in his unique way, acknowledges the deep "devotion" that Southerners have to not only their region, but even more to their local communities. He writes that "there is still in the South a level of devotion and commitment to local communities unparalleled elsewhere. In the past, this has often been expressed as mindless boosterism: in my Tennessee hometown, we used to brag about how high on the list of nuclear targets we were."[117] He notes that Southerners think their region is better than others, and they tend to like one another because of their Southernness.[118]

Like Bellah, Andrew M. Manis identifies Southern civil religion at the intersection of the civil and the religious. He argues that "[c]ivil religion is 'housed' exclusively in neither the religious nor the political systems. Rather, both appeal to it to help give meaning and integration to the

---

[116] Will Herberg, "America's Civil Religion: What It Is and Whence It Comes," in *American Civil Religion*, ed. Russell E. Richey and Donald G. Jones (New York: Harper & Row, 1974) 77.

[117] Reed, *My Tears*, 73.

[118] Ibid., 139.

society."[119] And, emphasizing the identity of culture with ultimate reality, Hill argues, like Herberg, that "Southernness has been the ultimate social good news. In a descriptive sense, society is God."[120]

Wilson notes that Southern culture has always blurred the distinction between the secular and the sacred.[121] He argues that civil religion in the South "has been embodied in the official religion of the churches, but it has also been diffused through southern culture, appearing at such rituals as football games, beauty pageants, and rock and country music concerts."[122] Of course, the key point here is the way that college football plays a role in the Southern civil religion. Others have noted this role. Michael Novak, for example, claims that in "Alabama, Arkansas, and Mississippi...college football is a statewide religion; it *does* celebrate the state and the region."[123] In other words, college football is an important ritual or set of rituals for Southern civil religion. "Somehow, in the South," he adds, "to play a good game is to honor one's state, one's university, the South, and the true spirit of the American nation."[124] The state university represents, as we have seen, the state, and the football team is a tangible expression of the strength and character of the university and thus the state, if not the South as a whole. If, then, college football comes to be a part of the civil religion of the South, it might be instructive for us to look more deeply at this Southern civil religion in order to understand better what college football has meant and still may mean for Southerners.

The socio-historical roots of Southern civil religion may go back further than the Civil War, but it was that conflict that marks its true genesis. As Kurt O. Berends observes, many Southerners considered the

---

[119] Andrew M. Manis, *Southern Civil Religions in Conflict: Civil Rights and the Culture Wars* (Macon GA: Mercer University Press, 2002) 21.

[120] Hill, *Religion*, 46.

[121] Wilson, *Judgment*, 4.

[122] Ibid., xvii.

[123] Novak, *Joy of Sports*, 242 (emphasis original).

[124] Ibid., 243.

Civil War a "holy war."[125] As in any holy war, sacrifices were demanded and made. The greatest sacrifice, of course, was of one's life. The sacrifices made on behalf of the Confederacy were salvific.[126] In other words, Southerners believed that those who died in the war had been eternally saved as a result of their participation. This belief represents well the fusing of Christianity with the South. In short, what it meant to be a Christian was the same as what it meant to be a Southerner. Berends concludes, "During the war, southern identity, with its emphasis on honor, became fused with Christian identity. For many southerners, saving the Confederacy became tantamount to saving Christianity."[127] The fusing of the institutional religion with a conception of a nation and its identity, however exaggerated it may be, was the precondition for the development of a civil religion, certainly along the lines envisioned by Bellah. This fusion of religious beliefs with civic identity seems to have been the case in the South. As Wilson so succinctly puts it, "Without the Lost Cause, no civil religion would have existed."[128]

The effect of the union of religion and state as embodied by the Confederacy on Christianity was to make the church, at least for much of the white majority, racist and an instrument in support of segregation. As Paul Harvey writes, "The era from the Civil War to the civil rights movement might be described for the South as God's long century, for it was in the South during this time that American Christianity was at its most tragic and its most triumphant."[129] It was a period during which

---

[125] Kurt O. Berends, "Confederate Sacrifice and the 'Redemption' of the South," in *Religion in the American South: Protestants and Others in History and Culture*, ed. Beth Barton Schweiger and Donald G. Mathews (Chapel Hill: University of North Carolina Press, 2004) 106.

[126] Ibid., 99.

[127] Ibid., 105.

[128] Wilson, *Baptized*, 13.

[129] Paul Harvey, "God and Negroes and Jesus and Sin and Salvation: Racism, Racial Interchange, and Interracialism in Southern Religious History," in *Religion in the American South: Protestants and Others in History and Culture*, ed. Beth

white Christians were, by and large, racists and, consequently, segregationists. Donald G. Mathews goes so far as to argue that one legitimately can study segregation *as* religion.[130]

As I have indicated, however, the civil religion of the South was different for whites than it was for blacks. Manis notes that *white* Southern civil religion was tied to notions of the "Old South"; it entailed "Yankee hating," believed that the preservation of the South was integral to the preservation of the nation, and had an inordinate fear of interracial marriage.[131] On the other hand, *black* Southern civil religion focused much more on the nation of the United States—a political entity that was thought to recognize and defend the dignity and equality of African Americans—while maintaining an allegiance to the South.[132] This division, of course, had its roots in a history of slavery and the Civil War. The federal government was welcomed as a liberator for blacks, while for whites it was a foreign intruder into "their way of life." The division continued into the twentieth century and through the Civil Rights era, when the federal government came to the defense of blacks to help end state-sanctioned segregation, while many whites perceived this intervention to be a violation of their political and cultural sovereignty. Because these differing views were bound up with ideas of what it meant to be a Christian in the South, one can understand why it led to what Manis describes as a "holy war"—with all the vehemence and violence that entails.

Without a doubt, divisions between whites and blacks in the South remain today, and, as a result, we still may speak of two civil religions. At the same time, though, much has changed to bring the two races together.

Barton Schweiger and Donald G. Mathews (Chapel Hill: University of North Carolina Press, 2004) 321.

[130] Donald G. Mathews, "Lynching Is Part of the Religion of Our People: Faith in the Christian South," in *Religion in the American South: Protestants and Others in History and Culture*, ed. Beth Barton Schweiger and Donald G. Mathews (Chapel Hill: University of North Carolina Press, 2004) 155.

[131] Manis, *Southern Civil Religions*, 116–23.

[132] Ibid., 49.

While college football has been a part of the culture and life of historically black colleges and universities throughout the twentieth century, college football at the major and predominantly white state institutions, which receive greater state funding and attention, can be described as an integral element of white Southern civil religion. Nevertheless, college football increasingly has become an integral part of the black Southern civil religion as well. It perhaps has functioned to lead to a broader Southern civil religion that transcends racial divisions.

The Civil Rights era was one of great division and violence. Shortly before the beginning of that dramatic transformation of Southern life, Cash concluded:

> Proud, brave, honorable by its lights, courteous, personally generous, loyal, swift to act, often too swift, but signally effective, sometimes terrible, in its action—such was the South at its best. And such at its best it remains today, despite the great falling away in some of its virtues. Violence, intolerance, aversion and suspicion toward new ideas, an incapacity for analysis, an inclination to act from feeling rather than from thought, an exaggerated individualism and a too narrow concept of social responsibility, attachment to fictions and false values, above all too great attachment to racial values and a tendency to justify cruelty and injustice in the name of those values, sentimentality and a lack of realism—these have been its characteristic vices in the past. And, despite changes for the better, they remain its characteristic vices today.[133]

Those vices included a blind acceptance of tradition and an ideal of Southern culture, including a fundamentally racist perspective and a commitment to segregation.

---

[133] Cash, *The Mind of the South*, 428–29.

As the Civil Rights era got underway, whites responded in part through a resurgence of Confederate and Lost Cause symbolism.[134] Many turned to their religious faith as a source of inspiration and support in the battle against federal intervention to end segregation, which they perceived as yet another Yankee invasion into Southern life. Major college football teams at the time were all white, and some remained so even until the 1970s. As James Meredith integrated the University of Mississippi in 1962, Governor Ross Barnett, an alumnus of Ole Miss, gave a staunch defense of segregation in a speech entitled "I Love Mississippi" and delivered to the fans just before an Ole Miss football game. Because the state college football teams were integral to the identity of white Southerners and to their Southern civil religion, integration of teams was a matter of central concern to them. Segregation on the major college football teams was a way of reaffirming the racial hierarchy and the white Southern (religious) worldview.

The pressures to end segregation were great, both from other regions of the country as well as from blacks and supportive whites in the South. Southern college football teams found it increasingly difficult to compete against integrated teams from other regions. Intersectional games were nearly impossible for many programs, given the proscription against playing integrated teams from other regions of the country. College bowl games—and the desire of Southerners to see their teams play in them—played a significant role in getting many Southerners to overcome their racism in order to participate in these important college football events. As Charles H. Martin observes,

> The triumph of pragmatism and self-interest that integrated bowl games embodied reflected a strong desire by most white southerners to participate fully in the national sporting culture, rather than maintain an extreme regional identity and risk further marginalization and isolation. Thus each year on the sacred day of

---

[134] Wilson, *Judgment*, 25.

January 1 [when many bowl games are played], if not necessarily on the other 364 days, Dixie had become "Americanized."[135]

Change was sometimes slow. After the height of the Civil Rights era had passed, racial tensions often were brought to the surface in frightening ways. Violence still erupted. Sometimes racial problems or issues were simply ignored, both in the broader society and in the world of college football. In Russ Bebb's book, *The Big Orange: A Story of Tennessee Football*, published in 1973, hardly a word is mentioned about the segregation and integration of the team. It is almost as if segregation never happened and integration, which had only just occurred in 1968, always was the case.

The changes that occurred at this time, though, were dramatic. Woodward writes, "Not overnight, to be sure, and not without exceptions and lingering relics of the past, but with remarkable speed, the bonds of the rigid, age-hardened code of racial 'etiquette' signifying white supremacy and black inferiority fell away."[136] Perhaps nowhere was this dissolution more dramatic than on sports teams. Certainly racism still existed during the last decades of the twentieth century, and blacks for a long time (in some cases even today) found it difficult to win certain starting positions, such as the quarterback position in football, or to become head coaches. Condredge Holloway was the first black starting quarterback in the Southeastern Conference, leading the Tennessee Volunteers in 1972— several years after integration of Southeastern Conference (SEC) football had begun. It was not until 2004 that there was a black head coach in the SEC, when former Alabama star Sylvester Croom took over at Mississippi State. Though these changes certainly did not occur as swiftly and justly as anyone would wish, the inherent meritocracy of sports still provided an

---

[135] Charles H. Martin, "Integrating New Year's Day: The Racial Politics of College Bowl Games in the American South," in *The Sporting World of the Modern South*, ed. Patrick B. Miller (Urbana: University of Illinois Press, 2002) 195.

[136] Woodward, *Burden*, 245.

important vehicle for blacks in the South to attain advances toward equality and acceptance in the mainstream culture.

Wilson argues that "[s]tudies of southern mythology have proliferated in recent years, but few of them deal with the modern period and none with the importance of sports to the regional psyche."[137] He adds that sports, especially football, "are providing images for a new pantheon of southern heroes. Sports figures, perhaps even more than musicians, are becoming prime icons of the modern South, the way the Confederate veterans were heroes in the late nineteenth century."[138] Unlike Confederate veterans, though, blacks and whites alike venerate today's sports heroes, regardless of the color of the hero's skin. Wilson argues that the 1970s and 1980s saw a revitalization of Southern culture, one that identified with the past—the Lost Cause—but embraced a more inclusive future. This revitalization could be seen in sporting life "and especially in college football. The god of southern football is a tribal god, a god of the Chosen People. When Alabama [integrated by this time] played Notre Dame in the 1970s, Southerners from many states waved the [Confederate] flag and rooted for their legions against the Yankees."[139]

Sports are central to Southern culture for both blacks and whites. Although recently challenged by stock car racing and collegiate basketball, football remains king. It is central to Southern civil religion—black or white. Anybody moving to the South should know this. As Reed observes, "Newcomers might want to pick a team and follow it. It doesn't greatly matter which one—it's like religion that way, too."[140] Nowhere perhaps is this more true than in the state of Alabama, where the flagship state university offers a compelling example of how college football can function as a crucial element of civil religion.

---

[137] Wilson, *Judgment*, 44.
[138] Ibid., 50–51.
[139] Ibid., 27–28.
[140] Reed, *My Tears*, 142.

If religion has been an integral part of the civil religion of the American South, college football has been as well. Perhaps this importance is no more evident than in the case of the University of Alabama Crimson Tide. The importance of Crimson Tide football in the lives of so many Alabama citizens is an exemplary illustration of the central role of college football in Southern history, culture, and its civil religion. Before looking at the university's football team, though, a brief description of the state during the twentieth century is in order.

There perhaps is no historian of Alabama more prominent than Wayne Flynt. In his *Alabama in the Twentieth Century*, we read a history of great tragedy, progress, hatred, and promise. Of course, like most of the South, one of the dominant threads in Alabama history is a pervasive racism. In the state constitution, which was drafted in 1901, racism was legalized and institutionalized. "The virulent racism of that original charter," Flynt writes, "reminded one and all that at the beginning of the century chief among the issues of governance in the minds of white citizens was the subordination and exclusion of black citizens."[141] That constitution, which continues to govern the state today, albeit with some amending, segregated schools and banned interracial marriages. It disenfranchised many poor people, including whites, but hit blacks much harder. In addition, impossible voter registration tests and their prejudicial application effectively excluded African Americans from voting. The constitution also gutted public service programs at the state level, again hurting the poor and particularly blacks. As a result, African Americans "would attend inferior schools, die more frequently of most diseases, experience worse health, and be overrepresented in the convict lease system."[142]

Another dominant thread running through Alabama history has been poverty, which, of course, was true for most of the South. From 1880 to

---

[141] Flynt, *Alabama*, 3.
[142] Ibid., 16–17.

World War II, per capita income in the South was only about half of the U.S. average. Even by the end of the twentieth century, it still was only about 80 percent of the U.S. average.[143] Because farming was so integral to the economy, agricultural mechanization dealt millions of farm laborers a devastating blow. Alabama often competed closely with other Southern states as the most destitute state in the country. In the "mid 1990s Alabama ranked 12th in one-parent families, 7th in child hunger, 5th in low birth weights, 3rd in births to teens, and 6th in infant mortality"[144]—all social indicators of poverty. In 2000, Alabama had eight of the nation's 100 poorest counties.[145]

The poverty in Alabama is brought to life in James Agee's *Let Us Now Praise Famous Men*, his classic account of poor, rural life in the state in the 1930s. Agee describes the living conditions:

> The water facilities are such as to hold laundering and personal cleanliness at or beneath its traditional minimum; to virtual nullity during the cold months of the year, and, in the case of the Ricketts and Woods [two families Agee spent time with], the water is very probably unhealthful. The beds, the bedding, and the vermin are such a crime against sex and the need of rest as no sadistic genius could much improve on. The furniture in general and the eating implements are all at or very near the bottom of their scale: broken, insecure, uncomfortable, ill-smelling, all that a man without money must constantly accept, when he can get it, and be glad of, or make do.[146]

---

[143] Ibid., 108–11.

[144] Ibid., 187.

[145] Ibid., 186.

[146] James Agee, *Let Us Now Praise Famous Men* (Boston: Mariner Books, 2001) 184.

This kind of poverty disappeared slowly and its lasting effects persist even today.[147]

Poverty was not restricted to the rural areas, however. Birmingham, the state's largest city, experienced "white flight," as did many U.S. cities at this time. Whites fled the encroachment of black populations, creating protected enclaves in the suburbs. This left much of the city to the poor and black, who were often one and the same. By 1985, the poverty rate in the city was at 20 percent, as was the percentage of residents living in substandard housing.[148]

Violence, of course, was the most extreme obstacle that blacks faced in Alabama throughout the last hundred years. Lynchings posed a serious threat in the early part of the century, but beatings and murders erupted throughout the century, particularly during the Civil Rights Movement. The violence, though, was a secondary concern in the daily lives of African Americans. What really made Alabama such a difficult place to live for blacks was the combination of racism and poverty. Flynt describes the decades from 1900 to 1930 as "arguably the worst in the twentieth century to be black and to live in Alabama. Denied the ballot by the new constitution, they were also denied equitable and adequate education."[149] It is little wonder, as Flynt notes, that blacks fled from the state when they could. In 1900, 45 percent of the population of Alabama was black. While the state's overall population increased, the number of blacks remained stagnant. Thus, by 1970 the black population in the state had dropped nearly 20 percentage points.[150] Towards the end of the century, black emigration from Alabama finally started to decrease, and black immigration into the state resulted in a net gain in the African American community. By

---

[147] The lasting effects of such poverty can be seen in the lives of the children and even grandchildren in Dale Maharidge's *And Their Children After Them: The Legacy of Let Us Now Praise Famous Men: James Agee, Walker Evans, and the Rise and Fall of Cotton in the South* (New York: Seven Stories Press, 1989).

[148] Flynt, *Alabama*, 188.

[149] Ibid., 51.

[150] Ibid., 177.

2000, blacks made up 26 percent of the population and projections had it at as great as 36 percent in 2025.[151]

While African Americans had it the worst, Alabamians in general struggled through the twentieth century. Alabama's health statistics were appalling.[152] Education statistics were equally so. Illiteracy in the state was always higher than the national average. In 1990, the state ranked dead last in percentage of high school graduates, moving up to 46th in the nation in 1997.[153] From 1970 to 1993, the state ranked 49th in terms of expenditures for education.[154] Even the major universities, Auburn and Alabama, were rated poorly by news magazines, educational journals, and higher education organizations.[155]

Despite the statistical abyss that separated Alabama from other regions in the country and the feeling that other Americans looked down on them, Alabamians nevertheless were and continue to be very patriotic. They also are militaristic. Total mobilization for World War II, Flynt notes, "reached a staggering 321,000, one-third of the state's adult male population."[156] Flynt adds, "As for the violence of war, Alabama was a violent society anyway, regularly ranking among the top states in homicide rates, casual physical assaults, and domestic violence."[157] This penchant for violence is consistent with trends in Southern history.

The patriotism Alabamians felt and still feel for their country is matched if not exceeded by the identification and pride that they feel about their region and their state. Such identification and pride perhaps are greater than what people seem to feel in many other regions of the country, although one could argue that Georgians, Tennesseans, and other Southerners feel similarly about their states. This sense of pride and

---

[151] Ibid., 177, 372.
[152] Ibid., 204.
[153] Ibid., 226.
[154] Ibid., 230.
[155] Ibid., 238.
[156] Ibid., 384.
[157] Ibid., 374.

identification may be psychological compensation in light of the lingering effect of the Civil War, Reconstruction, and a century of subordination and inferiority in relation to the North and other regions. Alabama novelist Charles McNair puts it this way: "It's like getting beat up in a fist fight when you're young. You never get over the grudge. Alabama has been beaten up in war—the Civil War—and beaten up ever since in one media or another. There is a deep resentment in having anyone tell them how to live, a contrarian pride."[158]

So the cloth of Alabama history in the twentieth century was woven with many threads. Racism and poverty were two dominant ones, but there also were patriotism, militarism, Southern pride, and more. And, of course, there was—and is—football. Flynt writes:

> As a fiercely proud people who perpetually found themselves at or near the bottom of many quality-of-life lists, Alabamians found one measure where they often ranked at or near the top: the final college football poll. This conservative population would begrudge every cent levied on their property for education but would spend lavishly to finish in the top 10. This Bible-believing citizenry would mobilize politically to pulverize advocates of a state lottery for education but would blithely ignore coaches and alumni who broke NCAA rules.[159]

Though life could be hard in Alabama, football offered a source of pride and diversion. "Towns that were losing industry, population, and even hope," Flynt argues, "rallied around local gridiron teams. Football and churches became the focus of local pride and community spirit." Indeed, in "many ways football and church merged."[160] Given this function and importance, it is little wonder that public funding for football programs, either at the high school or college level, has been high. Flynt

---

[158] Quoted in Flynt, *Alabama*, 151.
[159] Ibid., 408–409.
[160] Ibid., 422, 423.

adds, "If the Bible is correct when it states that where a person's treasure is there his heart will be also, then the state's true affection could be found at Bryant-Denny [University of Alabama] or Jordan-Hare [Auburn University] stadium."[161]

Football is a source of fierce devotion and even obsession in the state. In a highly religious state like Alabama, it is quite significant that a recent survey indicates that there are more atheists than non-football fans in the state.[162] Moreover, living in the state, one ultimately must pick a denomination or a team—usually the Auburn Tigers or the Alabama Crimson Tide. Dunnavant writes that from "an early age, children in the Heart of Dixie made a choice—Alabama or Auburn—and the decision tended to brand them for life."[163] He adds that because "the fans took their allegiances so seriously, the Alabama-Auburn rivalry routinely divided families and friends all across the state."[164] It does not matter if one attended the university or not. "At Alabama and Auburn, football extended beyond a game to become a process of community bonding, creating 'the Auburn family' and 'the Bama family,'" Flynt observes. "And one needed no diploma from either school to belong. College 'bloodlines' were determined by devotion to football teams, not by degrees earned."[165]

In this regard, one's favorite football team is like one's church. One is generally born into it. "Humorists insist that college football is the *unofficial* religion of most Alabamians," Flynt notes. "But if religion is defined as the object of a person's ultimate concern, a case could be made for Auburn or Alabama football as *the* state religion."[166] This assessment

---

[161] Ibid., 409.

[162] Warren St. John, *Rammer Jammer Yellow Hammer: A Journey into the Heart of Fan Mania* (New York: Crown Publishers, 2004) 1–2.

[163] Keith Dunnavant, *The Missing Ring: How Bear Bryant and the 1966 Crimson Tide Were Denied College Football's Most Elusive Prize* (New York: Thomas Dunne Books, 2006) 241.

[164] Ibid., 244.

[165] Flynt, *Alabama*, 423.

[166] Ibid., 449 (emphasis original).

does not mean, however, that football supplanted Christianity. "Rather than serving as a substitute for Christianity," Flynt argues, "football became its complement. The logic went like this: Christ did not select sissies to be disciples; he preferred real men, rugged fishermen and artisans."[167]

While Auburn has a rich tradition and its fans are as fervent as any others, the Alabama Crimson Tide stand out in the state and even the region. Much of the credit for this goes to an early twentieth century president of the university, George Denny. Football had already been introduced to the campus before Denny arrived and became president in 1912, but after he arrived, Denny strongly encouraged its development and the identification of the university with the team. As Flynt notes, Denny "made national football prominence the centerpiece of his plans to modernize and expand the university."[168] Central to achieving that prominence was to play the dominant schools from other regions of the country, especially, early on, the Northeast. In its first trip North in 1922, Alabama played the University of Pennsylvania, a powerhouse at the time, in Philadelphia. Southern teams, being inferior, almost always had to travel to the intersectional opponent's home field. Though clearly the underdog, Alabama pulled out the victory—one of the first of many significant victories in the 1920s. As Allen Barra writes, "Alabama papers touted the victory as a revenge for Gettysburg; the score—Alabama 9, Penn 7—was painted on the red brick side of a drugstore on University Boulevard. Locals claim that the score could still be made out on the wall even after World War II."[169] Inferior to Northern states in so many social indices, Alabama was at least superior in one—by a score of 9 to 7. Dunnavant writes that the win over Pennsylvania "was more than a football victory; it was a triumph of the Southern spirit—proof that the South, that Alabama, could compete and win against the best of the North in football and

---

[167] Ibid., 449.

[168] Ibid., 418.

[169] Allen Barra, *The Last Coach: A Life of Paul "Bear" Bryant* (New York: W. W. Norton, 2005) 41.

perhaps other things, a provocative, radical thought at the time."[170] Dunnavant adds:

> The Crimson Tide was no longer just a team. It was a symbol of pride, a symbol of hope, and in the years ahead, the vast majority of the state's residents would come to identify with it in ways many were not fully equipped to understand, bathing in the reflected glow of Alabama's glorious triumphs, and, in the process, feeling better about themselves and their beleaguered place in the world, when pride, like other life-sustaining commodities, was precious and hard-won.[171]

An even more important victory occurred four years later in the 1926 Rose Bowl against Washington, chronicled brilliantly by Andrew Doyle. As Doyle notes, it is difficult to overstate the significance of the game not only for Alabama fans and citizens of the state but for Southerners in general. He writes:

> The University of Alabama's stunning upset victory over the University of Washington in the 1926 Rose Bowl is arguably the most significant game in southern football history, but it did more than establish the legitimacy of southern football. This game possessed a multifaceted symbolic importance that illustrates the profoundly mixed emotions with which white southerners beheld their fitful and incomplete movement into the American cultural and economic mainstream.[172]

---

[170] Dunnavant, *Missing Ring*, 7.

[171] Ibid.

[172] Andrew Doyle, "Turning the Tide: College Football and Southern Progressivism," in *The Sporting World of the Modern South*, ed. Patrick B. Miller (Urbana: University of Illinois Press, 2002) 101.

On the one hand, lingering resentment from the Civil War and Reconstruction and feelings of inferiority in relation to those "damn Yankees" left Southerners alienated from other American citizens. But on the other hand, Southerners were beginning to seek greater assimilation into the dominant American culture, including into its sporting activities. The Rose Bowl at that time was the *only* college football bowl game, and for Alabama to be invited was a big step for the South with regard to greater cultural integration. On top of that, Alabama won! We will never know how an Alabama loss would have been received, but we do know that the Alabama victory was meaningful not only to Alabamians but to all Southerners. "[T]he Tide's trip to Pasadena captured the imagination not just of Alabama but of the entire South in an age where many could still personally recall the end of the Civil War,"[173] Barra writes. "The Crimson Tide's victory electrified the South.... The team's return to Alabama heralded the greatest statewide celebration since the shelling of Fort Sumter."[174]

The actual and perceived inferiority of the South was a major reason the game and the result were so meaningful. As Doyle asserts, a "Rose Bowl victory by Alabama would diminish the stigma of southern football inferiority, but it would also be a sublime tonic for a people buffeted by a historical legacy of military defeat, poverty, and alienation from the American political and cultural mainstream."[175] In his albeit partisan account of the game, Eli Gold writes, "In the early 1900s folks in the West, East, and Midwest had an elitist attitude in general. It's no secret there was bigotry directed toward southerners stemming from the Civil War. Many northerners looked down on the largely rural South and its relative poverty. They also looked down on their brand of football."[176] Thus, it is little wonder that the "press back home was building the game against

---

[173] Barra, *Last Coach*, 4.

[174] Ibid., 45.

[175] Doyle, "Turning the Tide," 103–104.

[176] Eli Gold, *Crimson Nation: The Shaping of the South's Most Dominant Football Team* (Nashville TN: Rutledge Hill Press, 2005) 46–47.

Washington to be nothing less than a Civil War rematch."[177] While the 20–19 victory prompted a huge celebration in Tuscaloosa, excited Southerners throughout the region celebrated the team's achievement at numerous stops along the way as the team's train made its way back from California. For example, one-thousand Tulane students reportedly cheered the team as it passed through New Orleans.[178] As Dunnavant claims, the victory "gave southerners the rare opportunity to claim national superiority in something other than historical angst."[179]

The 1926 Rose Bowl victory was the first of several such victories and national championships for Alabama in the coming decades. It was natural for so many in the state and throughout the region to identify with the Crimson Tide. "The Tide's Rose Bowl victory, and the national championships that followed in 1926, 1930, 1934, and 1941," Flynt notes, "proved a decisive rebuttal to negative northern publicity that depicted southerners as overly pious Bible Belters, hookworm-sapped weaklings, lazy slaggards, or incest-prone defectives."[180] Dunnavant concludes:

> In Alabama as throughout much of the South, college football is more than just a game. It is a kind of cultural glue that transcends class, race, sex, income level, and educational attainment, bonding the state's citizens in a way outsiders can never truly appreciate. In the absence of major league sports and other cultural activities, amid the drumbeat of statistics ranking the state among the nation's poorest and worst-educated, college football serves as the foremost extension of the state's pride and self-esteem. Deeply rooted in the southern traditions and a symbol of the state's tendency to favor the physical over the intellectual, the game is, for Alabamians, the great leveler. Football gives them an

---

[177] Ibid., 49.
[178] Ibid., 51.
[179] Dunnavant, *Coach*, 36.
[180] Flynt, *Alabama*, 419.

opportunity to truly compete against the rest of the country and, more often than not, to win.[181]

Football victories restored pride and were, according to Doyle, a "symbolic vindication of southern honor."[182] Given the importance of honor in Southern culture, it is little wonder that football could become such an important cultural activity.

Football victories were not merely revenge for the South's defeated past or an assault on behalf of the Lost Cause. They were also a way for the South to integrate into mainstream American culture and to claim that it was as modern and advanced as other regions. "Southern college football clearly illustrates how southerners expressed fervent devotion to the ideals of the past," Doyle writes, "while simultaneously transforming those ideals in the service of a radically new socioeconomic regime."[183] Thus, "Southerners may have extolled the Tide as a defiant symbol of a bygone era, but in virtually the same breath, they touted the team as proof that the region was every bit as modern and progressive as the rest of the nation."[184]

For many decades after 1926, the Alabama football team continued to be a source of pride and honor for its fans, for Alabamians, and for many Southerners. There were many great victories, important bowl game triumphs, and national championships. While there were great players and coaches throughout the years, none was greater than Paul "Bear" Bryant. Indeed, understanding Bryant's celebrated life tells us much about Alabama football and Southern civil religion.

Bryant was born in a poverty-stricken rural area in Arkansas called Moro Bottom on 11 September 1913. When he was a boy, other children, particularly those in Fordyce, the nearest town of any significance, often picked on him. The experience of growing up poor shaped both his own character as well as his legend. Poverty is something he shared in common

---

[181] Dunnavant, *Coach*, 184–85.

[182] Doyle, "Turning the Tide," 108.

[183] Ibid., 113.

[184] Ibid., 117.

with so many Southerners, and his rise from poverty was a story that resonated strongly with them. As an adult, he would tear a small hole in each of his tee shirts as a symbolic reminder of his humble beginnings.[185]

It was football that saved Bryant from an otherwise impoverished life. Recruited by Alabama, he had the opportunity to play for the legendary Frank Thomas in the mid-1930s. Those years included some great Crimson Tide teams, including conference champions, Rose Bowl champions, and a 1934 National Championship team. Bryant may not have been the most talented member of the team (his roommate was the great receiver Don Hutson, a future National Football League Hall-of-Famer), but he was known as one of the toughest. In the 1935 game against archrival Tennessee, Bryant played with a broken leg!

That toughness, even in the face of considerable physical pain, carried over into his coaching. As the head coach at Maryland in 1945, Bryant pushed a broken bone back into place in the finger of Joe Drach so the player could finish the game.[186] The students at Maryland were so enamored with Bryant that thousands of them demonstrated in front of the administration building when they heard he would be leaving to go to the University of Kentucky.[187] And he had been at Maryland for only one season at that point.

Bryant turned around the football program at Kentucky, a school better known for its basketball teams. He started to garner national attention. From 1946 to 1953, Bryant went 60–23–5, including an 11–1 team in 1950 that won the Southeastern Conference championship and defeated a powerful Oklahoma team in the Sugar Bowl. Bryant knew, however, that he always would play second fiddle to Adolf Rupp, the legendary basketball coach at Kentucky, so in 1954 he went to Texas A&M.

It was Bryant's first team at A&M that he took to the desolate town of Junction for a training period in the hot Texas sun that was so brutal that

---

[185] Barra, *Last Coach*, 3.

[186] Ibid., 97; Dunnavant, *Coach*, 58–59.

[187] Barra, *Last Coach*, 103.

less than a third of those who went out returned, the others having surreptitiously left in the middle of the night for bus rides back to College Station or home. While the "Junction Boys," subsequent subjects of both a book and a feature film, may be the most famous recipients (or victims) of Bryant's sometimes barbaric practices, all of Bryant's teams had similar experiences. As Tom Stoddard notes, "the degree to which he had defined and codified the techniques of controlled violence was exceptional."[188] This harsh discipline involved not only grueling drills on the practice field that pitted one player against another (or sometimes multiple players), but also the infamous "gym" classes, in which his Alabama players were locked in a hot room, wrestling for their positions, leaving bruised and bloodied and not infrequently with stains of vomit on their clothes. Like many coaches of that era, Bryant did not believe in water breaks, which he thought were a sign of weakness, and he probably was lucky that a player never died from dehydration.

The team that Bryant inherited at Texas A&M was terrible. Even he could only achieve a 1–9 record in 1954. But in the subsequent three years, he compiled a 24–5–2 record, including a Southwest Conference title in 1956. In 1958, however, Bryant heard "mama calling": He returned to Alabama, his alma mater. The preceding years had seen a significant decline in the fortunes of the Crimson Tide, and Bryant was hired to restore the program to national prominence. When he came, he told recruits that he would lead them to a national championship by the end of their four years with him. It only took three.

The 1958 team did not have to go to Junction or any such barren town for early season practice, but they immediately got a taste of what it was like to play for Bryant. The late summer/early fall in Alabama that year was one of the hottest on record. Before classes started, players practiced in both the morning and the afternoon. The summer heat was so intense that many players cried just thinking of having to go back for afternoon

---

[188] Stoddard, *Turnaround*, 68.

practice.[189] One afternoon, Bryant decided to test the players with a running drill. Players would get in their normal stances, run full-speed for some number of yards (10, 20, 30, or 40), and then return to their stance. They did this exercise again and again. One player recalls:

I believe everybody I can remember that day was down crawling on their knees.... They weren't only crawling, there was a lot of throwing up. I thought really that day that I was going to die, and I was in good shape. I came back [to school after the summer] in good shape...but not for that.... I saw coaches grab players by the seat of their britches and throw 'em because they were throwing up...they'd just make 'em go a little bit more.... I'll always remember that...you'd be on your all fours trying to finish, and your buddy over there would be throwing up, and the coaches would be yelling, "You're not going to quit, you can't quit, you'll quit in the fourth quarter if you quit here."[190]

This technique was a famous strategy for Bryant. He would push the players so strenuously in practice that by the fourth quarter of the game, his players had greater stamina and could close out the victory. This toughness was both mental and physical. Certainly the media scrutiny at the time was not nearly as great as it is today. And in later years, even Bryant adapted his techniques, abandoning, for instance, the prohibition against water. Even so, many people in Alabama and throughout the South saw, or would have seen, nothing terrible in his practices. Men were supposed to be tough. Life was tough. Bryant knew sacrifice and suffering from personal experience. Success came at a price, sometimes a high price. Stoddard notes that "[w]hen a high school athlete was actually offered a scholarship, he incurred a responsibility toward his family, town, and school that was a heavy one for an eighteen-year-old to carry. Success became important beyond its personal meaning."[191] If one was going to

---

[189] Ibid., 123.
[190] Quoted in Stoddard, *Turnaround*, 124–25.
[191] Ibid., 51.

succeed and preserve his honor and pride, as well as that of his family, town, school, and state, then he had to be willing to pay the price. This idea was not simply Bryant's philosophy; it was and still is, to some degree, the Southern ethos.

Bryant's methods clearly were successful. His 1961 team, the first national championship team he had at Alabama, allowed only 22 points all season. And that team was probably not even his best! Bryant not only had great teams, he had great decades. In the 1960s, he went 98–20–3, winning the SEC title four times and the national championship three times. And he was only getting warmed up. In the 1970s, he went 107–13 with eight conference crowns and three national championships. During a stretch from 1971 to 1975, the Crimson Tide went 53–2 overall and 35–1 in conference.

While Bryant was known for his toughness—he intimidated members of the media and others as well as his players—he was nevertheless a caring and compassionate man. One of his greatest players was George Blanda, a member of the team at Kentucky. Blanda had come from a relatively poor family and did not have money for adequate clothing or a decent pair of shoes. Bryant made sure he got what he needed, telling Blanda that as a star player on the team he really needed to be able to dress the part.[192] And while he was tough on his players on numerous occasions, he also knew when to lighten up. At halftime of the Alabama-Tennessee game in 1966, a game played in a driving rain and on a sloppy field, the Crimson Tide trailed 10–0. Instead of berating his players, Bryant told them that they had Tennessee right where they wanted them, that the second half would be Alabama's half, and that they would win the game. "With a few simple words," Dunnavant writes, "he demonstrated his faith in them, and to the players in that room, his faith was a powerful thing, a force of nature capable of rivaling the mighty rain itself."[193] Alabama won 11–10.

---

[192] Barra, *Last Coach*, 18.

[193] Dunnavant, *Missing Ring*, 160.

But Bryant's care for his players went beyond the playing field. He attended funerals of his players' parents. He continually helped former players in their lives after college and, for most of them, after their playing days were over. His assistance included advice, investments in their businesses, or simply well-placed telephone calls to people who could help them. For those who "stuck it out," who persevered through the grueling demands of being one of the Bear's players, he "would go out of his way to help with a small loan, or to intercede with a fellow coach, a principal, or a potential employer for a job."[194]

Bryant considered himself, first and foremost, a teacher, though one who taught young men through the game of football. He always refused to have a base salary greater than the president of the university (something that is not the case for most major college football coaches), because he felt that it would send the wrong message. Education had to take precedence over football. This educational priority meant not only intellect but character as well, what we might call moral education. "Instead of grooming his players to become pros," Barra notes, "for thirty-eight years Bryant coached as if he had a sacred obligation to make their lives better for having played football for him. And today, almost to a man, the men who played for him look you in the eye and tell you that that is indeed the case, that they are better men, that they lived richer, more responsible lives, because they played football for Bear Bryant."[195] He even supported players who decided that football was an obstacle to their academic success, as he did with John Paul Poole, an Alabama player who quit the team in order to finish his degree in electrical engineering.[196] In many ways, Bryant exemplified what we might call "tough love." He was a man of psychological strength (and physical, for that matter) who served as a fairly strict disciplinarian to young men. In this regard, he was the stereotypical *Southern* man, helping to form the character of other Southern young men.

---

[194] Stoddard, *Turnaround*, 219.

[195] Barra, *Last Coach*, xxiv.

[196] Stoddard, *Turnaround*, 108–109.

Bryant also found ways to help players from other teams on occasion as well as many people unassociated with his teams. After Kent Waldrep, a member of the Texas Christian University football team, was paralyzed during a game against Alabama, Bryant frequently visited him in the hospital, showing emotional strength when with Waldrep but weeping with his parents in the hallway.[197] After Waldrep's medical coverage through TCU ran out, it was Bryant who started a special fund (including his own substantial contribution) to pay for care and equipment. Bryant often was a visitor to the children's wards at area hospitals, an experience that must have been quite special for Alabama children in particular, even if difficult for Bryant. "On one occasion in the late 1970s," according to Dunnavant, "he showed up at the Children's Hospital in Birmingham and went to see a terminally sick little girl who had been asking for him, and he held her in his arms until she died."[198]

There undoubtedly are thousands of stories—some factual, some embellished, and some simply legend—from "average Joes" and "average Janes" about their encounters, brief as they might have been, with Bryant. In numerous boxes of letters to Bryant stored at the Paul W. Bryant Museum Library in Tuscaloosa, Alabama, one finds letter after letter from people asking Bryant for favors both big and small. One man asks that Bryant pay a visit to the man's friend in Mobile who was a huge Alabama fan. Bryant replied that he certainly would do so on his next visit to Mobile.[199] Another man shared a story of a young boy who had dreamed of playing football but recently lost three fingers on his right hand. Bryant wrote the boy about the many players he had who lacked a finger or two and even a hand. He added, "Sure it will be a little harder for you in some things, but just make up your mind that you will work harder than others

---

[197] Barra, *Last Coach*, 407.

[198] Dunnavant, *Coach*, 200.

[199] Correspondence between Paul Bryant and Graham B. Loper, 20 May 1966 and 15 March 1967, Bryant Papers, Paul W. Bryant Museum Library, Tuscaloosa AL.

and be more determined than the others. If you do this, and I am sure you will, you will succeed in athletics and everything else."[200]

Bryant seemed to understand his importance to people and responded accordingly. A father in Texas sent Bryant a telegram to let him know how much his fifteen-year-old daughter would appreciate and treasure an autographed Christmas card from Bryant. Bryant wrote the girl, "I just heard through a very reliable source that you are BAMA's Greatest Texan Supporter. Just want you to know how much we appreciate your support of the Crimson Tide."[201] He sent films of Alabama games to soldiers in Vietnam who rooted for the Tide[202] and an autographed football to a boy whose father had had to return a ball that had been kicked into the stands during a game.[203] People speak of his being "larger than life," of his kindness, of the fact that he was a Southern gentleman. Vicki Middlebrooks tells another typical story:

In the late spring semester of my junior year in 1971, I was worried and very concerned about getting enough money to go to summer school so I could take some extra courses in order to graduate in May 1972. It was raining and I had had a lot of tests and papers due. I was stressed to the max. I was walking in the pouring rain from the library across the quad with my head down, soaking wet and crying. Suddenly, I ran into a man. When I looked up, there was Coach Bryant. He was looking straight down at me as he said in that

---

[200] Fred E. Ingerson to Paul Bryant, 8 March 1967, and Paul Bryant to Stephen Brown, 13 March 1967, Bryant Papers, Paul W. Bryant Museum Library, Tuscaloosa AL.

[201] Harold Hendricks to Paul Bryant, 4 December 1967, and Paul Bryant to Kim Hendricks, 5 December 1967, Bryant Papers, Paul W. Bryant Museum Library, Tuscaloosa AL.

[202] Paul Bryant to Gene H. Williams, 10 October 1966, Bryant Papers, Paul W. Bryant Museum Library, Tuscaloosa AL.

[203] Correspondence between Cas Weinacker and Paul Bryant, 3 and 4 November 1968, Bryant Papers, Paul W. Bryant Museum Library, Tuscaloosa AL.

low, slow southern drawl…'Suck it up and go, Dahlin'.' He walked off, and I just stood there. It is amazing how a brief moment can teach you a lesson you remember for the rest of your life.[204]

What this and other stories present is a stereotype of the Southern, male ideal: tough and strict yet caring and compassionate. Bryant was not only a Southern gentleman, but for many he was *the* Southern gentleman—he was what Southern men aspired to be and what they hoped their sons would become.

Like all those Southern men who admired him, Bryant also struggled through the waning years of the segregationist South and the dawning of a new South. The Civil Rights Movement did not occur only in Alabama, though the state often stole the national spotlight. The process of integrating hotels, lunch counters, and schools was a struggle throughout the South. Even the integration of football teams was a significant struggle and an important one. Given the prominence of Bryant, the supremacy of Alabama football in the South and its national recognition as well as the conflicts, confrontations, and tragedies of the Civil Rights Movement in the state of Alabama, the integration of the Crimson Tide took on a significance and symbolic import that matched its successes on the football field.

Major college football in the South, including the Southeastern Conference, remained entirely segregated until 1963.[205] While other Southern schools began integrating at that time, the SEC was the last of the major Southern conferences to integrate, beginning with Kentucky in 1967 and Tennessee in 1968. The last SEC schools to integrate were Mississippi, Louisiana State, and Georgia in 1972.[206]

Like most Southern states, Alabama had its fair share of racist prejudice. Yet it also had many whites who recognized the injustice of

---

[204] Vicki Massler Middlebrooks, "The Winning Ticket," *Tales of the Tide: A Book by Alabama Fans…For Alabama Fans,* ed. Clint Lovette and Jarrod Bazemore (Birmingham AL: FANtastic Memories, 2004) 223.

[205] Oriard, *King Football,* 9.

[206] Ibid., 10.

segregation. They were distraught by the violence that whites perpetrated against blacks and foresaw a future that would be very different from the region's historical racism. Dunnavant states, "Alabamians approached the controversial issue of integration from various viewpoints, but the vast majority abhorred the violence, resented the pejorative image a small number of troublemakers were giving their state, and felt increasingly defensive about their place in the world."[207]

It took a great deal of courage and perseverance on the part of African Americans in Alabama finally to achieve change. As many blacks had returned from World War II to segregationist Alabama, they wondered why they had gone half way around the world to fight for liberty and justice when they did not have it at home. This generation would lead in the initial years of the Civil Rights Movement. Many whites, however, did not respond quietly or positively to the call for equality and justice. From 1949 to 1965, Alabama literally was a battleground. In Birmingham alone, there were at least 19 bombings of black churches, homes, and other buildings during that period.[208] As Flynt notes, "Had such a wave of terror been conducted by Islamic extremists after September 11, 2001, the nation would have declared war." Some Alabama Christians fought on the side of justice, but many (white) Christians supported the forces of segregation and, by implication, the violence that allowed it to continue. Flynt concludes, "That Klansmen could have conducted such violence in Birmingham amidst the virtual silence of white evangelical churches, associations, conventions, and conferences does not speak well of the capacity of Christians to transcend their culture."[209]

The Voting Rights Act of 1965 was a watershed moment in the Civil Rights Movement and the history of many Southern states, including Alabama. With increased voter registration and participation, the political dynamics in Alabama began to change. Federal court rulings accelerated the process of desegregation. It should be noted that sport frequently was an

---

[207] Dunnavant, *Missing Ring*, 78–79.
[208] Flynt, *Alabama*, 470–72.
[209] Ibid., 472.

agent of change. As Flynt notes, "Integrated sports came to Alabama before integrated churches, country clubs, or politics."[210]

It was in this highly charged racial context that Bryant returned to Alabama in 1958. While Bryant was not the last to integrate his team—he eventually was both head football coach and athletic director at Alabama—neither was he a leader on this issue. Doyle describes Bryant as a "racial moderate" who slowly moved toward a more liberal position,[211] not unlike, we imagine, many men in the South whose lives spanned across the middle of the twentieth century. Gold, a longtime broadcaster of Alabama football games, observes that "I have never heard or read one word about Bryant being a bigot."[212] He adds that "under the leadership of Coach Bryant, who virtually could do no wrong as far as Alabamians were concerned, the transition to an integrated football squad, when it finally happened, was surprisingly smooth."[213] Of course, the key phrase here is "when it finally happened."

While Bryant may not have been much of a racist—Dunnavant argues, somewhat unpersuasively, that he generally treated blacks paternalistically—he was late in championing the cause of African Americans. He wanted to recruit black athletes at Kentucky and would have done so at Alabama, but for a long time he did not feel the time was right.[214] "By nearly all accounts," Barra writes, "he was ahead of most southern whites of his generation in his attitude toward race. Nearly every comment that can be gleaned from his friends and associates over the years indicates that he was for the integration of the football teams he coached."[215]

---

[210] Ibid., 430.

[211] Andrew Doyle, "An Atheist in Alabama Is Someone Who Doesn't Believe in Bear Bryant: A Symbol for an Embattled South," in *The Sporting World of the Modern South*, ed. Patrick B. Miller (Urbana: University of Illinois Press, 2002) 253, 268–71.

[212] Gold, *Crimson Nation*, 110.

[213] Ibid.

[214] Dunnavant, *Coach*, 249.

[215] Barra, *Last Coach*, 378.

At the same time, though, he had the misfortune of being linked to the divisive and racist governor of the state, George Wallace. Wallace used white fear of black empowerment and integration to win office multiple times. Bryant avoided becoming embroiled in politics, especially the racial politics in Alabama and more specifically the question of integration on the University of Alabama campus. But he apparently did provide monetary support to at least one Wallace campaign—his presidential campaign of 1968. In a letter dated 17 December 1968, Wallace thanks Bryant for his "generous contribution" and "all [he] did for us during the campaign."[216] In addition, Bryant facilitated the adoption of Wallace as a member of Alabama's prestigious "A" Club Alumni Association.[217]

Although Bryant certainly had some kind of connection or relationship with Wallace, it was greater in the popular imagination of Southerners and Northerners alike than it was in fact. "To much of the outside world, which considered Alabama a pariah state," Dunnavant writes, "George Wallace and Bear Bryant were synonymous."[218] A letter writer from Los Angeles wrote Bryant in 1967: "Your scrappy but sound team shares the nation's spotlight with your Alabama Governor George Wallace and his wife and successor [Wallace's wife Lurleen was elected to a term as Alabama's governor.] as being well-schooled in their required respective fundamentals in their present lives. They have the secret admiration of many Northern 'Yankees'—and I'm not kidding either!!!"[219]

When asked about the integration of the Alabama football team, Bryant often argued that the time was just not right. He did not oppose integration per se, but he felt there were too many people not ready for it, and he was concerned about the safety of the black players who would break

---

[216] George C. Wallace to Paul Bryant, 17 December 1968, Bryant Papers, Paul W. Bryant Museum Library, Tuscaloosa AL.

[217] Correspondence between A. B. Elmore and Paul Bryant, 2, 7, 21, and 30 July 1965, Bryant Papers, Paul W. Bryant Museum Library, Tuscaloosa AL.

[218] Dunnavant, *Missing Ring*, 78.

[219] Carl M. Miciak to Paul Bryant, 4 January 1967, Bryant Papers, Paul W. Bryant Museum Library, Tuscaloosa AL.

the color barrier. As Dunnavant argues, "he may have been right, but his caution played into the hands of the forces who wanted to equate him with George Wallace."[220]

In 1963, Wallace stood in the doorway of Foster Auditorium on the campus of the University of Alabama in an effort to prevent federal troops from ensuring the integration of the school. Forever known as the "Stand in the Schoolhouse Door," this largely symbolic and failed act of desperation galvanized support for Wallace and his legion of segregationists. Dunnavant notes, "From the vantage point of four decades of history, the continued segregation of the Alabama football program three years after Wallace stood in the schoolhouse door is impossible to justify. Knowing what we know now, Bryant should have invested some of his hard-earned political capital to knock down the barrier for good, regardless of whether many of his fans were unprepared for the change. Some, after all, would never be ready."[221] Bryant can be faulted for his lack of leadership. Barra argues that Bryant's "greatest failure as a leader was his lack of moral force, his hesitancy to do the right thing—to do what he very clearly understood was the right thing—when it was time to racially integrate the most storied football program in the South." At the same time, Barra adds that perhaps "his greatest achievement as a leader was the thoroughness with which he integrated the team and the coaching staff once the commitment was made."[222]

By all accounts, Bryant believed that a football player should be judged by his performance on the field and not by the color of his skin. As Ozzie Newsome, one of Bryant's greatest African American players from the early 1970s, said, "Martin Luther King Jr. preached equality. Coach Bryant practiced it."[223] Nevertheless, it took a number of years and a certain sequence of events to bring Bryant's moral position and Alabama's racial climate into synchronicity. Only then could an African American put on

---

[220] Dunnavant, *Missing Ring*, 82.

[221] Ibid., 88.

[222] Barra, *Last Coach*, xxv.

[223] Quoted in Barra, *Last Coach*, 343.

the crimson uniform. "Exactly why it took a coach with as genuinely integrationist sympathies as Bryant's so long to integrate," Barra observes, "isn't easily explained."[224] Nevertheless, some of the events that precipitated integration can be identified and explained.

After winning back-to-back national championships in 1964 and 1965, Bryant perhaps had one of his greatest teams entering the 1966 season. The pre-season number one selection, Bryant's Crimson Tide team was prepared to face another challenging schedule. One challenge it may not have been prepared for, however, was the increasingly tense racial climate in Alabama and the increasingly negative view that most of the country had about the state, its government, and even its all-white football team. Assaulted in the media for their bigotry and violence, many white Alabamians—whether or not they supported segregation—found solace in the achievements of their football champions. "[T]he vast majority of Alabamians looked up to those young men and their legendary coach," Dunnavant writes. "Because in 1966, the Crimson Tide was more than a football team. It was also a mirror. And a shield. A source of inspiration. And validation."[225] He adds, "To people all across the state who felt beleaguered on the race issue, the Alabama football team was like a shield deflecting all those slings and arrows of contempt and disgrace. It was their defense not only against the national news media, but ultimately, against their own shortcomings, their own gathering sense of shame at allowing an otherwise wonderful place to be defined by one glaring weakness."[226] Much of the country outside of the South viewed Alabama as a backward cesspool of racism and hatred. Most Alabamians rejected that viewpoint, and in the Crimson Tide, they saw the best of themselves. "Watching the Crimson Tide on television or in their mind's eye, Alabama fans of various backgrounds believed they were looking at themselves," Dunnavant argues. "They saw a program defined by strength, class, and a pursuit of excellence not just as a representative of their state, but as a reflection of who they were

---

[224] Ibid., 370.

[225] Dunnavant, *Missing Ring*, 2.

[226] Ibid., 80.

and what they believed."[227] The pride that they had for the team was made that much greater by the fact that their team tended to be smaller than teams from other regions of the country. Bryant preferred quick and agile athletes, especially prior to the era of two-platoon football. So when Alabama played teams like Nebraska, the Crimson Tide players were often significantly outweighed. "To Alabamians who felt like underdogs and clung to the Crimson Tide as a validation of their little corner of the world," Dunnavant observes, "the stunning achievements of the undersized teams of the mid-1960s assumed a kind of David vs. Goliath higher truth, making the players seem even more heroic."[228]

Alabama began the 1966 season ranked number one in both of the major polls that determined the national champion at the end of the season. Despite winning week after week, the Crimson Tide slowly was surpassed by Notre Dame and Michigan State. Given the fact that their team continued to win, Alabamians could only interpret the changes in the polls as a slight at best and an outright insult and injustice at worst. While many perhaps recognized the social and political context in the country that was influencing the voters in the major polls, there were others who undoubtedly failed to see the connection. Dunnavant writes:

Many of the same people who voted for the enormously popular Wallaces lived and breathed Alabama football. As fans all across the Heart of Dixie gradually began to see the poll slight as yet another shot at the state by the national media, few probably considered the irony that their decision to twice elect the Wallaces effectively empowered their critics. The voters' continued validation of the politician who stood in the schoolhouse door did not excuse the behavior of any panelist who equated George Wallace with Bear Bryant, but it certainly enabled it.[229]

---

[227] Ibid., 81.
[228] Ibid., 135.
[229] Ibid., 206.

The situation was made even worse when Michigan State and Notre Dame played one another late in the season. While normally this would have resulted in one of them being knocked out from their position in front of Alabama, their 6–6 tie left the Crimson Tide ranked third. Late in the game, Notre Dame coach Ara Parseghian had a chance to try and win the game but meekly chose to run out the clock. Strategically, that decision probably guaranteed Notre Dame the national championship; ultimately, it was voted number one in both polls. But to Alabama fans, it was an act of Yankee cowardice. When asked about it, Bryant said, "Everything at Alabama is based on winning.... I couldn't go for a tie late in the game.... *In our region,* our football players have a far-reaching effect on young people. Some of them are going off to Vietnam everyday, and I hope they aren't going over there for a tie."[230] Approximately 40 years later, Alabamians' disdain for Parseghian's decision and for the decisions of the poll voters is represented well in Dunnavant's words. He describes the final polls as "an insult—an unmistakable slap at the 'Bama program. At the SEC. At the South. At the most sacred principles of college football."[231] It was not only Alabama fans, though, who felt slighted and insulted; many Southerners did as well. A letter writer from Arkansas wrote Bryant in January 1967: "The Northerners are always down grading the football in the SWC [Southwest Conference] and the SEC [Southeastern Conference], however, I believe this present team of yours could beat anyone in the U.S. and Canada (except the [Arkansas] Razorbacks). You deserve number one in the Nation. Therefore, we thank you for enhancing the football in the South."[232] Another correspondent from Louisiana, identifying his subject as "THE PREJUDICED NORTHERNER," wrote that "a southern powerhouse has to practically walk on water (as coach Bear Bryant is purported to do) to achieve a top rank," adding that while Southerners certainly have their prejudices, so do people in other sections

---

[230] Quoted in Dunnavant, *Missing Ring,* 222 (emphasis mine).

[231] Ibid., 232.

[232] Ped G. Magness to Paul Bryant, 4 January 1967, Bryant Papers, Paul W. Bryant Museum Library, Tuscaloosa AL.

of the country, though the "press and other news media" tend to ignore that.[233] Dunnavant's analysis seems powerfully accurate and is worth quoting at length:

> More than a century after the end of the Civil War, the divide between North and South still defined the country in a variety of ways, and many Southerners were still inclined to hear echoes of the lost cause in any conflict between the regions. The wound still ran deep, and in many ways, football was a kind of proxy for a hundred years of frustration. Viewed through the prism of the historic rivalry between North and South, the battle for the 1966 national championship took on even greater meaning to many Southerners....
>
> At a time when it remained acceptable in the North to look down on Southerners, to stereotype anyone living south of the Mason-Dixon Line as an ignorant, racist, inferior hick, when southerners invested football with even greater meaning because it gave the region an opportunity to compete against the North on supposedly equal footing, the 1966 vote [in the college football polls] struck many Southerners as yet another indignity foisted upon the region by the North's superiority complex.[234]

As one letter writer to Bryant put it shortly before the final polls, "I don't see how they can not vote Alabama #1 but if they do [not] I know the answer. Too many who command votes are on the opposite side of the fence."[235] It was clear to him that the final ranking would not be based on merit but on Yankee prejudice against the South. More than a year later, another supporter wrote, "You have to fight twice as hard because we are

---

[233] Frank A. Hava to Paul Bryant, 12 October 1967, Bryant Papers, Paul W. Bryant Museum Library, Tuscaloosa AL.

[234] Dunnavant, *Missing Ring*, 271–72.

[235] Len Watters to Paul Bryant, 4 December 1966, Bryant Papers, Paul W. Bryant Museum Library, Tuscaloosa AL.

from the SEC, not the Big 10 and not the Irish from Notre Dame who rather tie than go for the win when they had the chance! You will have to fight twice as hard too because you represent <u>Dixie</u>."[236]

The lost national championship of 1966 did not lead to the integration of the Alabama football team. Bryant already was on his way to beginning this practice. But it certainly helped to prepare a more favorable environment for him to do it. He had always said that he was waiting for the right time. The "missing ring" of 1966 helped to create the right time. Diehard, racist Alabama fans probably did not change their views; they simply accepted segregation and racial injustice unreflectively. But numerous people, including many white Alabama fans, became more open to changes that would benefit black Alabamians, perhaps because making those Yankees happy, especially those who had voted in the AP and UPI polls, might benefit the boys dressed in Crimson Tide uniforms.

It may be distasteful to many that a willingness to accept racial integration and justice could be tied to a winning football team; nevertheless, we should not ignore or downplay the role of Alabama football as a means to a worthy end. Certainly, we must see Bryant in such a way, for he was far more interested in winning football games than he was in any kind of social engineering. As teams in other regions and then other Southern universities integrated, Bryant realized that the pool of talent from which he drew was smaller than the pool from which the integrated universities drew. Even given his exceptional ability to train, prepare, and motivate a football team, Bryant knew that without integrating, Alabama would be unable to compete in the long run against integrated teams. He may have believed that integrating his team was the right thing to do, but the fact that it was a winning thing to do certainly helped.

Bryant's overpowering desire to win is part of the mythology surrounding one of the most memorable (or, from an Alabama perspective, forgettable) games in Crimson Tide history—the 1970 game against the

---

[236] Mrs. Joe F. Randall to Paul Bryant, 18 September 1968, Bryant Papers, Paul W. Bryant Museum Library, Tuscaloosa AL.

University of Southern California. A perennial football powerhouse, Southern Cal's integrated team came to Birmingham to kick off the 1970 season against the all-white Alabama squad. Southern Cal pounded the Crimson Tide, with black running back Sam "The Bam" Cunningham gaining 135 yards and another black running back, Clarence Davis, scoring two touchdowns. The 42–21 final score was one of the worst defeats of Bryant's career. While these are the basic facts about the game, a number of unsubstantiated myths have accompanied the story of the game ever since.[237] The first is that Bryant scheduled the game because he knew that losing to an integrated Southern Cal team would prepare the ground for his own integration of the Alabama squad. But it is hard to imagine that Bryant would ever set himself up to lose. As his longtime assistant Clem Gryska says, "Coach Bryant never scheduled a game in his life in order to lose it."[238] A more widespread myth involves Bryant going to the Southern Cal locker room after the game, "borrowing" Cunningham, taking the player back to the Alabama locker room, and telling his players something along the lines of "This is what a football player looks like." No Alabama player or coach remembers the incident and Bryant never mentions the story in his autobiography.[239] Even Cunningham seems incapable of confidently confirming the story.[240] Al Browning, a longtime reporter on Alabama football, surmises that Bryant may have shown Cunningham not to his players—nobody believes that Bryant would have embarrassed his players in that manner—but to people connected to the university "who wanted to drag their feet on integration."[241]

The final and most significant myth concerning the game is that it led to the integration of the Alabama football team. It certainly did not hinder the process of preparing the ground for integration, *but the team already had been and was integrated.* After the torturous ending to the 1966 season,

---

[237] See Barra, *Last Coach*, 366–70.

[238] Quoted in Barra, *Last Coach*, 366.

[239] Ibid., 367, 368.

[240] Ibid., 368.

[241] Ibid.

two black athletes walked-on to the football team in spring 1967, and one even played in the spring game. Other blacks also walked-on in subsequent years, but all of them failed to make the squad for the regular season, sometimes for personal or family reasons, other times undoubtedly as a consequence of the tense racial environment at the time. In December 1969, however, Alabama signed its first black football player in Wilbur Jackson. Jackson had been in the stands the day of the USC-Alabama game in 1970; he was not on the field during the game since freshmen were not eligible to play at that time.

Of course, myths are more meaningful and powerful than historical facts. The point to make here is that these are not Alabama or even Southern myths: These are myths from and for the rest of the nation. They not only were shared word-of-mouth but found their way into many publications, including the recently published *Turning of the Tide: How One Game Changed the South*. The subtitle is indicative of the overarching myth of which the USC-Alabama game is but one small part, which is the myth of Yankee or Northern superiority—economically, culturally, and, in this case, morally—and Southern inferiority. Although there is much truth to the impact of other regions on the South, an impact often for the good, it seems easy for non-Southerners to have delusions of grandeur when it comes to their role in Southern history and culture. Think about the subtitle—*How One Game Changed the South*. Not only was Alabama already on its way to integration, but several other Southern schools already were integrated and inevitably would be in the coming years. It is little wonder that Southerners and more particularly Alabamians take exception to the myths concerning the USC-Alabama game. They only seem to confirm a denigrating attitude against the South among those in other regions.

The myths about the USC-Alabama game also detract from the good works that Bryant already had set in motion and that he would accomplish in the subsequent years of integration. Frank Rose, the president of the University of Alabama at that time, gave Bryant significant credit for preparing the campus for integration.[242] Bryant may have been a few years "behind the curve," but his contributions to integration, nevertheless, were significant. Dunnavant argues that when Bryant signed Wilbur Jackson to a letter of intent to play football at Alabama, it "represented the final nail in the coffin of segregation. In the culture of the state, [Rosa] Parks and Jackson are forever linked, generational bookends in the struggle for civil rights. The decision by an instrument of the white establishment to recruit a black man for one of the most exalted positions in Alabama society slammed the door on the turbulent era of violence and resistance."[243] Though it may have taken a while, when integration occurred, it occurred quickly. By 1973, about one-third of the Crimson Tide football team was African American.[244] "Having blacks and whites compete together on the state's most important cultural asset closed the door on a turbulent era with more force than a thousand marches," Dunnavant argues. "It compelled the races to share something more personal: their heros [sic]."[245] Bryant not only was instrumental because of the power he wielded as head coach and athletic director, he bore great symbolic power as well. "If it was all right for Coach Bryant, many reasoned, it must be all right for the rest of us," Dunnavant notes, adding that "Alabama today is closer to a color-blind society than Martin Luther King could have imagined in his wildest dreams. In the 1970s, Bryant's example was rife with symbolism."[246] While many Alabamians at the time may not have recognized or appreciated Bryant's efforts, others did. In January 1966, one Alabamian wrote to Bryant:

> I wish to commend you for the liberal attitude I understand
> you have toward accepting Negroes for scholastic purposes into
> Southern institutions of learning, which attitude is indicated by

---

[242] Ibid., 330.

[243] Dunnavant, *Missing Ring*, 280.

[244] Ibid., 283.

[245] Dunnavant, *Coach*, 264.

[246] Ibid., 264, 265.

your predicting that those of both races will be playing side by side in Southern athletic competition.

I feel that those of your ability and influence can do much to help soften the sectional as well as racial prejudices that have been serious barriers to human progress in this nation; not just in the halls of learning but in all other important aspects of life here in America....

I hope that you will see fit to continue to use your good influence to the end of helping to bring about better race relations here in Alabama.[247]

In spring 1967, after several black players participated in spring practice, a Connecticut letter writer (signed "A White, 'Yankee' Fan") wrote "to congratulate you [Bryant] and the Crimson Tide players for giving those Negroes a fair chance to play ball.... As an explayer I know you should be judged on your ability and not your color."[248]

Bryant's actions and the legendary stories about him garnered tremendous respect and admiration. Bryant clearly was a tough taskmaster. Some of his players did not like him and never would. An overwhelming majority of his players, though, black and white, had and continue to have great admiration for him; perhaps not during one of his grueling practices, but certainly in the many years after their days at Alabama (or Kentucky, Texas A&M, or Maryland) were over. Dunnavant writes, "Young men wanted to follow him. Some players loved him and were determined to do whatever was necessary to please him, so they gave him everything, which often was more than they thought they had to give. Others hated him for the way he pushed them, and they were equally determined to prove that he couldn't run them off, so they reached deep inside and found the will to

---

[247] Henley H. Watson to Paul Bryant, 18 January 1966, Bryant Papers, Paul W. Bryant Museum Library, Tuscaloosa AL.

[248] Marty Loughlin to Paul Bryant, 14 April 1967, Bryant Papers, Paul W. Bryant Museum Library, Tuscaloosa AL.

show him. Either way, he won."[249] "Coach Bryant was respected. Some say he was feared," Eli Gold observes. "But one word that keeps cropping up when his former players speak of him, as unlikely as this may sound, is *love*."[250]

Players sometimes described Bryant in god-like terms. At Kentucky, George Blanda said, "This must be what God looks like" when he first met Bryant.[251] Texas A&M player Don Watson likewise said upon meeting Bryant, "I just saw God!"[252] In the end, however, it was more than his rugged good looks and towering stature that impressed players; it was his powerful will and ability not only to have people carry out his plans but to get them to carry them out in ways they never thought they could. Thus, Howard Schnellenberger, a former player for Bryant at Kentucky and a very successful coach as well, reports, "There were times when it was difficult for those around Paul Bryant to distinguish his will from God's."[253]

For some players, Bryant was not simply a distant, fatherly disciplinarian. He also was a savior of sorts. The story of Kenny Stabler, a star quarterback at Alabama, is not atypical. Stabler had a difficult childhood, including an abusive father. At Alabama, he sometimes had a hard time sticking to the rules of the program and teetered on the edge of having his career cut prematurely short as a result. "He [Bryant] knew my wayward ways would cause me to lose out on a great opportunity and he wouldn't let me do that," Stabler remembers. "I was so young and dumb but he figured out a way to grab me by the back of the neck and make me get back in school and make me play. Coach Bryant saved me. There's no doubt about it."[254]

Like many players, Christ Vagotis contemplated quitting at those times when Bryant pushed him to the edge of his willpower. Like a few

---

[249] Dunnavant, *Coach*, 51.

[250] Gold, *Crimson Nation*, 193.

[251] Dunnavant, *Coach*, 71; Barra, 109, 114.

[252] Barra, *Last Coach*, 161.

[253] Ibid., 145.

[254] Gold, *Crimson Nation*, xii.

players, he did quit. And like most of those who quit, Vagotis regretted his actions. In 1966, he wrote Bryant, "I am a boy who played two and half years of football under you, and this has been the greatest honor of my life. When I quite [sic] the team on Oct. 5, 1965, I felt as though I wasn't doing my job as a football player for the University of Alabama." He then asked to be allowed to come back in September.[255] While Bryant was a strict disciplinarian and even his greatest players were punished when they broke the rules, he seemed to have a penchant for second chances. He replied to Vagotis, "It seems that I have heard that same song before.... Anyway, if you will report to practice in real good shape, we will give you another chance. We will be unable to give you a place to stay or eat until you prove yourself."[256] Again, Bryant's "tough love" was tempered with a compassion for the players and a conviction that playing football and receiving an education were going to be central to a young man's success, displaying once more his commitment to the educational aspect of the athletic scholarship.

While Bryant certainly meant a lot to his players, he perhaps meant just as much to Southerners in general. Southerners viewed Bryant as "an affirmation of their own values and virtues," Andrew Doyle observes, noting that after integration Bryant even became a symbol of the values of the New South.[257] "In his last years, and especially after his death in 1983," Wilson argues, "Bear Bryant was as close to a southern saint as the modern South has produced, with frequent comparisons to General Lee."[258] Indeed, after losing to Tennessee in October 1967, a fan wrote, "Now, I'm sure you're feeling low but let me say Virginia had [Robert E.] Lee and [Stonewall] Jackson (they were beaten too) but Alabama has her shining

---

[255] Christ Vagotis to Paul Bryant, July 1966, Bryant Papers, Paul W. Bryant Museum Library, Tuscaloosa AL.

[256] Paul Bryant to Christ Vagotis, 30 July 1966, Bryant Papers, Paul W. Bryant Museum Library, Tuscaloosa AL.

[257] Doyle, "An Atheist," 253, 271.

[258] Wilson, *Judgment*, 28.

knight 'Bear Bryant' and will always have him."[259] While Lee and Jackson were nineteenth-century icons of the Lost Cause, Wilson's claim is that Bryant was a "modern icon of the southern civil religion" and a "modern saint of the civil religion."[260] Of course, it is hard to live up to a saintly standard, but it is less important for our analysis whether he was in reality saintly than that people viewed him that way. "In Alabama, the heart of the Bible Belt, where more than half the counties forbid the sale of alcoholic beverages and where many consider drinking a sin," Dunnavant notes that "a large segment of the population saw the man as a saint. They wanted him to be more than he was; they loved him so much that they wanted him to be perfect."[261] Robert J. Higgs and Michael C. Braswell argue that Bryant "has entered into apotheosis, and it is questionable whether or not there are any other gods before him, especially in football."[262] Indeed, one fan wrote of seeing Bryant at an Alabama practice session, poised in his familiar tower over the practice field: "[T]he guy in the tower was Bear Bryant, the greatest coach in college football, overseeing his world like Zeus on Olympus."[263] It is little wonder, then, that people treated him with "reverence."[264]

In considering Bryant's importance to many Southerners, it becomes extremely difficult to disentangle religious conceptions (like sainthood) from football from the Southern civil religion (the Lost Cause). What we see in his life and his place in Southern history and the state of Alabama is how these elements all work together. Take, for example, this fan's assessment: "It [Alabama football] is a [*sic*] like a religion and your Christlike figure is Bear Bryant. People talk about him as if he is a saint. He is

---

[259] Sara O. Newton to Paul Bryant, October 1967, Bryant Papers, Paul W. Bryant Museum Library, Tuscaloosa AL.

[260] Wilson, *Judgment*, 38, 39.

[261] Dunnavant, *Coach*, 196.

[262] Robert J. Higgs and Michael C. Braswell, *An Unholy Alliance: The Sacred and Modern Sports* (Macon GA: Mercer University Press, 2004) 345.

[263] David Olivet, "Larger than Life," *Tales of the Tide*, 68–69.

[264] Gold, *Crimson Nation*, 96.

beloved by all Bama fans. Many Alabama fans are Christians, but they worship in the house of Alabama football Saturdays in the fall."[265] It is not surprising, then, that one can easily find and purchase books with titles like *Bama, Bear Bryant and the Bible: 100 Devotionals Based on the Life of Paul "Bear" Bryant*[266] and *God Bless the Crimson Tide: Devotions for the Die-Hard Alabama Fan.*[267]

Like that of many religious figures, Bryant's impact on the lives of people is significant. We already have seen examples of his impact on the lives of players, but the same can be said for the everyday fan as well. This influence is seen in many of the letters Bryant received from fans. One boy was so inspired by him that he wrote "Bear Bryant's Tuscaloosa Address"—wonderfully modeled on Abraham Lincoln's Gettysburg Address and ending with the somewhat apocalyptic lines "That the Alabama Crimson Tide under God shall have a new crop of All-Americans and to be sure that any team which dares to challenge the Crimson Tide shall perish from the face of the earth."[268] A more typical letter is the one received from a history professor, an Alabama graduate, from Columbus College in Georgia. He wrote of Bryant's "philosophy of dedication and devotion to duty" and "the profound impact the Bryant philosophy has had on my ability to teach." He explained that he had tried to incorporate the Bryant philosophy into his work and that his "approach in class is to try and instill the winning philosophy in students, make them <u>want</u> to learn, drive them when they fall behind in their studies and to let them know I am interested personally in their success." He went on to describe his disappointment and then anger at being denied a prestigious teaching award at his institution. "I was going to tell them to go to hell and quit," he

---

[265] Fan, e-mail message to author, 10 October 2006.

[266] David Shepard, *Bama, Bear Bryant and the Bible: 100 Devotionals Based on the Life of Paul "Bear" Bryant* (New York: Writers Club Press, 2002).

[267] Ed McMinn, *God Bless the Crimson Tide: Devotions for the Die-Hard Alabama Fan* (New York: Howard Books, 2007).

[268] Tony Kimbro to Paul Bryant, 13 April 1967, Bryant Papers, Paul W. Bryant Museum Library, Tuscaloosa AL.

wrote, "and then I remembered how you took it on the chin without a complaint when our team was deprived of the number one rating that it deserved [after the 1966 season]. So to make it short I am returning next year." He concluded:

> I know that through the use of the Bryant Philosophy I have made academic winner[s] out of academic failures. I could never put into words the debt of gratitude that I owe to you. I could never over impress upon you how profoundly your philosophy has influenced me personally and through me literally hundreds of young men and women.
>
> You sir, could never again belong just to yourself, your family or your team. You belong to this nation of ours. I am sure you have been the key to many successful people engaged in all sorts of activities far removed from the field of athletics. I for one humbly Thank You.
>
> May God bless and guide you and your teams to many more continued successes.

Because of how important he was to them, people generally sought to please Bryant and to attain his approval. His players clearly did, but so did others. Even hard-nosed journalists like Allen Barra, a Bryant biographer, writes, "I suppose, in the end, like just about everyone else who knew him, in my own way I want Bear Bryant's approval."[269]

At the end of the 1982 season, Bryant, in ailing health, finally decided to retire. He once said that without football he would "croak in a week."[270] It took a bit longer than that, but less than a month after coaching his final college football game Bryant, who to many seemed invincible, passed away. On 26 January 1983, the death of Paul "Bear" Bryant was announced to Alabamians from television sets, radios, and through school

---

[269] Barra, *Last Coach*, 503.
[270] Dunnavant, *Coach*, 316.

public address systems throughout the state. "One future 'Bama quarterback," Dunnavant writes, "all of ten years old, was sitting in his fifth-grade classroom in suburban Birmingham when his teacher ran into the room, crying, and broke the news. Shivers ran down his spine."[271] Steadman Shealy, a former player, was sitting in a law school lecture when he heard; he then "ran out into the hall and cried like a baby."[272] Dunnavant notes that the "state of Alabama descended into an unofficial two-day period of mourning leading up to the funeral."[273]

Bryant's funeral was indicative of the elevated (saintly, god-like, et cetera) status that the man had attained in his life. A procession took the body from the services in Tuscaloosa to Elmwood Cemetery in Birmingham for the burial, a stretch of about 55 miles. Lined along the route, 250,000 people or more paid their respects. Dunnavant writes of the scene:

> The greatest testament to Bryant's life, however, was the thousands of ordinary citizens who lined the fifty-five-mile route between the Tuscaloosa churches and Elmwood Cemetery in Birmingham, where he was laid to rest. Their tribute was silent, but it was powerful. Some dressed in black, others in crimson. Some tacked signs onto overpasses.... As the funeral procession moved up Interstate 59, truckers could be seen standing in front of their rigs on the shoulder of the expressway, their ball caps pressed against their hearts.[274]

Various shirts, hats, and photographs with Alabama colors and symbols were pervasive.[275] The funeral not only was a celebration of the man, but of the Bryant myth.

---

[271] Ibid., 317.

[272] Ibid., 318.

[273] Ibid.

[274] Ibid., 319.

[275] Wilson, *Judgment*, 41.

Bryant was so highly regarded by both players and fans alike because he represented so much of what they were and what they valued, as did the Alabama football team itself. His life was a microcosm of the South or at least of what many thought about the South. He had experienced abject poverty and understood well the inferiority complex that so many Southerners—even today—have about their region. He believed in hard work, and he was convinced that those individuals who wanted success could achieve it. He wanted players with "guts" or courage who would be required to give their all—literally at the risk of life and limb—in order for the team to achieve its goals. Dunnavant summarizes this orientation well:

> In the South, where football coaches enjoy a status on a par with governors and movie stars, Bryant became the foremost icon of his time. No man ever dominated the game that lives so close to the southern heart. He considered football a metaphor for life, and southern fathers, who more often than not agreed, wanted their sons to grow up to become men of strength and honor like Bear Bryant. In addition to respecting his unmatched success, southerners of all stripes identified with him because, more than other Americans, they could relate to his struggles against poverty and for respect, and they admired his self-deprecation and humility, which were as much a reflection of their culture as his sandpaper drawl. He won and lost with a certain dignity and class that mirrored the noblesse oblige planter mentality that subtly dominated southern culture well after the age of the gentleman planter, and yet he was always the toughest son-of-a-bitch in the room.[276]

Of course, Bryant's level of importance to Alabamians was particularly high. "[The] Bear became the psychological antidote to Alabama's festering inferiority complex," Dunnavant argues. "To Alabamians who felt under

---

[276] Dunnavant, *Coach*, 183.

siege on the race issue, he was a source of tremendous pride when pride was in desperately short supply."[277] In short, "Bryant remains a giant, not just because of how often he won, but also because of how the sum of all his heroics made the people of Alabama feel about themselves."[278]

Some Final Words

The point of this chapter has been to show how college football in the South was woven closely into the very fabric of the culture and its history, at least for many Southerners. The University of Alabama Crimson Tide is an exemplary model of how this intertwining worked, epitomized during the career of Paul "Bear" Bryant, who became more than just a famous coach but also a figure of cultural and religious devotion.

What we get in the end is an understanding of a Southern civil religion that has college football as a key component. While a close examination of Southern history and the development and flourishing of college football was necessary in order to fully comprehend the phenomenon, we nevertheless could have *experienced* the phenomenon simply by attending a game on an autumn Saturday in the South. Here are three examples, highlighting the ways in which music and ritual bring various elements of the Southern civil religion together for fans in powerful moments of communal worship.

First, there is "Rocky Top" at Tennessee. No song is perhaps more associated with a school or played so often than is "Rocky Top," a country classic from the Osborne Brothers. The lyrics emphasize the simplicity and goodness of life on a mythical mountain in East Tennessee:

Wish that I was on ol' Rocky Top,
down in the Tennessee hills;
Ain't no smoggy smoke on Rocky Top;
Ain't no telephone bills;

---

[277] Ibid., 185.
[278] Ibid., 327.

Once I had a girl on Rocky Top;
Half bear, other half cat;
Wild as a mink, but sweet as soda pop,
I still dream about that…

Once two strangers climbed ol' Rocky Top,
Lookin' for a moonshine still;
Strangers ain't come down from Rocky Top;
Reckon they never will;
Corn won't grow at all on Rocky Top;
Dirt's too rocky by far;
That's why all the folks on Rocky Top
get their corn from a jar…

The final verse even compares the humble and rural life on Rocky Top to the very different life in America's cities, perhaps invoking Yankee cities in particular: "I've had years of cramped-up city life / Trapped like a duck in a pen; / All I know is it's a pity life / Can't be simple again." "Rocky Top" is played dozens of times during a Tennessee football game, especially after a score or critical defensive play. The result often is an ecstatic frenzy among the fans. While the verses of the song are rarely sung, fans enthusiastically join in with the chorus: "Rocky Top, you'll always be / home sweet home to me; / Good ol' Rocky Top; / Rocky Top, Tennessee; / Rocky Top, Tennessee." Here we have the typical defiance of the South and pride in its unique characteristics, affirmed in the communal ritual of the Southern college football game, and expressed by nearly 100,000 fans singing in unison their beliefs about who they are and supporting the team that represents those beliefs, their school, their state, and their region. *This is Southern civil religion.*

Next, there is the medley of the "Battle Hymn of the Republic" and "Dixie" played at Ole Miss. The irony, of course, is that a Yankee hymn like the "Battle Hymn of the Republic" is even a part of an Ole Miss medley played by the marching band. However, its themes, both religious

("Mine eyes have seen the glory of the coming of the Lord") and militaristic ("He hath loosed the fateful lightning of His terrible swift sword"), fit well with the Southern ethos. "Dixie," on the other hand, is perhaps the best-known musical celebration of the Southern past. "O, I wish I was in the land of cotton / Old times there are not forgotten / Look away! Look away! / Look away! Dixie Land." Combined, these two songs move the hearts and minds of fans in Oxford, Mississippi, home of William Faulkner, the Ole Miss Rebels, and perhaps the one place in the South that most embraces and celebrates the Southern identity. A particularly moving moment occurs at the end of a game. While some fans are leaving the stadium, a large portion, particularly the student section near where the band sits, stays for a final playing of the medley. It begins slowly, mournfully (particularly appropriate after a tough-fought loss), the "Battle Hymn of the Republic" and "Dixie" gently mixing together. One feels a sense of longing for a past more ideal than real but one that represents what so many Southerners think is so great about their culture and themselves. Midway through, the tempo picks up, hands are clapping, and the parts that include the fans singing (particularly the chorus of "Dixie") are louder and more boisterous. This all culminates with a yell, a hope, a declaration of defiance rising from all—"The South will rise again!" *This is Southern civil religion.*

Finally, we have the Southern anthem "Sweet Home Alabama," the Lynyrd Skynyrd classic played at Crimson Tide games. To understand the song, one first has to remember the historical and cultural context in which it was composed. In 1970, Neil Young recorded a powerful condemnation of Southern bigotry and violence called "Southern Man." The song reminds Southerners of their vicious past and their present debt to African Americans:

I saw cotton
and I saw black
Tall white mansions
and little shacks.
Southern man

when will you
pay them back?
I heard screamin'
and bullwhips cracking
How long? How long?

In addition, it suggests a deep hypocrisy among Southern whites, whose brutal treatment of blacks runs counter to what the Bible identifies as moral behavior.

Southern man
better keep your head
Don't forget
what your good book [the Bible] said
Southern change
gonna come at last
Now your crosses [the burning crosses of the Ku Klux Klan]
are burning fast
Southern man

Lynyrd Skynyrd's "Sweet Home Alabama," first recorded in 1974, was written partly in response to Young's song along with his later song "Alabama," but it was also written in response to the harsh (even if deserved) media attention of the 1960s and early 1970s. In some ways, the song is an apology for the South, an insistence that good people were trying to do the best they could: "In Birmingham they love the governor [controversial segregationist George Wallace] / Now we all did what we could do...." The song also points out an apparent contradiction of those outside the South, specifically those in Washington, D.C., who condemn the moral waywardness of the South but regularly engage in immorality or acts of corruption: "Now Watergate does not bother me / Does your conscience bother you? / Tell the truth...." But mostly the song strikes a chord of defiance and, in stereotypical fashion, seeks to defend the honor of the South: "Well I heard Mister Young sing about her / Well, I heard ol' Neil put her down / Well, I hope Neil Young will remember / A southern man don't need him around anyhow...." Booming through the public address system at Bryant-Denny Stadium in Tuscaloosa, tens of thousands of Alabama fans roar their approval when the song is played, which occurs frequently throughout the game. In the middle of the chorus, the fans declare their identity not only with their beloved Crimson Tide but with their state and culture as well, inserting "Roll Tide Roll" into breaks in the chorus.

> Sweet home Alabama;
> (ROLL TIDE ROLL)
> Where skies are so blue;
> Sweet home Alabama;
> (ROLL TIDE ROLL)
> Lord, I'm coming home to you.

With all its foibles, the South is still a good place to be. It is good; and, just like the Crimson Tide, it can achieve greatness. *This is Southern civil religion.*

Southern civil religion is music—hymns and Southern rock, country and traditional/folk. It is church (particularly charismatic and emotional) and community (and food, lots of food). It is a history of courage, shame, stubbornness, and honor. It is the Lost Cause: sometimes racist, despicable, and divisive, and sometimes uplifting and uniting. Woven into this civil religion is college football, drawing from and adding to these various elements and often holding them all together at once on beautiful Saturdays in towns and cities all across the South.

6

Marx Is in the House!
Football as the Opiate of the
Southern Masses and Other Political Musings

The previous chapter concluded with the triumph of integration and a vibrant and more inclusive Southern civil religion. Obviously, the situation is less ideal than the conclusion to that chapter suggests. Race, for instance, continues to be a stumbling block to a more harmonious society. The Southern civil religion still has not resolved centuries of racial division, even with the integration (in law, if not always in practice) of schools, public facilities, and football teams. What we see in the South are the limitations that its civil religion has with regard to social or political reform. This chapter will examine the limitations of college football as one aspect of Southern civil religion and highlight the ways that college football has been a part of Southern civil religion's failures.

Lingering Issues of Justice in the American South

A significant portion of the previous chapter included details about the central role of race in Southern history and culture. While much changed through the Civil Rights era and the end of the twentieth century, race still matters. We see its importance in a number of different circumstances. While schools legally are integrated, the fact of the matter is that many Southern communities largely have segregated education. If nothing else, the flight of whites from Southern cities to outlying suburbs meant that many white children were in completely separate school districts from their black peers. In addition, many white parents simply pulled their children out of public schools and enrolled them in the predominantly segregated private schools that burst upon the scene at that time.

The persistent tension in racial relations occasionally explodes, as it did in Jena, Louisiana, in late 2006 and through 2007. In September 2006, a black student broke a school tradition by sitting under the "white tree" outside of Jena High School. The name of the tree did not denote its color, but the color of the students who sat beneath it. After the violation of this racial code, three nooses were found dangling from the "white tree." These acts set in motion several other events, including the beating of a white student and the arrest of six black students on the charge of attempted murder of that white student. The boys, ranging in age from 15 to 18 years old, were all charged as adults. The charges ultimately were reduced and the individuals taken to juvenile court instead. But the initial charge created a firestorm. Many black citizens and leaders in Jena and elsewhere believed that this incident and its initial prosecution were a return to old-time Southern justice—the kind of justice that applied the law differently depending on the color of one's skin.

The display of the Confederate flag is another lightning-rod issue in the South and reveals the continuing tension in race relations. The University of Mississippi, with its nickname (Rebels), Confederate colors (red, white, and blue), and a band that plays "Dixie" almost continuously, is a prominent example. James C. Cobb writes of the 1981 incident when a black cheerleader refused to carry the Confederate flag at an Ole Miss sporting event. His action "set off a more-than-decade-long dispute that finally led university administrators to disavow the flag as the official symbol of the university and attempt with little success to get white students to wave a new banner bereft of Confederate insignia or implication."[1] The Confederate flag and race in general continue to be difficult issues at Ole Miss. In 1993, 700 black undergraduates refused to sit in the student section because of Confederate flag waving, and three members of the band put down their instruments rather than play

---

[1] James C. Cobb, *Redefining Southern Culture: Mind & Identity in the Modern South* (Athens: University of Georgia Press, 1999) 135.

"Dixie."[2] The atmosphere at Ole Miss frequently has made it difficult for the school to recruit the black athletes who could help the team win—an objective that is central to the mostly white alumni.

Of course, Ole Miss is not alone with regard to continuing problems centering around race. Other examples often do not get front-page coverage or even end up in the newspaper. Most day-to-day racism occurs in unsuspecting and surprising ways. Warren St. John tells the story of going back with some acquaintances after an Alabama victory to watch the television reports of the game. Instead, the lead story involved a scandal in which an Alabama state trooper had been "fixing" or eliminating traffic tickets for Alabama players, in this case, a particular black player. St. John's acquaintances proceeded to talk about "stupid niggers," how they "are always getting us [the Alabama football program] in trouble," and that "Them niggers always doin' sumpin' stupid."[3] St. John, who is an Alabama fan and at the time was doing research on Alabama football fans, was devastated. He could not understand how he could feel so close to these fellow fans in one moment and then so distant the next when race so easily inserted itself into the relationship.

Race need not enter so starkly or abruptly. A fan and knowledgeable observer of Alabama football tells the story of leaving the spring game and walking behind a father and son. At the time, there was a heated competition between a black quarterback and a white quarterback for the starting job. The black quarterback had an excellent game, and the son was telling his father how impressed he was. His father indicated, however, that they were supporting the white quarterback for the starting position. When the son asked why this was so, the father simply stated that that was the way it was. There was no further explanation. No derogatory or racist comments were made. Yet it was clear that race was fundamental to the situation.

---

[2] Andrew M. Manis, *Southern Civil Religions in Conflict: Civil Rights and the Culture Wars* (Macon GA: Mercer University Press, 2002) 173.

[3] Warren St. John, *Rammer Jammer Yellow Hammer: A Journey into the Heart of Fan Mania* (New York: Crown Publishers, 2004) 149.

These examples illustrate that while the Civil Rights Movement led to significant changes, the issue of race and racism has never wholly disappeared. This persistence has had implications for Southern politics. As "Dixiecrats," conservative, segregationist Democrats, drifted into insignificance in the party, the national Republican Party came in to capitalize on the void in Southern politics. Southerners, whites in particular, were drawn to the Republican party's platform espousing small government (even suspicion of government) and social conservatism. Whereas once the South was solidly Democratic, it soon became, especially from the Reagan years on, solidly Republican. The Republican Party also became the home for the whites who were uncomfortable with integration—from the mildly uncomfortable to the fervent racists. As David Goldfield notes, the "revitalized Republican Party in the South has been the primary beneficiary and instigator of the camouflaged racial rhetoric."[4] Or, as Andrew M. Manis puts it, the Republican Party has been like "George Wallace without the southern accent."[5]

The persistent presence of racism in Southern politics has had practical implications and has thwarted the region's ability to achieve genuine integration. Wayne Flynt notes that the four largest cities in Alabama all rank in the top third of segregated cities in the United States.[6] As Flynt concludes, the "final four decades of the twentieth century experienced a cycle of desegregation and stability, followed by resegregation."[7] Nowhere, perhaps, has resegregation been more striking than in the educational systems, where disparities in funding and opportunity persist. White flight to suburbs have left many inner-city schools predominantly black and under-funded. Even where schools are integrated, Flynt observes, blacks and whites often are "segregated by

---

[4] David Goldfield, *Still Fighting the Civil War: The American South and Southern History* (Baton Rouge LA: Louisiana State University Press, 2002) 260.

[5] Manis, *Southern Civil Religions*, 188.

[6] Wayne Flynt, *Alabama in the Twentieth Century* (Tuscaloosa AL: University of Alabama Press, 2004), 361.

[7] Ibid.

different curriculum (whites in precollege, blacks in occupational tracks), sports (whites in soccer, swimming, cross-country, wrestling, golf, tennis, blacks in football and basketball), and social activities."[8] Some high schools, for example, even have black and white homecoming queens.[9] The pattern, of course, continues into the colleges and universities. As Flynt notes, it was not until the twenty-first century that the white fraternities and sororities at the University of Alabama admitted a black student.[10]

While the South statistically is the most racially mixed region in the country, this fact does not mean that the relationships between whites and blacks are very substantial. The "prevailing race relations in the South today are actually none at all," Goldfield argues. "The instances of interracial contact that we see all around us, in restaurants, businesses, and schools, are for the most part superficial."[11] He argues that the South is "still fighting the Civil War," in part because blacks and whites cannot talk productively about the Southern past.[12] In *Confederates in the Attic: Dispatches from the Unfinished Civil War*, Tony Horwitz describes the problem in this way:

> Everywhere, it seemed, I had to explore two pasts and two presents; one white, one black, separate and unreconcilable. The past had poisoned the present and the present, in turn, now poisoned remembrance of things past. So there needed to be a black Memorial Day and a white Veterans Day. A black city museum and a white one. A black history month and a white calendar of remembrance. The best that could be hoped for was a grudging toleration of each other's historical memory.[13]

---

[8] Ibid., 362.

[9] Goldfield, *Still Fighting*, 290.

[10] Flynt, *Alabama*, 363.

[11] Goldfield, *Still Fighting*, 289.

[12] Ibid., 295.

[13] Tony Horwitz, *Confederates in the Attic: Dispatches from the Unfinished Civil War* (New York: Vintage Books, 1998) 208.

The inability to come to terms with the Southern past has given rise to a distinct problem of Southern identity. Blacks have their understanding of Southern history and culture as well as their place in them. Whites, obviously, have a somewhat different understanding. When blacks poured out of the South in the late nineteenth and early twentieth centuries, the identity of the South hardly seemed like it would be a problem. Most blacks would not even be around. However, the latter half of the twentieth century saw a migration reversal as blacks came into the South and increasingly identified themselves as Southerners.[14] Cobb writes:

> [M]any of the most energetic and purposeful participants in the process of constructing a new southern identity are black southerners whose spirited attacks on the Confederate flag, "Dixie," and other symbols of the New South's racial order complement their efforts to establish monuments to their own crusade to overturn that order. Meanwhile, finding little else of substance in which to ground their claim to a distinctive identity, many white southerners continue to cling to "Dixie" and the Confederate banner, insisting that they represent more than a sordid history of slavery and racial repression.[15]

In addition, the disappearance of "the negative northern reference point" in the post-Civil Rights era made the finding of a Southern identity even more challenging.[16] It is not enough anymore simply to identify oneself as a Southerner through an opposition to Yankees.

As an important element of the civil religion of the South, college football has been bound with this struggle to define what the South is and what it means. We saw in the previous chapter how segregation of Southern college football teams would have perpetuated white understanding of the

---

[14] Cobb, *Still Fighting*, 127.
[15] Ibid., 185.
[16] Ibid., 209.

South and its history and culture. Through the 1960s and into the 1970s, though, the integration of major college football teams in the South had a great impact on both whites and blacks and their conceptions of and feelings about their region.

Although the meaning of Southern college football originally was shaped greatly by the Lost Cause (see previous chapter), the game was capable of developing new meanings and significance for Southerners both black and white. In that way, college football could be a means by which to form a new Southern identity. As Andrew Doyle writes:

> The bellicose assertions of sectional pride and the ceaseless allusions to the glories of the southern past that were an integral part of the dramaturgy of southern college football dovetailed nicely with the Lost Cause and made the sport an invented tradition in its own right. Yet the Lost Cause and the myth of the Old South were the progeny of southern defeat.... The invented tradition of southern college football was more flexible. It perpetuated the mythology of the southern past while embodying a progressive vision of the future.[17]

Thus, we have a paradox of sorts. College football once served the interests of Southern whites to the exclusion of blacks. It then became an agent, albeit belatedly, of change, serving to unite blacks and whites around a common cause—in this case, not the Lost Cause, but the Crimson Tide Cause, the Volunteer Cause, et cetera. However, as already noted, tensions between races in the South continue, and integration in many areas is either incomplete, superficial, or simply more an idea than a reality. How can we explain this lack of success in race relations?

---

[17] Andrew Doyle, "Turning the Tide: College Football and Southern Progressivism," in *The Sporting World of the Modern South*, ed. Patrick B. Miller (Urbana: University of Illinois Press, 2002) 120.

Karl Marx described religion as the "*opium* of the people."[18] This phrase is perhaps the most famous criticism of religion ever made. To understand it and how it might apply to something like college football in the South, we must examine Marx's general theory of society and ideology.

Marx, along with his frequent co-author Frederick Engels, argues that the character of a society is fundamentally shaped by the way in which it produces what it needs and how it organizes people through those means of production. This fundamental economic base then gives rise to the superstructure. This superstructure is what we might call culture. It includes art, religion, literature, and philosophy (social or political, most importantly). In these various cultural manifestations, we can find the dominant ideology of a culture, that core set of interconnected beliefs and values that shape a society.

Marx claims that the ideology of a culture is not neutral with regard to the various constituencies in that society. Ideology tends to support or justify the unequal distribution of goods and wealth in a society. In other words, ideology tends to justify the superior position of the "haves" over against the "have nots." This assertion makes sense because it is the "haves" who are in control of the means of production, not only for the most basic necessities of life, but also the means of cultural production. The "haves" control art, religion, literature, philosophy, and much more. We might wonder, then, why the "have nots" put up with such disparity. The reason is that they, in addition to the "haves" themselves, do not see the ideology and the elements of culture as simply humanly created and in the service of distinct economic classes. They see the ideology and the elements of culture as natural and obvious parts of the universe, not subject to refutation or even questioning. Alienation is the word that describes this condition in which people create elements of their culture that they then do not

---

[18] Karl Marx, *Karl Marx: The Essential Writings*, ed. Frederic L. Bender (Boulder CO: Westview Press, 1972) 46.

recognize as their own creation. In short, they are alienated from the products of their own consciousness.

From a Marxist perspective, religion is the classic example of such alienation and of how a cultural institution comes to serve the hegemonic aims of the ruling class(es). Religion is not taken to be a human construction that serves some people better than others. Rather, it or its central concepts (for example, God) are taken to be parts of the universe—indeed, the most important parts of the universe. Its rules or laws are not those imposed by the "haves" but are handed down by God. The commandment against stealing protects the property of the "haves" because the "have nots" fear eternal damnation if they break God's law (and, of course, the "haves" also have police and armies to guard their stuff). This fear still may not be enough for the "have nots" to accept economic and social disparity. Fortunately, in a sense, religion offers one important consolation. Despite the struggles of living as a "have not," as long as one follows along and accepts the status quo, one at least can look forward to an eternal reward in heaven. In the face of the injustice of economic forms like capitalism, religion acts as an "opiate" to pacify the justified anger—if, in fact, the "have nots" are able to reflect critically enough on their situation to even experience anger—of the "have nots" and preserve the advantages of the "haves."

This Marxist critique has been central to the work of many scholars attempting to describe and evaluate contemporary popular culture. Guy Debord's *Society of the Spectacle* is a great example. Spectacles are cultural productions that act upon the masses like an opiate, leading people through a life detached from the real processes of existence and from real relationships. Spectacles also function to the benefit of the "haves" rather than the "have nots," since spectacles implicitly or explicitly support or justify the existing socio-economic order. The spectacle thus functions in much the same way that religion does. In the society of the spectacle, the "illusory paradise that represented a total denial of earthly life is no longer projected into the heavens, it is embedded in earthly life itself."[19] The spectacle gives the illusion of "heaven on earth," leaving people unconscious to the real world, particularly the world of capitalist exploitation, alienation, and general social injustice. Debord concludes:

> The spectacle keeps people in a state of unconsciousness as they pass through practical changes in their conditions of existence. Like a fictitious god, it engenders itself and makes its own rules. It reveals itself for what it is: an autonomously developing separate power, based on the increasing productivity resulting from an increasingly refined division of labour into parcelised gestures dictated by the independent movement of machines, and working for an ever-expanding market.[20]

The consequence of the society of the spectacle for the workers or the "have nots" is that the fundamental structure of the socio-economic world remains outside of one's control. He or she is simply a cog in the structure, with little dignity or respect, except, Debord notes, as a consumer. "Once his workday is over, the worker is suddenly redeemed from the total contempt toward him that is so clearly implied by every aspect of the organization and surveillance of production," he writes, "and finds himself seemingly treated like a grownup, with a great show of politeness, in his new role as a consumer."[21] He is the consumer of spectacles, ranging from the hottest concert experience to the newest technological gadget. These are all designed to usher the worker through life without ever confronting reality—that is, the socio-economic structure itself, genuine human relations not distorted by that very structure—or even questioning it. Thus, the spectacles are not real. "The real consumer has become a

---

[19] Guy Debord, *Society of the Spectacle* (London: Rebel Press, 2005) 12.
[20] Ibid., 14.
[21] Ibid., 22.

consumer of illusions," Debord argues. "The commodity is this materialized illusion, and the spectacle is its general expression."[22]

Our desires for these commodities also are produced and sold to us. In other words, the manufacturing of commodities, of spectacles, goes hand-in-hand with the manufacturing of the desires for those commodities. We see here the "replacing [of] the satisfaction of primary human needs (now scarcely met) with an incessant fabrication of pseudoneeds."[23] He adds, "Consumers are filled with religious fervour for the sovereign freedom of commodities whose use has become an end in itself. Waves of enthusiasm for particular products are propagated by all the communications media."[24] This propagation is ubiquitous today, given the wide range of media vehicles for advertisers and marketers. Human desires or needs are actually being generated on a daily if not hourly basis. The *real* need that is met, of course, is the need of the system or structure itself. The "pseudoneeds" all "ultimately come down to the single pseudoneed of maintaining the reign of the autonomous economy."[25] This need is met quite well, while the needs of the workers/consumers are met sporadically and unsatisfactorily. Debord concludes, "The image of blissful social unification through consumption merely *postpones* the consumer's awareness of the actual divisions until his next disillusionment with some particular commodity. Each new product is ceremoniously acclaimed as a unique creation offering a dramatic shortcut to the promised land of total consummation."[26]

Of course, from a consumer perspective, twenty-first-century advanced capitalism seems to provide a cornucopia of wonderful commodities. The society of the spectacle indeed seems spectacular. But the incredible range of goods and services provides us simply with choices among illusions, for they ultimately prevent us from directly confronting or even

---

[22] Ibid., 24.
[23] Ibid., 25.
[24] Ibid., 33.
[25] Ibid., 25.
[26] Ibid., 34.

seeing the real world. Even our sense of choice is illusory. We choose what we desire or need, yet the desire or need is not a matter of choice. It increasingly is thrust upon us by the culture industry.

This Marxist critique also is an element of contemporary approaches to the study of sport. Like other cultural productions, sport serves ideological and hegemonic purposes. Sportswriter Frank Deford suggested in the 1970s that if Marx lived in twentieth century America, he would have viewed sports as the opiate of the people. Allen Guttmann lays out this case, though he is critical of it, in his 1978 work *From Ritual to Record: The Nature of Modern Sports.*[27] Author David L. Andrews has extended it more recently in *Sport-Commerce-Culture: Essays on Sport in Late Capitalist America.*[28] In Debord's terms, we can say that sport is a principal spectacle of twentieth and twenty-first century capitalism.

Given Marxist analysis, it might make sense to ask the following: If college football in the South functions religiously, is it susceptible to the kind of critique Marx levels against religion in general? Sport certainly is bound with the dominant ideology of American society. As Andrews writes, "contemporary American Sport culture must be considered as both a product, and producer, of the social formation (contemporary American society) in which it is situated."[29] Harry Edwards, for instance, argues that a "winning team reinforces the societal values upon hard work, discipline, good character, mental alertness, hard but honest competition, the 'American way of life,' and so forth. Its performance is evidence that the system is still capable and viable, despite occasional or even frequent contradictions."[30] As Guttmann concludes, "Capitalist society is essentially

---

[27] Allen Guttmann, *From Ritual to Record: The Nature of Modern Sports* (New York: Columbia University Press, 1978).

[28] David L. Andrews, *Sport—Commerce—Culture: Essays on Sport in Late Capitalist America* (New York: Peter Lang, 2006).

[29] Ibid., 4.

[30] Harry Edwards, *Sociology of Sport* (Homewood IL: Dorsey Press, 1973) 245.

achievement-oriented and competitive and sports present to us the purest model of that society."[31]

While sport brings the dominant ideology of the culture to our consciousness at some level, it also obfuscates the divisions and injustices within our society. Echoing Debord, we can say that sport provides us with excellent spectacles that gloss over the economic and social disparity among those who participate and watch. As C. Richard King and Charles Fruehling Springwood note, "Sporting spectacles make it easy to forget. They distract the masses from their troubles and struggles in everyday life as the play of bodies and signs absorbs them into a libidinal economy of excess. Beyond the individual subject, spectacles also hide the relations that make them possible"[32]—relations that may not be equal or just.

What is true of sport in general is true of college football in particular. College football reflects the society in which it exists the same way that the superstructure reflects, in a distorted way, the base in Marxist analysis. At the same time, college football implicitly supports the dominant ideology of the society just as the superstructure legitimates the base, the fundamental "means of production" or economic structure of society. Michael Oriard suggests this kind of argument when he writes, "Football is a text in which the social and political and economic histories of our century are written indirectly, not altogether consciously. A cultural history of football would not reveal what Americans have openly proclaimed about certain fundamental issues of their time, but it would perhaps bring us closer to their deepest responses to them."[33]

If college football in the South is like other spectacles, then what reality does it obfuscate? The standard Marxist approach would be to look at issues of economic class, and this approach certainly would yield some

---

[31] Guttmann, *Ritual to Record*, 69.

[32] C. Richard King and Charles Fruehling Springwood, *Beyond the Cheers: Race as Spectacle in College Sport* (Albany NY: State University of New York Press, 2001) 18.

[33] Michael Oriard, *Reading Football: How the Popular Press Created an American Spectacle* (Chapel Hill: University of North Carolina Press, 1993) 279.

insight. In chapter two, we saw how anthropologist Victor Turner's concepts of *communitas* and *structure* could help make sense of what is happening in the formation of game-day communities on college campuses throughout the South. Structure refers to the predominant social roles, relationships, and stratifications in the society. *Communitas* refers to the transcendence of this structure through powerful and emotional ritual behavior. From a Marxist perspective, the rituals of the game-day experience are part of the superstructure of the society. They give rise to *communitas*. There is nothing inherently wrong with the experience of *communitas*, except for the fact that it blinds us to the persistent injustices within the social structure.

The typical stadium at a major university in the Southeastern Conference is the site of many rituals and the experience of *communitas*. At the same time, though, it is very much structured along the lines of economic class and social status. While fans may chat about the game and "high-five" one another as they enter the stadium (an example of *communitas* where social interaction is not prescribed or coded by social structure), many of them inevitably will head to separate seating sections. Some of these will be in the "nose-bleed" sections in the upper deck, while others may be lower level on the 50-yard line. Clearly, there is an economic and social structure within the stadium. Those lower-level seats will be much more expensive than those in the upper deck, sometimes by thousands of dollars. Others, still, will spend the game in "luxury" or "sky" boxes. There also are the class divisions manifested in the simple fact that some people can afford tickets to the game but many cannot (in 2007, Tennessee football tickets were $40 to $50 each). And there is no guarantee that one could even get a ticket if he or she had the money. Many games "sell out," and the only way to be assured of getting a ticket for a game is to be a season ticket holder. Eligibility for this privilege usually entails a significant contribution to the school's athletic fund that can run into the thousands of dollars. So when a season ticket holder talks football with a fellow fan working at the gas station, the genuine bond (or *communitas*) they share is real but it conceals, probably for the season ticket holder more than for the gas station worker, the economic structure that results in the disparity of wealth between them.

The creation of community across economic class is based on the exclusion of others. The season ticket holder and gas station attendant may come together out of their devotion to their team, but this camaraderie entails the exclusion of those who are devoted to other teams, especially to bitter rivals.

Of course, the us-versus-them dichotomy is an inherent aspect of human beings and human collectivities. Regina Schwartz explicates this split in the context of Biblical traditions in her book *The Curse of Cain: The Violent Legacy of Monotheism*.[34] Schwartz argues that a scarcity of resources (God's favor) culminates in violence, for example, in Cain's slaying of Abel. In a college football game, only one team can win. (Note that college football's adoption of an overtime system in 1996 eliminated the possibility of ties.) Significantly, only one team can earn the honor and adulation that comes with victory. Only one team can have "bragging rights" after the game. This situation undoubtedly contributes to the fervor and even violence of the game. Little wonder that violence breaks out occasionally among fans, especially when combined with a tradition of violence in the South. It is not unusual, then, to have stories like the one where the South Carolina fan shot his friend, a Clemson fan, when they argued about a $20 bet on the game (the game having been won by South Carolina). One would imagine that it was not so much the sum of money that was in dispute, but what the money signified: victory, honor, superiority, et cetera.

The sort of partisanship that divides the world up into "us" and "them," Rebels and Bulldogs, Tide fans and Tiger fans, may even be particularly prominent in the South. Goldfield notes that "southerners are quite fond of flag-waving, from flags snapping from car antennae on football Saturdays, proclaiming, 'My college is going to cream yours,' to a

---

[34] Regina Schwartz, *The Curse of Cain: The Violent Legacy of Monotheism* (Chicago: University of Chicago Press, 1997).

mindless patriotism that, like most southern religion, asks no questions and generates no doubts."[35] This somewhat blind devotion to one's team or region becomes particularly problematic when it blinds Southerners to the problems, like racism and economic disparity, that are right in front of them.

College football in the South provides an effective form of escape from problems, be those personal or social. This is true of most sports, religions, and forms of entertainment. They take our minds off the pressing problems of the day and allow us some peace of mind or at least diversion. A Tennessee fan writes that "going to UT games provides an escape for a few hours. It doesn't matter what is going on in the world, how bad the world is screwed up, who is fighting who [sic] in a war, when I am over there [at the game] everyone gets along with everyone and for those few hours everything seems ok."[36] Given such escapism, one might think, then, that diehard sports fans would be apolitical—basically apathetic. Apparently not. Guttmann concludes that when confronted "with the empirical data, the argument about apathy falls apart."[37] Daniel Wann and his collaborators note that there is little evidence that sports fans are any more or less political than non-sports fans.[38] The real question, however, is what kind of politics sports fans practice. Whether they are Democrats or Republicans, both parties fundamentally defend the status quo. Neither party seeks any immediate or radical remedies for the fundamental injustices, often accentuated in cases of racial or ethnic difference, of the socio-economic system. To this extent, it is hard to see sports as anything more than a support of the status quo.

---

[35] Goldfield, *Still Fighting*, 84.

[36] Tennessee fan, e-mail message to author, 28 August 2006.

[37] Allen Guttmann, *Sports Spectators* (New York: Columbia University Press, 1986) 154.

[38] Daniel L. Wann, Merrill J. Melnick, Gordon W. Russell, Dale G. Pease, *Sports Fans: The Psychology and Social Impact of Spectators* (New York: Routledge, 2001) 203.

Cornel Sandvoss notes that being a sports fan is intertwined with being part of a capitalist order. "Being a fan is of course not a universal human condition," he writes. "It is based on forms of consumption and a separation between actor and spectator that are inherently intertwined with the rise of capitalism and industrial modernity and, more specifically, with twentieth-century mass consumerism."[39] Yet, paradoxically, being a fan also entails the possibility of escaping capitalist logic. "Through their fascination with their extension of self, fans, wittingly or not, withdraw themselves from the formal rational logic of capitalist exchange," Sandvoss argues. "It is because the object of fandom functions as an extension, and hence becomes part of one's identity and self, that fans engage in practices that evade, to use Weber's term, formal rational considerations."[40] In other words, being a fan sometimes leads one to behave in economically irrational ways, as when, for example, an individual spends thousands of dollars—money one cannot afford to spend—on game tickets. However, the fact that fans sometimes exceed the bounds of rational economic behavior does not mean they really question the capitalist logic; it simply means that they sometimes fail to manifest it. The truth of the matter is that sports fans rarely if ever are led to fundamentally question the social order as a consequence of their consumption. This lack of critical reflection does not necessarily have to be the case. Attention to the larger social context of sports might bring issues of social injustice to the fore and might even lead to efforts to address these issues. Andrews concludes:

> [W]hile as enthusiastic sport consumers we may be temporarily intoxicated by the intensity of a Dodgers' rally in the bottom of the ninth or a heroic feat by an American Olympian, we should not overlook the economic, technological, and political forces and relations that influence our understandings and experiences of contemporary sport. Whether we recognize it or not,

---

[39] Cornel Sandvoss, *Fans: The Mirror of Consumption* (Malden MA: Polity Press, 2005) 113.

[40] Ibid., 115.

the practice of sporting contextualization offers the possibility of nurturing a truly critical sporting and social consciousness, through which the consuming populace can begin to make sense of "the totality of its world."[41]

With regard to college football in the South, making sense of "the totality of its world" would mean coming to terms with the place of race in its history and current manifestations.

Returning to the Question of Race

Having taken a detour through some Marxist or neo-Marxist critiques of sport and their relevance to understanding college football in the South, we may be able to look more deeply and critically at issues of race in the South and in college football in that region.

As with economic class, race is a social structure obfuscated by major college football in the South. The racial divide in college football in the South will be apparent to anyone who has witnessed the pre-game walks of the football players to the stadium. They make their way through the crowd, as it forms a pathway for the athletes—the fans reaching out for "high fives" or handshakes or simply to touch the players. The fans are overwhelmingly white, while the players often are black. In the state of Alabama, 26 percent of the population is African American. At the University of Alabama, the student body is only 11 percent black—less than half the state percentage. The football team, however, is 53 percent black. In the state of Mississippi, 37 percent of the population is African American. At the University of Mississippi, the student body is only about 15 percent black—again, less than half the state percentage. The football team, however, is 64 percent black.[42]

---

[41] Andrews, *Sport*, 126.

[42] Data for school enrollment and racial make-up of the teams is from a 2006/2007 review of institutional websites and a review of photographs of players on the websites or in football media guides.

At Ole Miss, the racial climate often has made it difficult to recruit the best players. Dr. Charles Ross, director of African American Studies, suggested to me that some Ole Miss alumni and fans would rather maintain school traditions (the Rebel nickname, the frequent playing of Dixie, and the display of the Confederate flag) than win football games. Given how important winning football games is in the South, this comment perhaps reveals the depth of racism or at least racial insensitivity in Mississippi. On the other hand, many white fans expressed to me that perceptions of Ole Miss often were distortions created by the media. One fan described for me the intimacy that blacks and whites have in Mississippi. She said they live "elbows to assholes." Yet this physical proximity has not always translated into strong relationships across the racial divide. Another fan insisted that people simply need to be better educated about what the symbols of Ole Miss mean; that is, that they refer to pride in the South rather than to racism. While there undoubtedly is some truth to this position, it really is just another way of standing one's ground. In other words, someone arguing along these lines is saying, "If you were better educated about these matters, you'd adopt my position." Both of these Ole Miss fans agreed that sports, college football in particular, have helped to lessen the racial divide.

It *is* true that college football in the South helps to erase the distinctions between "us" and "them"—the rich and the poor, whites and blacks. It accomplishes this erasure on individual campuses by creating a larger "us" that is pitted against another, sometimes even demonized, "them." In Alabama, "us" and "them" means the University of Alabama and Auburn University. The rivalry is intense. As one fan suggests, the intensity or passion that fans have for their teams can even divide families.[43] In Mississippi, the primary rivalry is between Ole Miss and Mississippi State University. Each year they compete in what is called the Egg Bowl, named in honor of the trophy that the winner receives. As one Ole Miss official put it, "It's kind of like the situation in the Middle

---

[43] Fan, e-mail message to author, 10 October 2006.

East…. Fans of one grow up hating the other and really don't know why."[44] The fans, of course, are predominantly white (at least those who are able to attend the games) while the players are predominantly black. This racial division creates a perplexing situation. Michael Lewis writes of one locker room scene, "The circumstances were that the Ole Miss football team, like the Mississippi State football team, consisted mostly of poor black kids from Mississippi. When the Ole Miss defense gathered in a single room, the only white people were coaches. On the football field the players became honorary white people, but off it they were still black, and unnatural combatants in Mississippi's white internecine war."[45] This situation is inexplicable until one considers it at least roughly from a Marxist perspective. College football, as a social construction that supports the fundamental ideology of the society, temporarily blinds the white spectators to the problem of race. For an afternoon, the players are not white or black or brown. They simply are Rebels or Bulldogs. The *communitas* formed by the fans and the players (perhaps felt more by the fans than the players) allows them to ignore the issue of race. Yet the very formation of the group requires the exclusion of others. The formation of the supporters of the Rebels excludes all Bulldogs, though it includes black Ole Miss players. The same is true for the formation of the supporters of the Bulldogs. But when the game is over and the players are out of their uniforms, the Ole Miss player might be just another young black man to the white Ole Miss fan, and now that young black man becomes the excluded one while the Ole Miss fan goes off to play golf with his white Mississippi State friend.

Of course, this account of black football players in the South is simply one part of the complex, tragic, and victorious history of the African American athlete. William C. Rhoden chronicles much of it in his brilliant *Forty Million Dollar Slaves: The Rise, Fall, and Redemption of the Black Athlete*. Blacks started competing athletically in America as early as the

---

[44] Quoted in Michael Lewis's *The Blind Side: Evolution of a Game* (New York: W. W. Norton & Company, 2007) 272.

[45] Ibid., 280.

eighteenth century with black slaves performing athletically for their masters.[46] As slaves became free in the nineteenth century, they used sports, such as boxing and horse racing, to achieve levels of success not previously available to them. As they became more successful, however, whites tended to create obstacles to prevent blacks from being competitive in sports. This effort on the part of whites is what Rhoden calls the "Jockey Syndrome." The "Jockey Syndrome" is named for efforts in the horse racing industry to exclude black jockeys. It is "the primary mechanism in American sports for tilting the ostensibly level playing field of sport away from equal opportunity and toward white supremacy."[47] By the beginning of the twentieth century, interracial sports generally were non-existent, and a long process of re-integration (what many people assumed was integration for the first time) began—a process highlighted by Jackie Robinson breaking the color barrier in professional baseball in 1947, but one that included brave and tragic efforts throughout much of the first three quarters of the century.

Since re-integration, "black athletes have been at the core of some stylistic or structural innovation in sports"[48]—from the slam dunk to touchdown celebrations to much more. This development has been central to the growth of the multi-billion dollar sports industry.[49] It is here that we get to the idea of "forty million dollar slaves." While black athletes are compensated very well at the professional level, they are exploited in two ways. First, they only share in a fraction of the wealth created by their labor. Second, and this point is most critical for Rhoden, they have little opportunity (and have sought rarely to change this situation) to become the people who control the various branches of the sports industry at its various levels. Blacks are under-represented among owners, general managers, and coaches. While blacks make up an increasing percentage of

---

[46] William C. Rhoden, *Forty Million Dollar Slaves: The Rise, Fall, and Redemption of the Black Athlete* (New York: Three Rivers Press, 2006) 50, 51.

[47] Ibid., 68.

[48] Ibid., 152.

[49] Ibid., 153.

players on the field, less than four percent of college and university athletic directors are black and about the same percentage are head coaches of major college football programs.[50] So, Rhoden concludes, the "power relationship that had been established on the plantation has not changed, even if the circumstances around it have."[51] King and Springwood concur, writing that "American colleges and universities, intercollegiate athletics, and sporting spectacles structure and are structured by an insidious, if largely invisible, white supremacy."[52]

At the same time that re-integration was opening new opportunities, though still limited, for black athletes, it also was destroying black institutions. Integration in baseball, for example, led to the demise of the Negro Leagues, an institution where African Americans not only made money but had power and control over the industry in which they worked. "Integration in sports...was a winning proposition for the whites who controlled the sports-industrial complex," Rhoden argues. "They could move to exploit black muscle and talent, thus sucking the life out of black institutions, while at the same time giving themselves credit for being humanitarians."[53] In addition, blacks bought into the narrative of integration and equal opportunity. The ideology represented by the sports industry occluded, for many, recognition of the exact socio-economic and racial basis of the society. As Harry Edwards writes, "when the black athlete puts life, limb, and health on the line in sports, he becomes a *key* factor in a social *sedative process* whereby America dulls black consciousness and awareness of the totality of the impact of white racism and oppression."[54] In other words, sports become the opiate of the masses for blacks as well as whites.

College football is implicated in the history just summarized. As Oriard writes:

---

[50] Ibid., 140–41.

[51] Ibid., x.

[52] King and Springwood, *Beyond*, 9.

[53] Rhoden, *Forty Million*, 135.

[54] Edwards, *Sociology*, 265.

Racist stereotypes of black players as naturally talented but lazy, and of whites as harder working and tougher; the 'stacking' of black players at running back, receiver, and corner back, and their restriction from the central positions of quarterback, center, and middle linebacker; the dearth of black head coaches and management personnel—and the varied challenges to these stereotypes and practices—have generated narratives in which the full range of racial attitudes in the United States has been exposed and explored.[55]

From the start, racial and ethnic minority groups used sports like college football as a way of entering the mainstream of American culture and achieving economic success. Oriard argues that "success in football served primarily to validate outsiders' claims to being fully American."[56] For ethnic minority groups, football seems to have served its function well in this regard. Poles, Irish, Germans, and others have all been integrated into American society. But for blacks, the story has been different. "No one notices any more whether a white player has a Polish or Italian or Mayflower-stock British name," Oriard observes, "but everyone is conscious whether a player is white or black."[57] For black Americans, "college football resonated with the deepest hopes for the race, and for all readers of the black press the racial dramas of sport during the fall months took place mostly on football fields."[58] What blacks discovered in the early part of the twentieth century was that while college football offered opportunities for education and positive attention to their race, many schools excluded them from participation. This exclusion, of course, was

---

[55] Oriard, *Reading Football*, 281.

[56] Michael Oriard, *King Football: Sport & Spectacle in the Golden Age of Radio & Newsreels, Movies & Magazines, the Weekly & the Daily Press* (Chapel Hill: University of North Carolina Press, 2001) 36.

[57] Ibid., 365.

[58] Ibid., 39.

most prominent in the South and continued well into the latter half of the century.

Oriard's research reveals that between 1920 and 1960, the *Saturday Evening Post* and *Collier's*—two prominent, national magazines—had 113 covers that featured scenes related to football. Not a single one included a black face on it. In addition, of the 120 feature films that had football as a relevant part of the storyline, only one had a black leading character.[59] Cartoons from the 1890s to the 1920s suggested that blacks couldn't possibly understand the complexity of football.[60] This stereotype continued throughout the twentieth century, explaining in part why it was so hard for blacks to earn starting roles in positions like quarterback or middle linebacker, offensive and defensive positions respectively where the player calls for alignments, selects plays, and generally leads the team.

As African Americans found increased opportunities in college football through the middle part of the twentieth century, they continued to be excluded from college football in the South, at least in terms of the major educational institutions, public or private, but white nonetheless. Even blacks from other regions suffered, as arrangements regularly were made to bench black players on non-Southern teams when those teams played squads from the South. When teams from other regions traveled to the South to play, they often would leave their black players behind. According to Oriard, "no integrated team played in the South until Harvard's Chester Pierce was welcomed to Charlottesville by the University of Virginia in 1947" (a 47–0 Virginia victory).[61]

As we saw in the case of Paul "Bear" Bryant at Alabama, the integration of college football in the South had as much to do (if not more) with the desire to win than it did with the principle of equality. "The most powerful force for integration was not high-minded principle but the need to win football games, and integration, as future generations would learn, could mean recruiting ill-prepared young athletes with slight prospects of

---

[59] Ibid., 292.
[60] Ibid., 294.
[61] Ibid., 302.

graduating," Oriard concludes. "Opportunity and exploitation became deeply entangled. Football was a powerful force for racial justice, but powerfully limited as well."[62] Part of the limitation of integration in college football in the South and elsewhere is the extent to which it fools us into thinking that race issues have been resolved. As King and Springwood note, "Progressive interpretations of the desegregation of college sports exaggerate its effects, imposing a happy ending on ongoing struggles. They invoke race only to (dis)miss its continued significance."[63]

The issue of exploitation is critical, of course, for Rhoden, and again makes relevant the kind of Marxist critique raised earlier. A college education and an opportunity to play collegiate athletics certainly are important goods for the student-athlete at a major college or university. But many student-athletes, especially in major college football and basketball, never complete their college educations, and only a very small fraction "cash in" on their collegiate careers with big professional sports contracts. So while many student-athletes walk away from their careers with some wonderful athletic memories and an array of credit hours, major colleges and universities walk away with millions of dollars in ticket sales and proceeds from merchandising. In short, major college football and basketball are huge businesses for institutions that make millions of dollars off the labor of student-athletes who often fail to receive the promised compensation (a college education and/or professional contract). "Major intercollegiate sports function like a plantation," Rhoden argues. "The athletes perform in an economic atmosphere where everyone except them makes money off their labor."[64] "Exploitation" seems like an appropriate word to describe the situation.

One might reasonably object that it is the student-athlete's fault that he failed to complete his education. But this objection is naïve. The daily and weekly schedules of student-athletes are imposing. Practices and team meetings take up much of the time that otherwise could be devoted to

---

[62] Ibid., 313.
[63] King and Springwood, *Beyond*, 31.
[64] Rhoden, *Forty Million*, 240.

academic pursuits. Even off-season weightlifting and conditioning make significant demands on the student-athlete's time throughout the year. One also might reasonably object that it is the student-athlete's fault that he sets his hopes on attaining a professional contract. Yet, again, this objection is naïve. Many programs successfully recruit the best athletes *because* they are successful at moving their players to the professional level.

This process of bringing young athletes along through the system, from high school (or earlier) to college and then to the professional ranks, is what Rhoden calls the "Conveyor Belt." For blacks, the process began with integration. "The integration of intercollegiate sports in the mid-1970s created an insatiable appetite for black athletes," Rhoden notes, "which in turn triggered a strip-mining of black communities across the United States. Talented young black athletes and their families were wooed and pursued with the promise of scholarships and, often, material gifts."[65] In this process, young black athletes adapt their behavior in order to avoid making the whites in power feel uncomfortable. "On the Conveyor Belt," Rhoden argues, "young athletes quickly learn that easy passage through a white-controlled system is contingent upon not 'rocking the boat,' not being a 'troublemaker,' and making those in positions of power feel comfortable with the athletes' blackness."[66]

An excellent example of the Conveyor Belt can be found in the story of Michael Oher, a black adolescent from Memphis whose size and athletic skill brought him out of a nearly impossible situation into a private high school (almost all white), on to the University of Mississippi, and now on to the National Football League. Michael Lewis chronicles the story in his best-selling *The Blind Side: Evolution of a Game*. In it, we learn Oher's story: about the absentee father, the drug-addicted mother, stints in foster care homes, and even living on the street. By a strange twist of events, though, Oher meets a prominent Memphis figure named Sean Tuohy and his family, and is enrolled in the private, Christian (almost all white) high

---

[65] Ibid., 168–69.
[66] Rhoden, *Forty Million*, 178.

school that the Tuohy children attend. There, Oher becomes an athletic phenomenon, particularly in football, comes to live with the Tuohy family, and comes to play football at Ole Miss, Sean Tuohy's and his wife's alma mater. It is an amazing story, one that rightfully brought suspicion from the National Collegiate Athletic Association. As Lewis writes, the NCAA heard a "rumor that white families in the South were going into the ghetto, seizing poor black kids, and *adopting* them, so that they might play football for their SEC alma maters."[67] In the end, nothing came of the NCAA investigation, and there certainly is good reason to praise the Tuohy family for its generosity and genuine Christian charity.

But the Conveyor Belt that pulled Oher out of obscurity and possibly a life of poverty and violence does little for the greater African American family. While it is wonderful that Oher escaped, thousands of blacks remain behind in the destitute neighborhoods of Memphis. In celebrating Oher's story and that of the Tuohy family, we forget the others left behind and we neglect to address the socio-economic system that led to the Tuohy family's wealth, a wealth that allowed them to pull one child up and out of the bottom of that system. While Oher's talent and effort certainly helped, there is little doubt that luck played a significant role in his story. Lewis concludes:

Michael Oher might have been born to play left tackle in the NFL [National Football League], but if he had remained in the environment into which he was born, no one would have ever known about his talent. I still find this remarkable. When we list all the problems afflicting the American inner city we don't usually include its inability to identify its star athletes, and export them. But even boys with talent to play in the NFL can be born into circumstances so low that their talents are never noticed.[68]

---

[67] Lewis, *Blind Side*, 195 (emphasis original).
[68] Ibid., 334.

Such a conclusion reveals why it is problematic to naïvely accept the American myths of equal opportunity and individualism. No matter how great one's natural gifts may be, certain circumstances—some of which are endemic to our socio-economic structure—will prevent one from realizing full potential. Sports, and stories like those of Oher, keep us from soberly and seriously reflecting upon that socio-economic structure.

In his influential *Sociology of Sport*, Harry Edwards writes that "if American society is as obsessed with the alleged virtues of 'whiteness,' as Western civilization as a whole...then there is little ground for the expectation that this society, which does not tolerate an image of its sacred God cast in a Semitic [Jewish] body, would be strongly predisposed to tolerate black heroes and 'gods' in its secular religion of sport."[69] He even claims that if basketball were to become dominated by black athletes, then most whites would abandon the sport.[70]

Written in 1973, Edwards' book was, thankfully, wrong. Millions of white children and adults sport replica jerseys of their favorite baseball, basketball, and football heroes. And, in many cases, these jerseys are copies of those worn by black athletes. Edwards perhaps could not have imagined this development back in 1973, when the nation still was reeling from the trauma of great social change.

However, despite the great changes in the twentieth century and especially in the last few decades, sport fundamentally has maintained the status quo in regard to the socio-economic structure, a structure still distorted by race. Many African American athletes have struck it rich, but there still are a disproportionate number of poor black communities. Sport has created gods (black, white, and brown) for all of us to share, but the worship of them has not altered the fundamental living conditions of their admirers. In fact, if the above analysis is correct, they have prevented their admirers from achieving a greater understanding of the reality around them and generating the drive to change it.

---

[69] Edwards, *Sociology*, 267–68.
[70] Ibid., 257.

Ritual, Sport, and Social Structure

Whether explicitly Marxist in orientation or not, many scholars of religion have focused on the ways that religion becomes entangled with power, hierarchy, and the legitimating of power and hierarchy. Two prominent examples are Catherine Bell and Bruce Lincoln. Their work indicates the ways in which ritual, either sacred or secular, can serve ideological purposes.

Bell argues that rituals have both an explicit and implicit, even unconscious, message. When one participates in a ritual, one may very likely understand all the intended meanings and purposes. But often one does not. Yet these meanings and purposes still are expressed through the ritual. Few people probably understand all the meanings and purposes of their family's Christmas morning rituals, though they certainly know some. However, there are going to be other intended meanings and purposes, intended in the very structure or nature of the rituals, that still are expressed *and experienced* by the participants. For example, perhaps in a particular family, the father sits on the couch and orchestrates the opening of the presents while the mother provides refreshments, picks up the wrapping paper, and organizes the presents. Whether or not the family members *consciously* understand the importance of the different actions of the parents, the ritual nonetheless expresses the dynamic of the relationship between the parents and the role that each plays in the family. In this case, the ritual affirms the authority of the father in the family. What is true with this somewhat mundane example is true with nearly all rituals. Thus, Bell concludes that ritual "is designed to do what it does without bringing what it is doing across the threshold of discourse or systematic thinking."[71]

Many times, the intended meaning or purpose of a ritual has something to do with social hierarchies, as is apparent in the above example. Bell argues, "Ritualizing schemes invoke a series of privileged oppositions that, when acted in space and time through a series of

---

[71] Catherine Bell, *Ritual Theory, Ritual Practice* (New York: Oxford University Press, 1992) 93.

movements, gestures, and sounds, effectively structure and nuance an environment."[72] The grand ritual that takes place in the stadium includes numerous privileged positions from where one sits, to access to the field, to the role(s) one may play in the ritual. These various positions tend to work harmoniously to perform successfully the various elements of the ritual (the game, the spectator participation, et cetera), yet they clearly are in hierarchical opposition as well; for instance, players are subordinate to coaches, fans are restricted to the stands, and fans are segregated into specific seating areas. This hierarchy, however, is not revealed through the ritual for the purposes of potential critique. The ritual, in fact, affirms it. This affirmation and general agreement among the participants is even a central purpose of the ritual. In short, "[r]itualization sees the evocation of a consensus on values, symbols, and behavior that is the end of ritualization."[73] This consensus includes agreement among the participants of their appropriate place in the ritual and, further, in the more general social hierarchy. "The goal of ritualization as a strategic way of acting is the ritualization of social agents," Bell notes. "Whether ritual empowers or disempowers one in some practical sense, it always suggests the ultimate coherence of a cosmos in which one takes a particular place."[74]

Through the ways that ritual generates consensus regarding the hierarchical structure and the values and roles that it entails, we see the relationship of ritual to power. Accordingly, Bell insists that "ritualization is first and foremost a strategy for the construction of certain types of power relationships effective within particular social organizations."[75] Again, in the stadium, where one is positioned and what role one plays in the ritual is a reflection of one's power or lack thereof. Bell concludes that the "deployment of ritualization, consciously or unconsciously, is the deployment of a particular construction of power relationships, a particular

---

[72] Ibid., 140.
[73] Ibid., 110.
[74] Ibid., 141.
[75] Ibid., 197.

relationship of domination, consent, and resistance."[76] The resistance about which she writes is important to note. The relatively equal participation by spectators (perhaps doing the "wave" in the stands) serves as a counter to the otherwise hierarchical setting. The fans' rushing onto the field after a significant victory blatantly violates the restricted boundaries. In other words, rituals can both affirm the social hierarchy as well as offer opportunities to transcend it.

This dual function of ritual is central to the approach of Lincoln. He argues that "discourse and force are the chief means whereby social borders, hierarchies, institutional formations, and habituated patterns of behavior are both maintained and modified."[77] Discourse can be expressed in a great variety of ways, ranging from myth to philosophy, popular culture to ritual. The borders, hierarchies, formations, and patterns that Lincoln identifies are the very cleavages in a society that separate one person or group of people from another. Lincoln notes that "integration of any society depends on the peaceful management of cleavages such that sentiments of affinity predominate over those of estrangement."[78] Discourse can be central to this process of integration, and generally is much more effective than brute force. It should be no surprise that ritual discourse is effective in this regard. Lincoln concludes:

[F]or all its power and efficacy, ritual is never able either to eradicate cleavages or to resolve tensions between groups in competition for scarce resources of a material and nonmaterial nature. Rather, what ritual is competent to do...is to "cloak the fundamental conflicts," thereby permitting groups and individuals to forget them for a time (or at least to take them less seriously) so

---

[76] Ibid., 206.

[77] Bruce Lincoln, *Discourse and the Construction of Society: Comparative Studies of Myth, Ritual, and Classification* (New York: Oxford University Press, 1989) 3.

[78] Ibid., 173.

that some temporary measure of good will, common spirit, and stability may emerge.[79]

This account certainly is an illuminating way to look at the ritual(s) surrounding the game-day experience of Southern college football. Fundamental social "cleavages," such as class and race, are "cloaked" behind the "good will" and "common spirit" generated through the rituals.

But can religious activity, ritual activity, transcend the socio-economic structure? Bell and Lincoln both think so, and they certainly would find support from Victor Turner, whose distinction between *communitas* and structure applies to this question. This distinction was introduced in chapter two and has been utilized further in this chapter. The question here is whether or not *communitas* leads to change in structure. We have seen that it too often is simply a respite from the rigidity of structure. As Guttmann notes, modern sports allow us to "lose ourselves in play and forget the creative and sustaining (and restricting) social organization and cultural assumptions" of our society.[80] Additionally, we have seen that sports implicitly support the existing structure. If *communitas* does not provide the possibility for change in the structure, this inability may represent a significant limitation to the role that sports can play in society. "Spectators are linked solely by their one-way relationship to the very centre [the spectacle] that keeps them isolated from each other," Debord argues. "The spectacle thus reunites the separated, but it reunites them only *in their separateness*."[81] For him, contemporary spectacles are not capable of overcoming structural divisions in society. They, in fact, only re-affirm them.

Yet for all the shortcomings that sports have had in bringing about greater equality and opportunity for all, we cannot deny that they have had a positive influence. One reasonably can make the case that college football in the American South has helped to foster more positive racial relations.

---

[79] Ibid., 89.
[80] Guttmann, *Ritual to Record*, 160.
[81] Debord, *Society*, 16.

Take the example of Alabama. Keith Dunnavant argues that the "integration of the Alabama football program profoundly affected the state's culture. Martin Luther King, Jr., and others broke down the legal barriers, but the effort led by Paul Bryant reached into the hearts and minds of people across the Heart of Dixie."[82] Dunnavant adds:

> [King] probably could not have imagined a day when the sons of white people who voted for George Wallace would fight for the right to "be" African-American Alabama football players like Wilbur Jackson and Calvin Culliver in backyard pickup games. He could not have imagined the day white Alabamians who once believed in segregation as a just institution would cheer the descendents of slaves and take them to their hearts, because being an Alabama football hero ultimately was a stronger force than the legacy of hate and division.[83]

Dunnavant recognizes that many people might believe that Alabamians "invest too much meaning in football." But he insists that, at least at times, "the meaning Alabama people attach to the game has been harnessed for a profound purpose." In that regard, the "stats will never demonstrate how Alabama's obsession with football actually helped the state surmount the most formidable obstacle of all [racism and segregation]."[84]

Dunnavant primarily is talking about the role that football has played in the state of Alabama for *whites*—helping them to accept racial integration. In other words, it has helped whites broaden their understanding of community, breaking down parts of the structure of segregation, and welcoming African Americans into the broader, integrated

---

[82] Keith Dunnavant, *The Missing Ring: How Bear Bryant and the 1966 Crimson Tide Were Denied College Football's Most Elusive Prize* (New York: St. Martin's Press, 2006) 284.

[83] Ibid., 285.

[84] Ibid., 287.

Alabama community. However, this progress toward integration only occurred as African Americans also came to view themselves as part of a larger, integrated community. Perhaps the integration of college football was part of the movement in this direction, for there undoubtedly has been movement. In addition to a shift in the black migration pattern—towards the end of the twentieth century, more blacks tended to move *to* the South rather than *away* from it—sociologist John Shelton Reed notes that from 1964 to 1976, the heart of the period of integration of major college football teams in the South, there was a striking increase in the "tendency of Southern blacks to think of themselves as Southerners."[85]

The case may be made that college football in the South leads to experiences of *communitas* that successfully suspend the experience and power of structure (perhaps not completely, but to some extent) and that the very power of that *communitas* can effect some changes or even transformations in that structure.

Red State, Blue State (Okay, Just Red State)

Much of this chapter has grappled with the social and political issues of race and class in the American South and how the history and role of college football in that region has affected and been affected by race and class. But what does any of this have to do with the broader political culture in the exceedingly conservative American South?

For most of the twentieth century, conservatism in the South was bound with the Democratic Party, and, in fact, Democratic presidential candidates generally could count on sweeping many of the Southern states. Several factors contributed to a shift in the late 1960s and then through the rest of the century. There was a split in the Democratic Party between the Southern members, many of whom did not support integration, which was being supported strongly by Democratic presidents John F. Kennedy and Lyndon Johnson, and the members in other regions. In addition, the

---

[85] John Shelton Reed, *My Tears Spoiled My Aim...and Other Reflections on Southern Culture* (New York: Harcourt, 1993) 53.

Southern members, or Dixiecrats, found that the Republican Party increasingly stood for some fundamental conservative principles long held dear in the South: small government, cutting taxes, opposition to gun control, and general deregulation. In addition, the courting of conservative religious elements in American culture (for example, evangelicals) and the party's staunch opposition to abortion led many religious Southerners, primarily whites, to become Republicans. By the 1980 election, Republican candidate Ronald Reagan had built a solid coalition of support in the South, a coalition that ever since has strongly supported Republican presidential candidates.

While Democrats generally are characterized as liberal and Republicans as conservative in American political rhetoric, it is important to remember that Southerners did not become more conservative as they became more Republican. They simply found a different party home that reflected more accurately their long-held conservative views.

Harry Edwards argues that sports are fundamentally conservative. "While, unlike the political institution, sport is not directly involved in political implementation," he argues, "it does share with the polity the function of disseminating and reinforcing values that are influential in defining societal means and in determining acceptable solutions to problems, that is, goals to be attained."[86] In other words, "the values currently dominant within sport reflect the value emphases of the society at large."[87] The effect of sport on the fans is to affirm those values for him or her. As Edwards concludes, "Sport reaffirms the viability of the values or rules under which the fan must operate in his day-to-day instrumental pursuits—and may thereby sustain the individual's faith in and willingness to abide by those rules."[88]

To the extent that sport does not challenge existing values or rules but actually affirms them, it is conservative. In his historical account of sport and society, Guttmann notes that this conservativism has not always been

---

[86] Edwards, *Sociology*, 91.

[87] Ibid., 341.

[88] Ibid., 243.

the case. In the early nineteenth century, sports were fairly progressive, representing a democratic departure from the more elitist sporting life of the medieval period. Yet with the ascendancy of capitalism and commercialism, sports "began to play an increasingly conservative and reactionary role."[89] This development is borne out by a 1971 survey, cited by Edwards, that indicates that politically conservative regions tend to have an increased interest in sports.[90] To the extent that nationalistic attitudes or perspectives are conservative in nature (such attitudes or perspectives tend to celebrate national values rather than seek their critique, revision, or overthrow), it is easy to see how sport can have a nationalistic bent. "In one sense, the main thrust of the sports creed is 'nationalistic,' supporting as it does many of the general values and certain traditional political and economic philosophies of American society," Edwards observes. "In addition, there is the symbolism of flag ceremonies and the honor guards made up of military personnel that have become part of the opening show at important athletic events."[91] It is little wonder, then, that Michael Novak describes going to a sporting event as being similar to attending a political rally.[92]

Among the major sports in America, football may be especially conservative. We have seen the ways in which it has been limited in its ability to fundamentally change some of the entrenched racial issues in the country and especially in the South. We also have seen that this inability is true with regard to issues of class as well. While other major American sports are also complicit in racial and class injustices, football is unique in its male centeredness. There is no softball counterpart, as in baseball, and while women participate in basketball in professional leagues, this is not true for football. Except for the cheerleaders, women play little role in the

---

[89] Guttmann, *Ritual to Record,* 62.

[90] Edwards, *Sociology,* 92.

[91] Ibid., 125.

[92] Michael Novak, *The Joy of Sports: Endzones, Bases, Baskets, Balls, and the Consecration of the American Spirit,* rev. ed. (Lanham MD: Madison Books, 1994) 19.

rituals of football. The focus on men, then, reaffirms the social view that men are the primary agents of action in society, as they are in the game. In addition, Oriard notes, "If the football hero was fundamentally nonfeminine, not a woman, his female counterpart [e.g., the cheerleader] had to be everything he was not: slim, not muscular; weak, not powerful; soft, not hard; gentle, not tough; decorative, not substantial."[93] Football, then, seems conservative on multiple layers, and it perhaps is no coincidence that football, particularly college football, probably is more popular in the South, the most conservative region of the country, than in any other region of the nation.

Conclusion

As we have seen in this chapter as well as the previous one, college football in the South has had an interesting history with regard to its place in the social fabric of that region. Much of our focus has been on the issue of race and how college football has helped the South in moving forward on this issue, while at the same time we have recognized the limitations of college football to significantly address the issue. In this sense, the "mixed bag" we get with college football in the South is similar to the "mixed bag" we get when looking at the role that various churches have played in those same struggles.

As we conclude this chapter, it seems appropriate to look at the prospects for the future. While African Americans as a group tend to be near the bottom in a variety of social indices, things are changing and have been changing for quite some time. While Barack Obama's 2008 presidential campaign may be of particularly special historical significance, the fact of the matter is that blacks increasingly have come to hold public office, and not just outside the South. According to Reed, more blacks hold office *in the South* than in any other region.[94] In fact, the quality of life in the South has improved dramatically for blacks, explaining in part the

---

[93] Oriard, *King Football*, 351.
[94] Reed, *My Tears*, 138.

reversal of the black migration pattern (typically *out* of the South, but now *into* the South) beginning in the 1970s.[95]

It certainly is not the case that African American participation in sports is the cause of some dramatic increase in opportunities or enhancement in their quality of life. But that participation is not without its effect. Greater acceptance of African Americans on the field or the court *has* led to greater acceptance in other areas of Southern culture. Sports *are* helping to create change, even if it is slower than many would like. "Sports, and especially football, are providing images for a new pantheon of southern heroes," Wilson argues. "Sports figures, perhaps even more than musicians, are becoming prime icons of the modern South, the way the Confederate veterans were heroes in the late nineteenth century."[96] These heroes are "becoming fresh new representatives of a culture that managed to overcome legally imposed racial segregation."[97]

For Wilson, black and white sports heroes in the South express the idea of a united future. He argues that "at the mythic level, sports symbolism, and especially football, offers a new model for southern youth, a shared vision, unlike much earlier regional symbolism. It represents the reality of a South moving a bit closer to realization that its once segregated people, black and white, have, after all, shared interests."[98] This mythology and symbolism is foundational for thinking of sports as religious. Indeed, Wilson describes sports as a "new kind of religion" in the contemporary South.[99] As important as religion has been and continues to be in the South, we can hope that it will function at its best—whether that be in the church pews or on the stadium bleachers. For when religion functions at its best, it helps bring people of all races and classes together.

---

[95] Ibid.

[96] Charles Reagan Wilson, *Judgment & Grace in Dixie: Southern Faiths from Faulkner to Elvis* (Athens: University of Georgia Press, 1995) 50–51.

[97] Wilson, *Judgment*, 162–63.

[98] Ibid., 51.

[99] Ibid., 142.

Conclusion:

Sport as Religion?
A Summary and Final Assessment

So far, it seems like there is a compelling case to conclude that college football in the South is a form and expression of religious life. College football has its myths, symbols, and rituals, as well as sacred time, objects, and places. It seems to function religiously, whether we think about the individual's experience of game day or its communal aspects. College football in the South has become part of the civil religion of that region for many people. As part of the social fabric of people's lives, it also has stereotypically religious limitations—limitations that prevent communities or the region from taking on needed reforms.

That said, the reader no doubt may still think that college football in the South or really any sport anywhere cannot constitute religion, and that they are fundamentally two separate things. Such a reader would not be alone. As the number of books and articles about the relationship of sport to religion has proliferated, there have been dissenting voices. Before a final consideration of the broader implications of this particular study, it is imperative that we listen and respond to these dissenting voices.

In this concluding chapter, I want to consider more generally the idea of sport as religion. In short, I want to address the critics who would say, "This is just a bunch of nonsense. College football in the South or, for that matter, any sport, is not the same as religion." For example, Robert J. Higgs, one of the staunchest opponents of the equation of sport and religion, argues that they are "entirely different categories of human experience.... When they [sport and play] appear to take on the raiments of traditional religion, then heresy, we may conclude, is afoot in the land."[1]

---

[1] Robert J. Higgs, *God in the Stadium: Sports & Religion in America* (Lexington: University Press of Kentucky, 1995) 21.

To address Higgs and other critics, let me respond point-by-point to the objections they might have.

Objection 1: Sport is not religious because there is no God or ultimate reality.

This seems like an obvious objection and perhaps one of the most difficult to refute. Where is God in sports? In earlier chapters, I argued that we could find sacredness in college football, and, in particular, that there are sacred places, time, and objects. But in *An Unholy Alliance: The Sacred and Modern Sports*, Higgs and co-author Michael C. Braswell argue that the sacred is not the same as the holy, the latter referring to God or ultimate reality. They write, "To have any chance of understanding the rapid transformation taking place in our culture, we need to understand as best we can the differences, as opposed to the similarities, between the holy, the 'inconceivable,' that which according to Otto is 'peculiar to the sphere of religion,' and the sacred, that which is held in special esteem in *any* field of human endeavor, and of the distinctions between both the 'secular' and the 'profane.'"[2] Thus, while granting that we may be able to speak of the "sacred" in sports, the sacred is still very different from the holy, from God. In short, the holy certainly is sacred, but not everything sacred is holy. They describe the holy as "a reality wholly beyond our power. The sacred is always indicated by place, time, object, or word, while the holy is beyond place and time and language, that before which 'words and understanding recoil.'"[3]

The problem with the argument presented by Higgs and Braswell is that they posit the existence of an object of experience—the holy—for which they cannot provide any proof or argument other than that it is something "wholly other" than the sacred or anything else for that matter. This *via negativa* argument may be the best they can offer, but as a form of

---

[2] Robert J. Higgs and Michael C. Braswell, *An Unholy Alliance: The Sacred and Modern Sports* (Macon GA: Mercer University Press, 2004) 27.
[3] Ibid., 47–48.

argumentation, it is inherently weak. In fact, the existence of the holy, by their definition, is simply an assertion rather than an argument. There seems to be no rational criteria by which to validate their assertions about the sacred and holy against the assertions made by anyone else.

In short, Higgs and Braswell are engaged in a "protective strategy" for religion, much like Wayne Proudfoot identifies among post-Enlightenment theologians and religionists. Attempts to "naturalize" religion—to provide naturalistic explanations of it or to identify gods naturalistically (Emile Durkheim, for example, identified them with society)—simply are dismissed. For Higgs, Braswell, and others, identifying sport (a human construct) with religion implicitly reduces the latter to the natural as opposed to supernatural realm. "The danger of attempting to make sport a religion, even one qualified by the word 'popular,' is the distinct possibility of an opposite effect," Higgs and Braswell argue, "legitimizing religion as sports, trivializing the grand purposes of religions in spite of failures that all human institutions experience."[4]

In the end, religion for Higgs and Braswell must ultimately be about something other-worldly, so it cannot be about sports at all, for sport is worldly.

Objection 2: Religion is about the "big" and meaningful questions; sport is not.

Again, this seems like a reasonable objection. We often associate religion with "big" questions, such as the nature of the universe, the meaning of life, or the nature of God. Sports do not seem to ask or answer these questions.

We first need to make the distinction between various "big" questions and meaningful questions. Most "big" questions are meaningful, but not all meaningful questions are "big." The most meaningful questions and answers to me might have to do with my relationship to my family. These hardly inform me about the nature of the universe, at least not directly.

---

[4] Ibid., 27.

These questions and answers also may provide my life with purpose—and perhaps that is enough for me. In other words, I do not have to imagine that a divine being has an even greater purpose for me. There are plenty of ways that religious ideas can be bound up with these questions and answers, but not necessarily so, or only in such an abstract way that few people would ever care to know or understand. In a similar way, I would argue that for some college football fans in the South, and, by extension, many sports fans around the world, their devotion to their team and the broader community is such that *it does* lend meaning or purpose to their lives.

College football in the South may not ask the "big" questions, but it nevertheless is meaningful for many people. And while many religious people consider the "big" questions to be central to their understanding of religion, we need not accept those questions as central or even necessary to a definition of religion. Indeed, I would argue that religion is much more about meaning and purpose than it is about attempting to ponder and answer the "big" questions. Jesus apparently spent much more of his time trying to help people live meaningful and purposeful lives than helping them answer "big" questions. Similarly, the Buddha often avoided grappling with the "big" questions with his followers, concluding that it would only lead to confusion and take their attention off the (meaningful and purposeful) practice of living that he was teaching them.

Objection 3: Sport is not religious
because sport is too worldly.

Cornel Sandvoss claims, similarly to Higgs and Braswell, though in a less polemical way, that fan-generating activities or institutions lack the "transcendental points of reference" (God and heaven, for example) of religion. He writes:

> In contrast to religion, fandom lacks an absolute, other-worldly framework through which social realities are constructed and legitimized. If fandom differs so radically in its premises from

religion, it is difficult to juxtapose their consequences meaningfully. The pilgrimages of fans, for instance, lack the universal cultural acknowledgement of the places of pilgrimage of the monolithic world religions. Rather than a communal search for a future place in another world, they are individual journeys seeking a sense of place in *this* world.[5]

Two points need to be made in response, both of which respond to Higgs and Braswell as well. First, it is unclear whether or not such "transcendent points of reference" are central to the definition of religion or even necessary to it. Second, even granting this point, might not sport involve a transcendent point of reference? When fans join at the stadium or the arena and cheer for their team, do we not talk about the "spirit" of the crowd or "team spirit"? But where is that spirit? It is not in any single individual, it "transcends" the individual. One might respond that if all the fans were gone, however, then the spirit would be gone as well. Yet this raises a similar problem for the religionists: If there were no humans on earth, could we talk about the spirit of God here? Some undoubtedly would say yes, but that simply is an assertion of belief rather than an argument.

A related point involves the very distinction between the immanent and the transcendent, the natural and the supernatural. Identifying religion strictly with the latter is culturally relative and hardly necessary. As an example, look at ancient Greek religious practice, which is relevant to our concerns because, as Allen Guttmann notes, for the Greeks sport "became a part of the ordinary life of the *polis* as well as a means of worship."[6] Certainly, the Greeks had their gods, but they were not transcendent or other-worldly in the same way in which Higgs and Braswell would argue. Few people, though, would claim that the ancient Greeks did not have a

---

[5] Cornel Sandvoss, *Fans: The Mirror of Consumption* (Malden MA: Polity Press, 2005) 63.

[6] Allen Guttmann, *From Ritual to Record: The Nature of Modern Sports* (New York: Columbia University Press, 1978) 23.

religion or that they practiced a false religion, a charge that would strike many of us as ethnocentric at best and succumbing to the vice of pride—the most dangerous Christian sin—at worst.

Guttmann goes on to argue that modern sports are secular as opposed to the way that ancient Greek sports were sacred. This difference is due to the fact that modern sports have lost their connection to the "realm of the transcendent."[7] It is true that modern sports generally do not affirm a direct connection to the gods, but a connection with the gods represents simply one understanding of "transcendent"—one that we need not blindly accept and one that we reasonably can reject. Sport might be "worldly," but that does not exclude it from being religious. To the critic who says it is *too* worldly, we can respond, by which or by whose criteria is it too worldly?

Objection 4: Religion, unlike sport, has to do with goodness and living the moral life.

It is true that various moral virtues are a part of many if not most religious traditions. Therefore, if there is an absence of morality in sport, then this absence certainly could be a critical difference between sport and religion. Higgs and Braswell make this argument when they write that sports "are about the chosen ones, those who are able to make the team—the fit, the able, and the talented. All religions at their best are about caring for the unchosen, the rejects, those who don't qualify for any team."[8] One of the keys to being able to care for others is to restrain our own desires. Instead of seeking our own good, religion and morality direct us to seek the good of others. This regard for others requires overcoming our pride or hubris. But "in our sporting, corporate, militarized world, it [pride] has become the chief virtue of success or more accurately excess, seen regularly in the form of running up the score on hapless opponents for the purpose of national ranking."[9]

---

[7] Ibid., 26.
[8] Higgs and Braswell, *Unholy Alliance*, 236.
[9] Ibid., 55.

The importance of the moral virtues to the religious life, however, can vary greatly depending on the given tradition. Even when the moral virtues are emphasized within a given tradition, there is a big difference between what people say about them and whether or not they practice them. Every major religious tradition probably has had moments in its history when its leaders condoned or even encouraged violence against others, even when this action clearly was contrary to the religion's teachings. As D. Stanley Eitzen and Charles H. Sage note, sport shares this characteristic with religion. "The emotional attachment of some fans for their teams verges on the religious fanaticism previously seen in holy wars against heretics and pagans," they write. "Opposing teams and their fans, as well as officials, are occasionally attacked and brutally beaten."[10]

My point here, however, is not that sports fans can become as despicable as some religious fanatics. Certainly, they can. My point, though, is that there are moral virtues within the sporting world. In describing the development of the young athlete, Randolph Feezell writes that participation "requires a certain honesty about himself, a respect for coaches who embody the tradition [of the sport], a sense of who deserves or merits playing time, a feeling about the need for cooperation to achieve shared goals, courage in the face of failing to achieve standards, and persistence or determination in the attempt to achieve his goals."[11] While virtues like honesty, cooperation, courage, and persistence are manifested in the game in specific ways, they nevertheless are virtues applicable to other aspects of the athlete's life.

In short, sports teach us much about morality—from sportsmanship to sacrifice for the team. Can virtue get lost in the pursuit of athletic victory or in excessive boosterism? Of course it can. But this shortcoming is no different than any other institution in human societies. We should not let

---

[10] D. Stanley Eitzen and Charles H. Sage, "Sport and Religion," in *Religion and Sport: The Meeting of Sacred and Profane*, ed. Charles Prebish (Westport CT: Greenwood Press, 1993) 92.

[11] Randolph Feezell, *Sport, Play, and Ethical Reflection* (Chicago: University of Illinois Press, 2004) 129.

the excesses of a few—whether they are religious fanatics or sports hooligans—distort our assessment of a social institution. Sports can lead to excessive behavior, but they also play a role in the moral education of citizens. As Michael Novak concludes, "I sometimes wonder what we would do for the moral education of our children if they did not have sports. Where else do they learn so much about enduring pain and defeat? Where else are they driven to strive for perfection?"[12]

One other aspect of this objection deserves our attention. Many religious traditions have a long and continuing history of charitable work, both through their individual members and institutionally. Sports also have their charities as well. Professional franchises regularly conduct benefits for charitable organizations, and professional athletes often become extensively involved with particular charities, contributing both their time and significant amounts of money. At the collegiate level, amateur athletes may not have the financial resources to support charities in the same way, but they often donate their time as part of a team or university commitment. Fans also engage in charitable giving. As noted in chapter two, a University of Georgia football game (as was the case at a number of venues) was the occasion for a significant fundraising effort on behalf of Louisiana and Mississippi victims of hurricane Katrina. Do sports provide the same kind of opportunities to practice the virtue of charity as do religions? Probably not. Yet sports certainly are not devoid of those opportunities.

Objection 5: Religion is about how we can get to heaven; sport is not.

This objection is related to the previous one, since many people believe that following the moral code of their religion is the way that they *will* get to heaven. We need not imagine, however, that the affirmation of an afterlife

---

[12] Michael Novak, *The Joy of Sports: Endzones, Bases, Baskets, Balls, and the Consecration of the American Spirit*, rev. ed. (Lanham MD: Madison Books, 1994) 358.

in heaven or elsewhere is a necessary element of religious life. It certainly is for many. But for a good number of religious people (many Buddhists, for example, but also many contemporary Christians) there is doubt about the existence of an afterlife, and concerns about getting to heaven are minimal or non-existent. In other words, many people consider themselves religious or spiritual, and I think there is no reason to doubt their self-assessment, yet believe that the practice of their religion is mainly, if not exclusively, about this world and not the afterworld. So the fact that sports do not lay out a path to heaven certainly should not prevent us from recognizing their religious elements or functions.

Of course, one might also respond that for a Tennessee fan a victory over Alabama *is* heaven. In one sense, this is hyperbole. But keep in mind that there legitimately may be experiences of *communitas* among fans during game day, times when social structures drift away and people transcend their "selves" to join with *all* others in a unified ecstatic experience. Is this not heaven on earth? This concept is related to the next objection.

Objection 6: Religion, unlike sport, is about peace and harmony with others.

Higgs and Braswell put great stress on this point. They argue that "sports are a story of power."[13] In contrast, the cross in Christianity "is not based upon victory over others in contests but on a much more important premise, that loss in the name of love is gain and compassion, not conquest, points the way to what is sought."[14] More generally, they conclude:

> As a human endeavor, religion is more versatile than sports in that it is possible in religion, and indeed preferable, for people to be joined together in admission of weakness (including moral

---

[13] Higgs and Braswell, *Unholy Alliance*, 73.
[14] Ibid., 111.

weakness) rather than strength; seeking salvation rather than attempting to display it, knowing that salvation is a process rather than a destination or a "goal," which, in contrast, is essential for all athletic contests, as is a "record."[15]

The shepherd symbolizes genuine religion, whereas the knight is the symbol of the victorious athlete, the battlefield hero, and the successful corporate executive. In his earlier work, Higgs sees a contemporary trend in the United States toward the glorification of the knight rather than the shepherd: "Our national orthodoxy has become tilted far toward the sword of honor and conquest and away from the staff of care and toleration."[16] The connection with the military and militarization is central. "Sports took on religious significance in America not because they were fun for a growing number of civilians in the 1850s," Higgs argues, "but because they became intimately connected with the ideal of the complete officer committed to duty, honor, and country."[17] Consequently, the effect of the military mindset on sports is to rob them of their joy and spontaneity, just as it also warped religion, Christianity, in particular, by putting it in the service of nationalism.

As usual, Higgs and Braswell compare an idealized version of religion (primarily Christianity) with excesses and abuses from the sporting world. It hardly is the case that religion is free from the excesses and abuses of power, and various religions have been used to justify oppression and violence against others (or even their own adherents!). Again, my point is not to highlight the failings of religion or religions, which are all too apparent; my point, rather, is a constructive one: *Sports provide training in the peaceful resolution of competitive relationships.* We unavoidably are in competitive situations—vying for honors, wealth, and goods. Sports allow us to learn how to engage in these competitive situations without resorting to unregulated and excessive violence. This capacity is true even in the

---

[15] Ibid., 126.

[16] Higgs, *God in the Stadium*, 6.

[17] Ibid., 96.

more physically aggressive sports. While football may include violence as part of the game, it is bound by certain rules, and once the game is over the competitors stop engaging in violence. Sports fans may heap verbal abuse upon one another before the big game but almost always return peacefully to the parking lot after the game is over. The exceptional instances of fans engaging in violence against one another prove the rule that they generally support their teams in a peaceful manner. Daniel L. Wann and his co-authors perhaps get it right when they conclude:

> [S]port has the potential to model several values regarded as crucial to a democratic and humane society, such as legitimization of authority, honesty, justice, equality, respect for the rule of law, respect for the rights of others, cooperation, competition, and fair play, to name just a few.... However imperfect, sport typically offers spectators and fans demonstrable evidence of the ideological elements that constitute the dominant value structure in American society.[18]

In other words, sport has the potential to teach the values of civic life, values that very practically can lead to more peaceful and harmonious communities.

Objection 7: Religion, unlike sports, is a private matter.

For many people, religion is a private matter, a matter of individual conscience. Religion is about solitude, about getting away from the crowd—nothing like the spectacle of a major sporting event. "There is...a theater side to religion as in all other forms of human drama," Higgs and Braswell argue, "but what has distinguished it from other forms of entertainment is a private side evident in every religion on earth, the solitude needed for

---

[18] Daniel L. Wann, Merrill J. Melnick, Gordon W. Russell, Dale G. Pease, *Sports Fans: The Psychology and Social Impact of Spectators* (New York: Routledge, 2001) 190.

respite from a society talking to itself, for meditation, and—who knows?—for listening in private to something wholly other."[19]

For many religious people, solitude is a primary good of their practice. But this is culturally relative. For many other people around the world, religion is first and foremost a communal activity: Religion is not about isolation, it is about community. Certainly, Higgs and Braswell would not want to rely on solitude as a key distinguishing characteristic of religion. For some individuals, fishing or hunting by themselves is an enjoyable and entertaining activity. They prefer to do it alone. Yet surely Higgs and Braswell would not want to call that religious.

Once again, this objection is too culturally specific to carry much weight in an argument against sport as religion.

Objection 8: What about fair-weather fans? They do not seem very religious.

"Fair-weather fans" are those who support their team (wearing the paraphernalia, talking about the team, and going to the games) when the team wins but do not support the team when it loses. Such fans certainly do not seem to display the kind of faith or devotion that we expect of religious people.

Two points need to be made here. First, we need to keep in mind that there are millions upon millions of fans every year who continue to support teams that not only are having bad seasons but also are perennial losers. Chicago Cubs fans have gone 100 years since last winning a World Series championship, yet they are considered to be some of the most supportive and devoted fans in baseball. My uncle is a season-ticket holder for Vanderbilt University football games, and they have never won a Southeastern Conference championship. Yet he continues to support the team. He is not alone. While college football reigns supreme in the South, many teams have had only modest success over the years. Yet their fans remain quite faithful.

---

[19] Higgs and Braswell, *Unholy Alliance*, 93.

Second, fans who are fair-weather are not unlike those who attend religious services at one church and then switch to another or eventually stop attending religious services all together. In other words, religious people can be fair-weather as well, perhaps by not supporting their church when it challenges them too much or asks too much of them. As a result, this objection hardly seems to discount sport as religion.

Objection 9: Many fans do not take sports very seriously, unlike religious people.

This objection is related to the previous one. Even as you can find fair-weather fans in religion as well as sports, so can you find people in both who do not take it very seriously. Many people go to church, for example, because they think it is good for their families or to please their parents or to enjoy the food at the potluck after the service. They often "go through the motions" of the religious service, but without any real commitment or dedication. In short, we live in an age when many people do not take their religion very seriously. Obviously, this lack of devotion is true with sports as well. Many people do not take it very seriously and are suspicious of those who do, much like some people are suspicious of religious fanatics. Yet many people do take sport seriously, even as there are many dedicated and fervent religious believers. In short, the degree of belief or seriousness depends much more on the particular individual than it does on the practice (sports or religion) itself.

Objection 10: Sport is subject to so much corruption. It is nothing like religion.

Sports' very public abuses (steroids, violations of rules regarding amateur athletes at the collegiate level, "hooligan"-style violence by fans, et cetera) might lead one to this objection, but even a cursory review of religious history would show that religious traditions have not been immune to various abuses or even to genocidal practices. Of course, many might argue that such abuses by religious institutions or leaders were not really religious. Higgs and Braswell insist, "the cruelties committed in the name of religion are not at all what religion, by common understanding, is about."[20] Once again, however, it is not a "common understanding" with which they are working so much as an "idealized understanding." The supporter of sport could just as easily posit an idealized vision of sport and insist that all that falls outside of that idealized vision simply is not what sport is about.

The fact of the matter is that all human institutions are subject to corruption—religion, politics, sport, you name it. Individuals and groups seeking power, wealth, or prestige easily manipulate institutions. In this sense, sports are no more corrupt than religions. Indeed, one could make the case that sport is actually less subject to abuse in certain areas than religions, since those within sport tend not to be complicit in the sexual abuse of children or in genocide.

Money, of course, is a corrupting influence for many institutions, and that is the case in sports as well. When winning has such significant financial implications, it is little wonder that athletes and management will do whatever it takes, even cheating, in order to win. The emphasis on winning is one of the causes of the rampant use of steroids in professional sports. At the collegiate level, we often see the corrupting influence of money in the recruitment of star athletes and the willingness to cut academic corners in order to keep those athletes eligible to play. Here again, though, we should not ignore the fact that plenty of religious institutions have been corrupted by money. Many certainly have not been shy in their efforts to build massive fortunes—one need look no further than the Roman Catholic Church. Nevertheless, there still is need of a cautionary note here: Sports are often viewed as a moneymaking business rather than an important social institution that serves a public good. Religious institutions often are viewed as the latter rather than the former. This important difference certainly works to the detriment of sport. Recognizing

---

[20] Ibid., 365.

the sacred nature of sports would entail being more diligent in our efforts to prevent money from corrupting them.

Objection 11: Being a sports fan is a passive activity and, thus, unlike religion.

We often talk about religious life in active terms, such as when we describe someone as a "practicing" Christian. Being a spectator at a sporting event, however, is usually seen as a passive activity, especially compared with the active role the athletes play. But is there really such a difference between the religious adherent and the sports spectator?

What do we mean when we say that someone "practices" a particular religion? In Christianity, for example, it probably entails attending church services, participating in certain rituals (singing hymns, taking communion, et cetera), reading appropriate texts, and joining in certain social functions associated with the church. Certainly there is more, but these activities at least would be the minimum. Yet none of these is particularly active. Generally, the officials of the church perform most of the action. But that does not mean that the people in the pews are passive spectators. As Novak observes, at a liturgy (in this case, religious or sporting) "elected representatives perform the formal acts, but all believers put their hearts into the ritual. It is considered inadequate, almost blasphemous, to be a mere spectator. Fans are not mere spectators."[21]

In short, it is not the case that the typical Christian is any more active than the typical fan attending Southeastern Conference football games. Such a fan attends home games and often away games on a regular basis, participates in the various rituals that revolve around the game (see chapter one), reads profusely about his team (perhaps reads more about his team than the typical Christian reads the Bible), and joins in many social functions associated with game day (primarily tailgating or even meeting up with friends at a local bar).

---

[21] Novak, *Joy of Sports*, 24.

Of course, the opponent might argue that the typical Christian incorporates the teachings of the religion into many aspects of his or her daily life in a way that the sports fan does not. This is what "practicing" the religion could mean. Many Christians do incorporate the tradition into their lives in some substantial way, but the previous chapters of this book should make clear that for many sports fans (in this case, especially college football fans in the South), their devotion and dedication to their teams are central to how they identify themselves and how a good deal of their lives are structured. The way that devotion and dedication to a team permeates the lives of fans would seem to be a distinguishing characteristic of what it means to be "practicing" a religion, albeit one that we typically do not call religion.

Objection 12: The sporting event is like a carnival or festival, not a religious event.

Here is another objection that relies upon a very culturally specific understanding of what religion is supposed to be like. In particular, it betrays a predominantly Christian (particularly Protestant) bias that sees religious services as austere and solemn affairs. Certainly, that *is* religion for many people, but only blind prejudice would restrict religion to this model.

In her book *Dancing in the Streets: A History of Collective Joy*, Barbara Ehrenreich traces the history of carnival and festival in Western history, including its roots in ancient religions and subsequent ambivalent relationship with institutional Christianity. Carnivals and festivals have been occasions for ecstatic experiences among those who participate. Often these occasions have been accompanied by religious practices or, in some cases, the carnivals and festivals were considered religious practices. In looking at the anthropological evidence concerning ancient and contemporary practices from around the world, Ehrenreich concludes, "It is not clear that this distinction between ritual and festivity, religion and recreation, is always meaningful to the participants."[22] While this distinction *is* meaningful to many Christians, it is not for all. We have no need to cede the definition of proper religious decorum to any particular religious tradition or portion thereof.

The "core elements" of the ecstatic practices that one might find at a carnival or festival are "the dancing, the feasting, the artistic decoration of faces and bodies."[23] These, of course, are elements found at sporting events as well, and throughout the early chapters of this book, we saw how central they are to the rituals of college football in the South. As a consequence of one's participation in these elements, the participant loses his or her "self," and the participant has the experience of *collective effervescence* (Durkheim) or *communitas* (Turner) that was described in chapter two.

Ehrenreich affirms this experience of losing the self. Such experiences are psychologically beneficial to the individual and build community; one loses one's self in the greater good of the community. Yet, in Western history, these experiences, and the carnivals or festivals that gave rise to them, were seen as a threat to the public order. Ecstatic crowds of people who abandoned all social and hierarchical distinctions were perceived—rightfully—as potentially revolutionary, and this represented a threat to the authority and preeminence of the church itself. Peter Stallybrass and Allon White write, "In the long-term history from the seventeenth to the twentieth century...there were literally thousands of acts of legislation introduced which attempted to eliminate carnival and popular festivity from European life."[24] Such actions were supported not only by the powerful elite but by the growing bourgeois class as well. "Carnival was too disgusting for bourgeois life to endure except as sentimental spectacle," Stallybrass and White argue. "Even then its specular identifications could

---

[22] Barbara Ehrenreich, *Dancing in the Streets: A History of Collective Joy* (New York: Metropolitan Books, 2006) 19.

[23] Ibid., 18.

[24] Peter Stallybrass and Allon White, "Bourgeois Hysteria and the Carnivalesque," in *The Cultural Studies Reader*, ed. Simon During (New York: Routledge, 1993) 385.

only be momentary, fleeting and partial—voyeuristic glimpses of a promiscuous loss of status and decorum which the bourgeoisie had had to deny as abhorrent in order to emerge as a distinct and 'proper' class."[25] Consequently, carnival and festival finally were marginalized in the church and heavily controlled by the political establishment. Ehrenreich concludes:

> At some point, in town after town throughout the northern Christian world, the music stops. Carnival costumes are put away or sold; dramas that once engaged a town's entire population are canceled; festive rituals are forgotten or preserved only in tame and truncated form. The ecstatic possibility, which had first been driven from the sacred precincts of the church, was now harried from the streets and public squares.[26]

In addition to the threat that carnival or festival posed to church and political leadership, Western history has been dominated by a fixation on the self rather than on efforts to transcend it. Thus, Ehrenreich claims, to "the 'self'-admiring Western mind, any form of self-loss—other than the kind associated with romantic love—could only be pathological."[27] The reverse, however, is really the case. "The loss, to ordinary people, of so many recreations and festivities is incalculable," she argues, "and we, who live in a culture almost devoid of opportunities either to 'lose ourselves' in communal festivities or to distinguish ourselves in any arena outside of work, are in no position to fathom it."[28] But, in fact, many people can fathom it: Millions of people can, because millions of people every year have ecstatic experiences at sporting events across the country (they have them in other settings as well, but sport is our focus). They are all too aware of the psyche-sapping banality of much of our day-to-day existence,

---

[25] Ibid., 388.
[26] Ehrenreich, *Dancing*, 97.
[27] Ibid., 15.
[28] Ibid., 99.

because they can compare it to the ecstasy experienced at a basketball game at the University of North Carolina, at a Red Sox game in Boston, or (of course) at a football game at Bryant-Denny Stadium in Tuscaloosa, Neyland Stadium in Knoxville, or Tiger Stadium in Baton Rouge.

Ehrenreich notices that the sports venue is one place where the carnival or festival lives on. She observes that in the 1960s spectators "began 'carnivalizing' sports events, coming in costume, engaging in collective rhythmic activities that went well beyond chants, adding their own music, dance, and feasting to the game."[29] If she spent a game day at a major university in the South, she would see many of the practices and experiences that she laments have been diminished in Western society.

The long and the short of it is that the wild and sometimes ecstatic scene of a college football game in the South may not look very religious to a lot of people, but there are many people historically and even today in other parts of the world who would recognize the scene as religious in some way.

Objection 13: If sports are religious, it is a primitive form of religiosity, at best.

The hierarchization of religious experience into primitive and advanced, usually meaning indigenous as opposed to, say, Christianity, is so antiquated and even offensive that one might not imagine anyone using it to argue against sport as religion. But Higgs and Braswell do just that. They describe sport as a "primitive religion" at best.[30] They even blame television, in part, for the current situation. "If modern sports are a religion, as apologists claim and as they certainly were in ancient Greece," Higgs and Braswell argue, "they are today increasingly pagan thanks to television, which has returned us to the mentality of children, the psychological worldview of primitive man."[31]

---

[29] Ibid., 227–28.
[30] Higgs and Braswell, *Unholy Alliance*, 158.
[31] Ibid., 102.

As proponents of a religion (Christianity) that regularly engages in symbolic cannibalism (communion), one might see Higgs and Braswell's judgment as a case of the "pot calling the kettle black." The larger point is that there are no objective criteria for determining "primitive" and "advanced." All criteria are culturally specific. In this case, Higgs and Braswell assume that Christianity or something like it embodies an advanced form of religion. Thus, anything else that looks like religion (sport, for example) but that differs from their ideal type must be primitive. This poor form of argument, which is more assertion than anything else, contributes to an ethnocentrism that historically has led to oppression and violence against those deemed primitive.

Given the good reasons for rejecting the primitive/advanced dichotomy, there seems little reason to entertain this objection further.

Objection 14: By your account, almost everything can be religious.

To some degree, this charge is not problematic. An underlying assumption of this book is that human beings act religiously in ways other than those restricted to institutionalized religion, that the sacred is not restricted to one's church, and that spiritual communities can be formed outside of stereotypically religious congregations. As Mircea Eliade would say, human beings are *homo religiosus* through and through, not merely on Sundays, or whatever day or days one stereotypically worships.

Not everything, though, is religious. In this work alone, there are certain characteristics that one would expect to find in any phenomenon that one would want to call religion. In chapter one, we saw the role played by myth, symbols, and rituals as well as sacred spaces, objects, and time. In chapter two, we saw how one of the primary functions of religion is the creation of community. In chapter three, we saw the often-complicated relationship that exists between religion, violence, and sacrifice. In chapter four, we saw that religious experiences tend to involve the transcendence of the self. And in chapter five, we saw how religion becomes involved in the larger social and historical fabric of a people. The argument of this book is that these characteristics and others can be found in college football in the South and, by extension, in other sports examples. Neither the argument nor the extension entails, then, that almost everything can be considered religious.

Objection 15: I just don't get it!

"Sports is [sic], somehow, a religion," Michael Novak writes. "You either see or you don't see what the excitement is."[32] Some people are going to look at sports and always see *just* games. Of course, many people look at a wide variety of practices generally called religious and simply do not "get it."

At this point, I am not sure there is much more to say in response to this objection. Given the arguments of the preceding chapters and the summary here, some people simply will not recognize any validity in the argument. I would ask even the staunchest opponent that we not see this strictly as an either/or issue, stating that sport is either fully a religion or it is not in any way. My hope is that even the most skeptical reader will acknowledge that there is some religious dimension to sport and to college football in the South in particular, even if he or she does not want to equate sport with Christianity, Hinduism, or another world tradition.

Finally, let me conclude by saying that expanding our viewpoints and extending our categories can be difficult. Religion is extremely important to many people, and a person's particular religion is, well, sacrosanct. It can be threatening to have sport compared to religion for such people. At the same time, I would encourage these people to embrace the idea that human religiosity can transcend not only one's particular tradition (I hope most people grant this point today) but also even institutionalized religion in general. In that case, the argument that I make in this book is not a diminution of religion but a broadening and deepening of it.

---

[32] Novak, *Joy of Sports*, xvi.

Is Sport Replacing Religion?

This is an intriguing question with which to conclude this book. The possibility that sport could be replacing institutional religions clearly is of great concern to Higgs and Braswell and many others.

At least in the South, Charles Reagan Wilson sees peaceful coexistence rather than competition with these concepts. He claims that for "the modern, middle-class, urban and suburban South," sport "is a new kind of religion but one closely allied with traditional Evangelicalism."[33] My nine-year-old daughter's recent experience certainly is not exceptional and illustrates Wilson's point. We live in the South, though on its northern fringes. This past year, she eschewed my encouragement to play basketball and chose to try cheerleading instead, which is a whole other story. Nevertheless, the cheerleading squads cheered at the basketball games. The whole thing was run by an organization (Upwards) with an explicitly religious dimension, and the games were held in a gymnasium at the local Baptist church. At halftime of each game, an adult gave a short talk about Christianity or witnessed to his or her spiritual experience. A prayer followed this testimony. Though I did not conduct a survey, I do not think many of the parents or friends in the stands thought there was any great disjunction between the competitive nature of the games on the court and the values of Christianity. In fact, the religious point of the whole enterprise was to bring these two things together.

I suspect that most Americans who are religious do not think there is any great divide between their love of sports and their religious commitments. In my meetings with college football fans in the South, I talked with many very devout individuals who also were extremely devoted to their team. It may even be the case that the type of person who is energetic and passionate about religious life is the same type of person who has a similar experience with college football. In short, the person who has the personality type of a "passionate devotee" can be found in a stadium or

---

[33] Charles Reagan Wilson, *Judgment & Grace in Dixie: Southern Faiths from Faulkner to Elvis* (Athens: University of Georgia Press, 1995) 142.

in a church and, more often than not, in the former on Saturday and the latter on Sunday.

Such peaceful coexistence between sport and religion, however, is very different from the prospect that sports could be replacing institutional religion in the lives of many people. I believe that sport is replacing religion, though, based on the argument in the preceding chapters, I would argue that this is a substitution of form rather than substance. Human beings can express their religiosity in the sporting world or in church or in both. In this sense, expressing one's religiosity predominantly in the context of one's college football team in the South is really no different from being a Methodist or Baptist.

As mentioned earlier, my perspective is shaped greatly by the work of Mircea Eliade, who writes:

> The longing for Paradise can be traced even in the most banal actions of the modern man. Man's concept of the *absolute* can never be completely uprooted: it can only be debased. And primitive spirituality lives on in its own way not in action, not as a thing man can effectively accomplish, but as a *nostalgia* which creates things that become values in themselves: art, the sciences, social theory, and all the other things to which men will give the whole of themselves.[34]

Now we have to excuse his use of "primitive" given Eliade's historical context; that language was standard in the mid-twentieth century. We also should take his value judgment—the debased comment—with some caution. As argued earlier, what is debased or not is greatly a matter of historical and cultural context. But the passage does signal to us what Eliade means by *homo religiosus*. Even if all institutional religions were to disappear tomorrow, human religiosity still would exhibit itself in a

---

[34] Mircea Eliade, *Patterns in Comparative Religion* (New York: Sheed & Ward, 1958) 434.

multitude of "secular" forms. Eliade identifies art, science, and others, but I would insist that sport be included as well.

"For me, it is not just a parallel that is emerging between religion and sport, but rather a *complete identity. Sport is religion* for growing numbers of Americans, and this is no product of simply facile reasoning or wishful thinking," Charles Prebish argues. "Further, for many, sport religion has become a more appropriate expression of personal religiosity than Christianity, Judaism, or any of the traditional religions."[35] Prebish was an early proponent of the notion that sports could function religiously. While his focus is primarily on the athlete, I think much of what he has to say is applicable to fans as well. It is within the sporting world that they transcend their "selves," that they form community, that they can see and experience human excellence, and much more.

Joseph Price, one of today's most prolific and interesting writers on sport and religion, argues that "sports constitute a popular form of religion by shaping their world and sustaining their ways of engaging it."[36] He adds, "Through their symbols and rituals, sports provide occasions for experiencing a sense of ultimacy and for prompting personal transformation."[37] Apropos of our interests in college football in the South, Bonnie J. Miller-McLemore writes that "the sacred makes itself known through the ordinary and through the temporary suspension of the ordinary. Such is the case with modern football. Noticed or not, football expresses a complex system of coherent affirmations about ultimate reality through its myths and rituals—through its creation of sacred time and sacred space."[38] Allen Guttmann, a leading authority on modern sports and sports spectators, concludes:

---

[35] *Religion and Sport: The Meeting of Sacred and Profane,* ed. Charles Prebish (Westport CT: Greenwood Press, 1993) 62 (emphasis original).

[36] Joseph L. Price, editor, *From Season to Season: Sports as American Religion* (Macon GA: Macon University Press, 2001) 216.

[37] Ibid., 223.

[38] Bonnie J. Miller-McLemore, "Through the Eyes of Mircea Eliade: United States Football as a Religious 'Rite de Passage,'" in *From Season to Season: Sports as*

We can debate Michael Novak's proposition that sports have become a substitute for conventional religious faith, but how else can we understand the Nebraskan's ecstatic tears or the remark of an adolescent German girl who shocked her pious mother by saying of the local soccer team, 'The HSV is greater than God'? When we speak lyrically as Novak does (at epic length) about the 'sacred trinity' of baseball, basketball, and football, we indulge ourselves in hyperbole, but the fact remains undeniable that many (by no means all) sports spectators experience something akin to worship.[39]

Even social scientists like Daniel L. Wann and his co-authors conclude that "as a civil, secular, natural, or humanistic religion, both analogy and functional analysis suggest that there is much that is religious about sport fandom."[40]

All of the authors quoted above affirm either explicitly or implicitly the fundamental Eliadean concept of *homo religiosus*. They recognize that sport is not simply one activity among others; it is one of those special activities that help us express our religiosity or spirituality in powerful and meaningful ways.

Theologian William Dean sees football, along with other cultural elements like jazz and movies, as an important part of "American spiritual culture."[41] Religion scholar David Chidester argues more broadly that American popular culture does "religious work." "Traces of religion, as transcendence, as the sacred, as the ultimate, can be discerned in the play of

---

American Religion, ed. Joseph Price (Macon GA: Mercer University Press, 2001) 121.

[39] Allen Guttmann, *Sports Spectators* (New York: Columbia University Press, 1986) 178.

[40] Wann et al., *Sports Fans*, 200.

[41] William Dean, *The American Spiritual Culture: And the Invention of Jazz, Football and the Movies* (New York: Continuum, 2003).

popular culture," he argues. "As a result, we can conclude that popular culture is doing a kind of religious work."[42] Michael Mandelbaum concurs when he writes that "team sports provide three satisfactions of life to twenty-first-century Americans that, before the modern age, only religion offered: a welcome diversion from the routines of daily life; a model of coherence and clarity; and heroic examples to admire and emulate."[43] Novak even argues that sports may be more effective at one religious function (building community) than institutional religions: "Our other religions are all, despite their universal aims, sectarian; their symbols and liturgies cannot unite as many as sports do…. Where, then, can a secular society turn, if not to sport, as the chief communal ritual of its citizens?"[44]

What these authors indicate is not only that sports increasingly have functioned like religions, perhaps even replacing institutional religions for many people, but also that this is not the catastrophe that authors like Higgs and Braswell and others might imagine. The warnings and exhortations of the latter may not do much to change the situation either. Perhaps we are dealing with historical and social forces that simply are irreversible. Wann and his co-authors note that "record attendance at U.S. sporting events in recent years has coincided with the lowest levels of attendance at U.S. houses of worship since before World War II…. It may well be that new 'houses of worship,' sport stadia and arenas, are beginning to challenge the drawing power of traditional houses of worship in American society."[45] They conclude, "As societies grow increasingly more secular and theological beliefs become less salient and all pervasive…we should expect to see sport fandom assuming greater religious importance at

---

[42] David Chidester, *Authentic Fakes: Religion and American Popular Culture* (Berkeley: University of California Press, 2005) 231.

[43] Michael Mandelbaum, *The Meaning of Sports: Why Americans Watch Baseball, Football, and Basketball and What They See When They Do* (New York: PublicAffairs, 2004) 4.

[44] Novak, *Joy of Sports*, 292.

[45] Wann et al., *Sports Fans*, 200.

both the individual and societal levels."[46] This may turn out to be true and it reminds us of the prediction (cited earlier) made by Emile Durkheim. In *The Elementary Forms of Religious Life*, first published in 1912, he writes:

> If today we have some difficulty imagining what the feasts and ceremonies of the future will be, it is because we are going through a period of transition and moral mediocrity. The great things of the past that excited our fathers no longer arouse the same zeal among us, either because they have passed so completely into common custom that we lose awareness of them or because they no longer suit our aspirations. Meanwhile, no replacement for them has yet been created.... [However:] A day will come when our societies once again will know hours of creative effervescence during which new ideals will again spring forth and new formulas emerge to guide humanity for a time.[47]

Sporting events are not the only "feasts and ceremonies" that have come to provide the "creative effervescence" so critical to individual and communal life, but they are important ones in today's world. Thus, we may conclude that college football in the South, with all of its faults, nevertheless nourishes the soul.

---

[46] Ibid.

[47] Emile Durkheim, *The Elementary Forms of Religious Life* (New York: The Free Press, 1995) 429.

Circle appropriate answer:

Age: 18-25   26-40   41-55   56+

Sex: Male   Female

Average number of home games attended per year:

1 or less   1-3   3-5   all

Average number of games watched per year:

1 or less   1-3   3-5   all

What words best describe your experience of attending a LSU football game?

_____

_____

Rank the following (1 is most important; 8 is least important) in terms of the importance that they have in your life:

___ Church   ___ Family   ___ Job/Career
___ Friends   ___ School   ___ LSU Football
___ Spouse/Significant Other   ___ Hobbies/Recreation

Rank these in terms of the percentage of your income that you spend on each (1 is most; 4 is least):

___ Church   ___ Hobbies/Recreation
___ LSU Football   ___ Other Entertainment

Rank these in terms of where you experience the greatest sense of community (1 is most; 7 is least):

___ Church   ___ Family   ___ Job/Career
___ Friends   ___ School   ___ LSU Football
___ Other Clubs or Associations

Rank theses in terms of where you experience the deepest and most positive emotional experiences (1 is most; 8 is least):

___ Church   ___ Family   ___ Job/Career
___ Friends   ___ School   ___ LSU Football
___ Spouse/Significant Other   ___ Hobbies/Recreation

THANK YOU FOR PARTICIPATING IN THIS SURVEY.
ENJOY THE GAME!

Bibliography

Agee, James. *Let Us Now Praise Famous Men*. Boston: Mariner Books, 2001.

Andrews, David L. *Sport—Commerce—Culture: Essays on Sport in Late Capitalist America*. New York: Peter Lang, 2006.

Baker, William J. *Playing with God: Religion and Modern Sport*. Cambridge MA: Harvard University Press, 2007.

Barnhart, Tony. *Southern Fried Football: The History, Passion, and Glory of the Great Southern Game*. Chicago: Triumph Books, 2000.

Barra, Allen. *The Last Coach: A Life of Paul "Bear" Bryant*. New York: W. W. Norton, 2005.

Bebb, Russ. *The Big Orange: A Story of Tennessee Football*. Huntsville AL: Strode Publishers, 1974.

Bell, Catherine. *Ritual Theory, Ritual Practice*. New York: Oxford University Press, 1992.

Bellah, Robert. "Civil Religion in America." In *American Civil Religion*, edited by Russell E. Richey and Donald G. Jones. New York: Harper & Row, 1974.

Berends, Kurt O. "Confederate Sacrifice and the 'Redemption' of the South." In *Religion in the American South: Protestants and Others in History and Culture*, edited by Beth Barton Schweiger and Donald G. Mathews. Chapel Hill NC: University of North Carolina Press, 2004.

Blanton, Al Davis. "A Prayer for the Tide." In *Tales of the Tide: A Book by Alabama Fans...For Alabama Fans*, edited by Clint Lovette and Jarrod Bazemore. Birmingham AL: FANtastic Memories, 2004.

Cash, W. J. *The Mind of the South*. New York: Vintage Books, 1991.

Chidester, David. *Authentic Fakes: Religion and American Popular Culture*. Berkeley CA: University of California Press, 2005.

Cobb, James C. *Redefining Southern Culture: Mind & Identity in the Modern South*. Athens GA: University of Georgia Press, 1999.

Csikszentmihalyi, Mihaly. *Flow: The Psychology of Optimal Experience*. New York: HarperCollins, 1990.

Dean, William. *American Spiritual Culture: The Invention of Jazz, Football, and the Movies*. New York: Continuum, 2003.

Debord, Guy. *Society of the Spectacle*. London: Rebel Press, 2005.

Doyle, Andrew. "An Atheist in Alabama Is Someone Who Doesn't Believe in Bear Bryant: A Symbol for an Embattled South." In *The Sporting World of the*

Modern South, edited by Patrick B. Miller. Chicago: University of Illinois Press, 2002.

Doyle, Andrew. "'Fighting Whiskey and Immorality' at Auburn: The Politics of Southern Football, 1919–1927," *Southern Cultures*. 10/3 (Fall 2004): 6–30.

Doyle, Andrew. "Turning the Tide: College Football and Southern Progressivism." In *The Sporting World of the Modern South*, edited by Patrick B. Miller. Chicago: University of Illinois Press, 2002.

Dunnavant, Keith. *Coach: The Life of Paul "Bear" Bryant*. New York: Thomas Dunne Books, 2005.

Dunnavant, Keith. *The Missing Ring: How Bear Bryant and the 1966 Crimson Tide Were Denied College Football's Most Elusive Prize*. New York: Thomas Dunne Books, 2006.

Durkheim, Emile. *The Elementary Forms of Religious Life*. Translated by Karen E. Fields. New York: The Free Press, 1995.

Edwards, Harry. *Sociology of Sport*. Homewood IL: Dorsey Press, 1973.

Ehrenreich, Barbara. *Dancing in the Streets: A History of Collective Joy*. New York: Metropolitan Books, 2006.

Eitzen, D. Stanley and Charles H. Sage. "Sport and Religion." In *Religion and Sport: The Meeting of Sacred and Profane*, edited by Charles S. Prebish. Westport CT: Greenwood Press, 1993.

Eliade, Mircea. *The Myth of the Eternal Return: Or, Cosmos and History*. Translated by Willard R. Trask. Princeton NJ: Princeton University Press, 1954.

Eliade, Mircea. *Patterns in Comparative Religion*. Translated by Rosemary Sheed. New York: Sheed & Ward, 1958.

Eliade, Mircea. *The Sacred and the Profane: The Nature of Religion*. Translated by Willard R. Trask. New York: Harcourt Brace Jovanovich, 1959.

Feezell, Randolph. *Sport, Play, and Ethical Reflection*. Chicago: University of Illinois Press, 2004.

Flynt, Wayne. *Alabama in the Twentieth Century*. Tuscaloosa AL: University of Alabama Press, 2004.

Girard, Rene. *Violence and the Sacred*. Translated by Patrick Gregory. Baltimore MD: Johns Hopkins University Press, 1977.

Gold, Eli. *Crimson Nation: The Shaping of the South's Most Dominant Football Team*. Nashville TN: Rutledge Hill Press, 2005.

Goldfield, David. *Still Fighting the Civil War: The American South and Southern History*. Baton Rouge LA: Louisiana State University, 2002.

Guttmann, Allen. *From Ritual to Record: The Nature of Modern Sports*. New York: Columbia University Press, 1978.

Guttmann, Allen. *Sports Spectators*. New York: Columbia University Press, 1986.

Harvey, Paul. "God and Negroes and Jesus and Sin and Salvation: Racism, Racial Interchange, and Interracialism in Southern Religious History." In *Religion in the American South: Protestants and Others in History and Culture*, edited by Beth Barton Schweiger and Donald G. Mathews. Chapel Hill NC: University of North Carolina Press, 2004.

Herberg, Will. "America's Civil Religion: What It Is and Whence It Comes." In *American Civil Religion*, edited by Russell E. Richey and Donald G. Jones. New York: Harper & Row, 1974.

Higgs, Robert J. *God in the Stadium: Sports & Religion in America*. Lexington KY: University Press of Kentucky, 1995.

Higgs, Robert J. and Michael C. Braswell. *An Unholy Alliance: The Sacred and Modern Sports*. Macon GA: Mercer University Press, 2004.

Hill, Samuel S. *Religion and the Solid South*. Nashville TN: Abingdon Press, 1972.

Hill, Samuel S. *Southern Churches in Crisis Revisited*. Tuscaloosa AL: University of Alabama Press, 1999.

Horwitz, Tony. *Confederates in the Attic: Dispatches from the Unfinished Civil War*. New York: Vintage Books, 1999.

I'll Take My Stand: The South and the Agrarian Tradition (various contributors). Baton Rouge LA: Louisiana State University, 2006.

James, William. *The Varieties of Religious Experience*. New York: Collier Books, 1961.

Juergensmeyer, Mark. *Terror in the Mind of God: The Global Rise of Religious Violence*. Berkeley CA: University of California Press, 2000.

Kerr, John H. *Rethinking Aggression and Violence in Sport*. New York: Routledge, 2005.

King, C. Richard and Charles Fruehling Springwood. *Beyond the Cheers: Race as Spectacle in College Sport*. Albany NY: State University of New York Press, 2001.

Lewis, Michael. *The Blind Side: Evolution of a Game*. New York: W. W. Norton & Company, 2007.

Lincoln, Bruce. *Discourse and the Construction of Society: Comparative Studies of Myth, Ritual, and Classification*. New York: Oxford University Press, 1989.

Maharidge, Dale. *And Their Children After Them: The Legacy of Let Us Now Praise Famous Men: James Agee, Walker Evans, and the Rise and Fall of Cotton in the South*. New York: Seven Stories Press, 1989.

Mandelbaum, Michael. *The Meaning of Sports: Why Americans Watch Baseball, Football, and Basketball and What They See When They Do.* New York: PublicAffairs Books, 2004.

Manis, Andrew M. *Southern Civil Religions in Conflict: Civil Rights and the Culture Wars.* Macon GA: Mercer University Press, 2002.

Martin, Charles H. "Integrating New Year's Day: The Racial Politics of College Bowl Games in the American South." In *The Sporting World of the Modern South*, edited by Patrick B. Miller. Urbana IL: University of Illinois Press, 2002.

Marx, Karl. *Karl Marx: The Essential Writings*, 2nd ed. Edited by Frederic L. Bender. Boulder CO: Westview Press, 1972.

Mathews, Donald G. "Lynching Is Part of the Religion of Our People: Faith in the Christian South." In *Religion in the American South: Protestants and Others in History and Culture*, edited by Beth Barton Schweiger and Donald G. Mathews. Chapel Hill NC: University of North Carolina Press, 2004.

McMinn, Ed. *God Bless the Crimson Tide: Devotions for the Die-Hard Alabama Fan.* New York: Howard Books, 2007.

Miller, Patrick B. "The Manly, the Moral, and the Proficient: College Sports in the New South." In *The Sporting World of the Modern South*, edited by Patrick B. Miller. Urbana IL: University of Illinois Press, 2002.

Miller-McLemore, Bonnie J. "Through the Eyes of Mircea Eliade: United States Football as a Religious 'Rite de Passage.'" In *From Season to Season: Sports as American Religion*, edited by Joseph Price. Macon GA: Mercer University Press, 2001.

Morgan, William J. "An Existential Phenomenological Analysis of Sport as a Religious Experience." In *Religion and Sport: The Meeting of the Sacred and Profane*, edited by Charles Prebish. Westport CT: Greenwood Press, 1993.

Novak, Michael. *The Joy of Sports: Endzones, Bases, Baskets, Balls, and the Consecration of the American Spirit*, rev. ed. Lanham MD: Madison Books, 1994.

Oriard, Michael. *King Football: Sport & Spectacle in the Golden Age of Radio & Newsreels, Movies & Magazines, the Weekly & the Daily Press.* Chapel Hill: University of North Carolina Press, 2001.

Oriard, Michael. *Reading Football: How the Popular Press Created an American Spectacle.* Chapel Hill: University of North Carolina Press, 1993.

Otto, Rudolf. *The Idea of the Holy: An Inquiry into the Non-Rational Factor in the Idea of the Divine and Its Relation to the Rational.* Translated by John W. Harvey. New York: Oxford University Press, 1958.

Ownby, Ted. "Manhood, Memory, and White Men's Sports in the American South." In *The Sporting World of the Modern South*, edited by Patrick B. Miller. Urbana: University of Illinois Press, 2002.

Price, Joseph. "From Season to Season: The Rhythm and Significance of America's Sporting Calendar." In *From Season to Season: Sports as American Religion*, edited by Joseph Price. Macon GA: Mercer University Press, 2001.

Proudfoot, Wayne. *Religious Experience*. Berkeley: University of California Press, 1985.

Reed, John Shelton. *My Tears Spoiled My Aim…and Other Reflections on Southern Culture*. Orlando FL: Harvest Book, 1993.

Religion and Sport: The Meeting of Sacred and Profane, edited by Charles S. Prebish. Westport CT: Greenwood Press, 1993.

Rhoden, William C. *Forty Million Dollar Slaves: The Rise, Fall, and Redemption of the Black Athlete*. New York: Three Rivers Press, 2006.

Sandvoss, Cornel. *Fans: The Mirror of Consumption*. Malden MA: Polity Press, 2005.

Schleiermacher, Friedrich. *On Religion: Addresses in Response to Its Cultured Critics*, translated by Terence N. Tice. Richmond VA: John Knox Press, 1969.

Schwartz, Regina. *The Curse of Cain: The Violent Legacy of Monotheism*. Chicago: University of Chicago Press, 1997.

Sensbach, Jon F. "Before the Bible Belt: Indians, Africans, and the New Synthesis of Eighteenth-Century Southern Religious History." In *Religion in the American South: Protestants and Others in History and Culture*, edited by Beth Barton Schweiger and Donald G. Mathews. Chapel Hill: University of North Carolina Press, 2004.

Shepard, David. *Bama, Bear Bryant and the Bible: 100 Devotionals Based on the Life of Paul "Bear" Bryant*. New York: Writers Club Press, 2002.

Slusher, Howard. "Sport and the Religious." In *Religion and Sport: The Meeting of the Sacred and Profane*, edited by Charles Prebish. Westport CT: Greenwood Press, 1993.

St. John, Warren. *Rammer Jammer Yellow Hammer: A Journey into the Heart of Fan Mania*. New York: Crown Publishers, 2004.

Stallybrass, Peter and Allon White. "Bourgeois Hysteria and the Carnivalesque." In *The Cultural Studies Reader*, edited by Simon During. New York: Routledge, 1993.

Stoddard, Tom. *Turnaround: Paul "Bear" Bryant's First Year at Alabama*. Montgomery AL: Black Belt Press, 2000.

Tales of the Tide: A Book by Alabama Fans...For Alabama Fans, edited by Clint
  Lovette and Jarrod Bazemore. Birmingham AL: FANtastic Memories, 2004.
Turner, Kevin. "Some Things Never Change." In *Tales of the Tide: A Book by
  Alabama Fans...For Alabama Fans,* edited by Clint Lovette and Jarrod
  Bazemore. Birmingham AL: FANtastic Memories, 2004.
Turner, Victor. *Dramas, Fields, and Metaphors: Symbolic Action in Human Society.*
  Ithaca NY: Cornel University Press, 1974.
Turner, Victor. *The Ritual Process: Structure and Anti-Structure.* New York: Aldine
  de Gruyter, 1995.
Wann, Daniel L., Merrill J. Melnick, Gordon W. Russell, Dale G. Pease, *Sports
  Fans: The Psychology and Social Impact of Spectators.* New York: Routledge,
  2001.
Wilson, Charles Reagan. *Baptized in Blood: The Religion of the Lost Cause, 1865–
  1920.* Athens: University of Georgia Press, 1980.
Wilson, Charles Reagan. *Judgment & Grace in Dixie: Southern Faiths from Faulkner
  to Elvis.* Athens: University of Georgia Press, 1995.
Woodward, C. Vann. *The Burden of Southern History.* Baton Rouge: Louisiana
  State University Press, 1993.

Index

Davis, Sam 91
Dean, William 65, 237-238
Debord, Guy 183-186, 206
Deford, Frank 186
Democratic Party 178, 208-209
Denny, George 137
Dixiecrats 178, 209
Doyle, Andrew 10, 138-139, 141,
    151, 164, 181
Dunn, Winfield 88
Dunnavant, Keith 11, 39, 106, 137-
    138, 140-141, 145, 147, 150-
    158, 161-163, 165, 168-170,
    207-208
Durkheim, Emile 28-36, 43, 47, 51-
    52, 54-55, 58, 85, 239

ecstasy 69-85, 229-231
Edwards, Harry 42-43, 45-47, 51,
    52, 84, 186, 196, 202, 209-210
Ehrenreich, Barbara 228-231
Eitzen, D. Stanley 219
Eliade, Mircea 2, 4, 5, 11-12, 13-14,
    17, 23-24, 76-77, 232, 235-236
emotions 75
evangelicalism 116-119

Faulkner, William 111-112
Feezell, Randolph 219
festivals 57-58, 228-231
Flynt, Wayne 112, 118, 121, 131-
    137, 140, 150-151, 178-179
fundamentalism 104, 119

Gammon, Richard Vonalbade 8
Georgia, University of 8, 15, 17, 18-
    19, 23, 41, 149, 220
Girard, Rene 55-59, 61, 62

God, gods and goddesses 7, 30, 31,
    53-54, 72, 214-215, and the
    South 85, 89-90, 94, 95, 115
Gold, Eli 7, 19-20, 139-140, 151,
    163
Goldfield, David 91-99, 115, 120,
    178, 179, 189-190
Gryska, Clem 159
Guttman, Allen 186-187, 190, 206,
    209-210, 217-218, 237

Harvey, Paul 125
heaven 220-221
Herberg, Will 123-124
heroes and heroines 7
Higgs, Robert J. 11, 32, 53, 61, 62,
    63-64, 65, 165, 213-215, 218,
    221-222, 223-224, 226, 231-232
Hill, Samuel S. 117-118, 120-122,
    124
Hinduism 53-54
Holloway, Condredge 129
homo religiosus 5, 232, 235, 237
honor 98-100, 108-109, 141, 173-
    174, 189
Horwitz, Tony 179
Hutson, Don 9, 142

individualism 43, 99
Islam 54

Jackson, Stonewall 91-92, 164-165
Jackson, Wilbur 160-161
James, William 76
Jena, Louisiana 176
Jesus 216
"Jim Crow" (see segregation)
Jones, Harry 9

race (racism) 95-97, 120-122, 125-130, 149-162, 175-181, 192-202, 206-209, 211-212
Ransom, John Crowe 102-103
Reagan, Ronald 209
Reconstruction 93, 97, 103, 117
Reed, John Shelton 99-100, 114-115, 123, 130, 208, 211
religious experience 69-85
Republican Party 99, 178, 209
Rhoden, William C. 194-196, 199-200
Richmond, Virginia 92-93
ritual(s) 20-26, 28-43, 57-68, 203-208
Ross, Charles 193

sacred 2-26, 29-36, 84, defined 2, morphology of 2-26, objects 15-17, opposed to profane 2, order 4, space 17-20, time 23-26, transcendence 3
sacrifice 33-34, 55-58, 60-61
Sage, Charles H. 219
Sandvoss, Cornell 44, 191, 216-217
Schachter, Stanley 80
Schleiermacher, Friedrich 75-76, 77-78
Schnellenberger, Howard 163
Schwartz, Regina 189
segregation 96, 120-122, 126-130, 149-162, 175, 178-179, 208-209, resegregation 175, 178-179
Sensbach, Jon F. 116-117
Shealy, Steadman 168
Slusher, Howard 3-4, 60, 83-84
Smith, Loran 110-111
soul 30-31

South Carolina, University of 189
Southern Agrarian movement 101-103
Southern California, University of 159-160
Southern religion 92-97, 103-104, 113, 114-130
Springwood, Charles Fruehling 187, 196, 199
St. John, Warren 73-74, 177
Stabler, Kenny 163
Stallybrass, Peter 229-230
Stoddard, Tom 106, 143-144
symbols 13-17

tailgating 21, 39-40
Tennessee, University of 7-8, 9, 14, 22, 49-50 72-73, 88, 129, 149
Texas A&M University 9-10, 142-143
Texas Christian University 147
"Third Row Tailgaters" 39-40
Tuohy, Sean (and Tuohy family) 200-201
Turner, Victor 32, 34-36, 38, 51, 84, 187-188, 206

Vagotis, Christ 163-164
Vandegraaf, W.T. "Bully" 7-8
Vanderbilt University 224
violence 53-68, 98, 189
Virginia, University of 8, 198

Waldrep, Kent 147
Wallace, George 152-153, 155
Wann, Daniel L. 40, 42, 47-51, 52, 62, 190, 223, 237, 238-239
Warren, Robert Penn 112

White, Allon 229-230
Wilson, Charles Reagan 10-11, 89-
    99, 116-122, 124-125, 130, 164-
    165, 212, 234
women 98, 210-211
Woodward, C. Vann 100-101, 129

Young, Neil 172-174